# CAMBRIDGE LIBRARY COLLECTION

*Books of enduring scholarly value*

## Women's Writing

The later twentieth century saw a huge wave of academic interest in women's writing, which led to the rediscovery of neglected works from a wide range of genres, periods and languages. Many books that were immensely popular and influential in their own day are now studied again, both for their own sake and for what they reveal about the social, political and cultural conditions of their time. A pioneering resource in this area is Orlando: Women's Writing in the British Isles from the Beginnings to the Present (http://orlando.cambridge.org), which provides entries on authors' lives and writing careers, contextual material, timelines, sets of internal links, and bibliographies. Its editors have made a major contribution to the selection of the works reissued in this series within the Cambridge Library Collection, which focuses on non-fiction publications by women on a wide range of subjects from astronomy to biography, music to political economy, and education to prison reform.

## An English Carmelite

Catharine Burton (1688–1714) was an English Carmelite nun who in 1697 was inspired to write her autobiography following visions of her patron saint, Francis Xavier. During a severe illness in her teenage years which had brought her near death, Burton underwent a spiritual conversion and resolved to enter a religious order should she survive. After her recovery she entered the English Carmelite convent in Antwerp in 1693. She was elected Superior of the convent in 1700. This volume, first published in 1876, contains her autobiography as edited by her confessor, Father Thomas Hunter (1666–1725). Burton describes her childhood and spiritual struggles in fascinating detail, and provides a vivid account of her daily life, bodily sufferings and religious practices as a nun. This volume combines elements from medieval accounts of female religious experiences with early modern philosophical ideas, providing valuable information concerning changes in the representation of female spirituality. For more information on this author, see http://orlando.cambridge.org/public/svPeople?person_id=burtca

T0372688

Cambridge University Press has long been a pioneer in the reissuing of out-of-print titles from its own backlist, producing digital reprints of books that are still sought after by scholars and students but could not be reprinted economically using traditional technology. The Cambridge Library Collection extends this activity to a wider range of books which are still of importance to researchers and professionals, either for the source material they contain, or as landmarks in the history of their academic discipline.

Drawing from the world-renowned collections in the Cambridge University Library, and guided by the advice of experts in each subject area, Cambridge University Press is using state-of-the-art scanning machines in its own Printing House to capture the content of each book selected for inclusion. The files are processed to give a consistently clear, crisp image, and the books finished to the high quality standard for which the Press is recognised around the world. The latest print-on-demand technology ensures that the books will remain available indefinitely, and that orders for single or multiple copies can quickly be supplied.

The Cambridge Library Collection will bring back to life books of enduring scholarly value (including out-of-copyright works originally issued by other publishers) across a wide range of disciplines in the humanities and social sciences and in science and technology.

# An English Carmelite

*The Life of Catharine Burton,*
*Mother Mary Xaveria of the Angels,*
*of the English Teresian Convent at Antwerp*

CATHARINE BURTON
EDITED BY THOMAS HUNTER

CAMBRIDGE
UNIVERSITY PRESS

CAMBRIDGE UNIVERSITY PRESS

Cambridge, New York, Melbourne, Madrid, Cape Town, Singapore,
São Paolo, Delhi, Dubai, Tokyo, Mexico City

Published in the United States of America by Cambridge University Press, New York

www.cambridge.org
Information on this title: www.cambridge.org/9781108020916

This edition first published 1876
This digitally printed version 2010

ISBN 978-1-108-02091-6 Paperback

# 𝔔uarterly 𝔖eries.

EIGHTEENTH VOLUME.

———

*AN ENGLISH CARMELITE.*

ROEHAMPTON :

PRINTED BY JAMES STANLEY.

# AN ENGLISH CARMELITE.

## THE LIFE OF

## CATHARINE BURTON,

MOTHER MARY XAVERIA OF THE ANGELS,

*Of the English Teresian Convent at Antwerp.*

COLLECTED FROM HER OWN WRITINGS AND OTHER SOURCES

BY

## FATHER THOMAS HUNTER,

OF THE SOCIETY OF JESUS.

LONDON:
BURNS AND OATES, PORTMAN STREET
AND PATERNOSTER ROW.
1876.

✠

EN · DILECTUS · MEUS · LOQUITUR · MIHI
SURGE · PROPERA · AMICA · MEA
COLUMBA · MEA · FORMOSA · MEA · ET · VENI
JAM · ENIM · HIEMS · TRANSIIT
IMBER · ABIIT · ET · RECESSIT
FLORES · APPARUERUNT · IN · TERRA · NOSTRA
TEMPUS · PUTATIONIS · ADVENIT
VOX · TURTURIS · AUDITA · EST · IN · TERRA · NOSTRA
FICUS · PROTULIT · GROSSOS · SUOS
VINEÆ · FLORENTES · DEDERUNT · ODOREM · SUUM
SURGE · AMICA · MEA · SPECIOSA · MEA · ET · VENI

*(Ex Canticis Canticorum).*

# NOTICE

[BY THE EDITOR.]

————

THE volume which is here presented to the reader is printed from a manuscript in the possession of the Teresian Community at Lanherne in Cornwall. That Community is the same with that to which Catharine Burton, known in religion as Mary Xaveria of the Angels, herself belonged. It came, as it were, by direct descent from St. Teresa herself, inasmuch as its first Prioress was Mother Anne of the Ascension, an English lady of the Worsley family, who had been trained in the Spanish Teresian Convent at Brussels, under the famous Anne of St. Bartholomew, St. Teresa's constant companion, in whose arms the Saint expired. After flourishing for several generations as the home of a succession of holy English ladies who left their country in order to dedicate themselves to our Lord in the Order founded by St. Teresa, the Community left Antwerp, on account of the troubles occasioned by the Revolution, in 1794, and finally settled in their present abode at Lanherne, a spot where it is believed the Holy Sacrifice has been offered and the Blessed Sacrament reserved uninterruptedly through all the centuries of persecution since the change of religion in England.

The manuscript in question was compiled by Father Thomas Hunter, as is clear from internal evidence, at the request of the Community, within a few years of the death of the holy nun whose life it relates.

Father Hunter was of about the same age with

Mother Mary Xaveria, having been born in 1666. He made his early studies in the English Jesuit College at St. Omers, and entered the Society in 1684. He was a professed Father early in the eighteenth century, and was for many years chaplain and missioner to the Sherbornes of Stonyhurst. He died in 1725, not long, as it would seem, after the compilation of the manuscript. He is said to have been a man of powerful mind, and extensive information, and a reader who is versed in spiritual literature will easily see in the following pages many traces of his learning, experience, and judgment.

The work of Father Hunter is here reproduced, with the exception of a few of the notes which he has inserted in the autobiography of Mother Mary Xaveria. The orthography has been conformed to the standard of our own times, and in a very few cases a phrase has been altered where the manuscript was obscure or evidently faulty, or where a word has now lost the meaning attached to it in Father Hunter's time. Two chapters, with which the present narrative begins, have been transposed from their place in the manuscript, as Father Hunter, writing for the religious of the Convent, naturally put the autobiography of Mary Xaveria first, and his own collections as to her parents, family, and early years, second. This transposition has made it necessary to give up the division of the narrative into parts, but the chapters are all in their places, with the exception of the two already mentioned. For the biographical information contained in the short editorial notes which are here and there subjoined, I have to acknowledge my obligations to the kindness of two of my religious brethren, the Rev. John Morris and Brother Henry Foley.

H. J. C.

*London, Feast of our Lady of Mount Carmel, 1876.*

# PREFACE.

I PRESENT the public with a book which will be dif-
ferently received, according to the different dispositions
of those into whose hands it shall chance to fall. The
mentioning of visions, revelations, and other supernatural
favours, will raise the curiosity of some and prove a
jest to others, and in all probability will relish with
very few in an age so little inclined to believe anything of this nature. However, since I am persuaded
that those who are piously disposed will reap advantage
by it, I see no reason why it should not be published
for their sakes, notwithstanding whatever less favourable
reception it may meet with. I am very willing to give
so far in to the sentiments of those who declare against
the publishing anything which appears singular, as to
agree that nothing in this kind should be made public
which is not grounded upon sufficient testimonies to
secure the reader from being imposed upon. Though
this caution is always necessary, yet more particular
regard must be had to it when we treat of anything of
this nature with relation to women. There are not
wanting those, and in great number, who exaggerate
so much in them the weakness of nature and the force
of imagination and fancy, that they value themselves

upon discrediting everything in this kind, and they seem
persuaded that the only way not to be imposed upon
is to believe nothing; but these persons, as is observed
by a moderate author, do not seem to reflect that as
it would be a simplicity to take everything upon trust
without sufficient proof, it is no less a weakness of
judgment not to assent when proof exists. 'It would
be very pleasant,' says he, 'if in common discourse or
conversation you light upon a man who valued himself
upon believing nothing you could tell him. A person,
for example, comes directly from Court, he tells you
what he saw there. I suppose he is a man of probity,
known for such, who has no interest in deceiving the
company in these circumstances; but still our cautious
man, who is resolved not to be deceived, is upon his
guard; he fancies there is a plot laid to impose upon
him, that everybody aims at deceiving him, and upon
this, applauding himself in proceeding so warily, and
laughing at the simplicity of others, he tells them plainly
he does not believe one word of what is said. Such
a one would pass for an original, and it would be very
diverting to see him take his wise precautions.'[1]

This too great precaution would indeed appear most
absurd in common conversation upon ordinary subjects,
and yet perhaps it will not seem so unreasonable in
extraordinary events which are out of the common
course, such as are revelations and supernatural favours,
for here every one seems to have a right to suspect
or dispute the truth of them, and by consequence has

[1] The Author of the Dissertation about the belief of miracles.

great reason to be upon his guard lest he let himself
be imposed upon. I am far from blaming any reasonable methods which ought to be employed in an exact
search of the truth in these uncommon events, and I
shall by-and-bye lay down some reasons which induced
those concerned in publishing the life of this virtuous
woman to believe the favours mentioned in it were from
Almighty God; but I must first observe that if we have
any regard to religion, or indeed to common sense, we
can in no ways doubt but that God has in all times
had some favourite souls, as I may call them, whom
He has been pleased to admit to a more intimate
familiarity, and who, by a constant fidelity in complying
with the Divine grace, have deserved in a singular
manner to be favoured and caressed by Him. We find
so many examples of this in Holy Writ, and in the
most approved ecclesiastical histories of all ages, that
to call this in question is to make both our reason
and our religion suspected. I am very sensible that
an assent to this general notion that God has in all
times had His chosen souls does not plead for the
truth, of particular facts which may now be brought
upon the stage. However, it gives reason to hope that,
as His hand is not abbreviated, He may also in our
times find some who, by a faithful correspondence with
His grace, may deserve to feel the same effects of His
goodness.

I cannot but think that one reason which makes some
so apt to discredit anything of this nature is the mean
opinion they have of those who by their duty are

employed in treating with persons whom we judge
singularly favoured by Almighty God.  These good
men say they are too credulous in these matters, they
are too apt to be led away with every imaginary dream
or fancy.  Upon this supposition, which they take as
granted, they immediately give sentence and raise themselves as umpires in the case, pass their verdict, and
declare these favours are not to be credited.  It will
be questioned by some whether this peremptory decision
be grounded more on the profoundness of their judgment
or on their want of sense and religion, and I believe
upon examination it will be found that persons consecrated to God, and who make virtue their study, are
the properest judges in this case.  I should easily
persuade my reader he has reason to believe that persons
thus employed do not proceed rashly nor give in too
easily to everything which has the appearance of a
supernatural favour, if I should here transcribe these
solid rules laid down by the greatest masters of spirit
for the direction of such persons who, as we are chari-
tably to suppose, comply with their duty in giving serious
attention to what is prescribed in those circumstances.
Though this is not my present task, it will not be
amiss to say a word or two of the danger there is in
giving too easily credit to these supernatural favours;
it will prevent the mischief which some of weaker judgment might be apt to take from the lecture of this
book, by letting themselves be carried away with a
desire of entering into these extraordinary ways, and it
may help to convince others that those who are con-

cerned in publishing these papers would never have consented to it unless they had believed there were sufficient grounds to give credit to what is here related. It is very clear from the notions we have of visions, revelations, and supernatural favours, that these are things, as we may say, out of the common course, and though it cannot be denied but that God, as supreme Lord, may work wonderfully in regard of His creatures, yet considering the weakness of human understanding, and how little capable it is of judging of these things which are out of its reach, no wonder it should easily be deceived and take that for a Divine operation which is only the effects of imagination or fancy, heightened by some exterior cause, or by an innate propensity towards that which seems extraordinary or singular. If we reflect besides on the artifices of the enemy, who, as the Apostle says,[2] transforms himself into an angel of light to seduce unwary souls, we shall find still greater danger of delusion in these uncommon paths; hence it is that all those who have either experienced these effects in themselves, or who pretend to treat as masters of this mystical science in the direction of souls, lay this down as a certain maxim—that all these visions, whether interior or exterior, imaginary or intellectual, are always to be suspected as dangerous, never to be desired or sought for, and not easily to be relied upon, unless accompanied with certain effects and signs which may secure a director of souls that they are the operations of the Divine Spirit. What happened to St. Teresa in

[2] 2 Cor. xi. 14.

this kind was very notorious. We know this blessed Saint was left for several years in a great uncertainty, and all the help she could get from the most experienced men of her age was little enough to secure her that the favours she received proceeded from the Spirit of Almighty God.

The holy man, Joannes d'Avila, in the fiftieth chapter of his book, *Audi filia*, warns a devout soul under his charge to be very careful never to desire any of these supernatural favours. He proves there, by the authority of St. Augustine and St. Bonaventure, the danger of this temptation, which often draws souls into folly and error, and concludes, with the latter, that these extraordinary favours are more to be feared than desired. He alleges the example of one of the Fathers of the desert, who, upon the appearing of our Saviour crucified, shut his eyes, saying, 'I will not see Jesus Christ in this world, it shall serve my turn to see Him in heaven.' And of another, who in the like apparition of an angel presently cried out, 'I have no need nor am I worthy to receive messages by the mouth of angels, and therefore consider well to whom it is that you were sent, for it is not possible they should send thee to me, nor will I so much as hear thee.' Upon both which humble answers, says he, the proud devil betrayed himself and fled away. Blessed John of the Cross, a most spiritual man, and director of St. Teresa, in his second book of the *Ascent to Mount Carmel*, chap. xi., discoursing of interior visions and the satisfaction a soul feels in them, declares that a soul desirous of perfection ought absolutely to reject them all as in themselves most dangerous, and, even though there be a certainty that they come from God, yet he shows at the same time that to adhere to them with too much satisfaction is infinitely prejudicial. He there reckons up several inconveniences to which a person is subject who relies too much on these exterior favours, and in his eighteenth chapter he blames very much those directors who seem to put too much value upon these supernatural operations, which, unless great care be taken, may easily engage a soul in most dangerous errors.

This being the common sentiment of those who treat this subject, we may reasonably conclude that there is great danger in giving too easily credit to supernatural favours. What has been said may serve to deter souls desirous of perfection from engaging too carelessly or rashly in these extraordinary ways. The constant practice of Christian virtues, of humility, submission, patience, &c., are the solid means to please God and gain His favour, which is the only thing a pious soul ought to aim at; yet we must not pretend to prescribe laws to Almighty God. When He speaks it is our duty to attend His voice and to follow Him through those paths by which He is pleased to lead us to Himself. Avila, in the place above-mentioned, observes that it would be a great misfortune to seek darkness and error instead of truth, or which is worse, to follow the devil in place of God, of which, says he, there is great danger, when with facility of belief we accept of the instinct of an evil spirit as if it were the Holy Ghost. But on the

other hand it would be a kind of blasphemy to reject
the impulses which come from the Holy Ghost, manifested to us in these supernatural operations, as if they
came from the wicked spirit of the devil; and by this,
he says, we should make ourselves like those miserable
Pharisees, contradictors of the truth of God, who attributed to an evil spirit the works which Christ Jesus
our Lord did by the Holy Ghost.   On both sides, says
he, there is a great danger, either holding God for the
devil or the devil for God.   At the same time we must
confess that when these supernatural favours proceed
from God they are of infinite advantage to a soul which
knows how to make a due use of them.   Hence it is
St. Teresa, in her *Sixth Mansion*, chap. iv., tells us how
much she is touched with compassion and grief to see
what we lose by our own faults, by not preparing our
souls as we ought for the operation of the Holy Ghost;
for though it be true that they are things which our
Lord bestows on whom He pleases, yet did we but
love His Divine Majesty as He loves us, He would give
them to all.   He desires nothing else but some to bestow
them on, since His riches are not diminished thereby.
We have reason to believe the person we here treat of
was one of those whom God found disposed for His
favours.   I shall here lay down some reasons which
convinced those who dealt with her that they might
securely rely on her visions, revelations, &c., as effects
of the Divine Spirit.

The person whose life is here published was Mrs.
Catharine Burton, born in Suffolk in the year 1668.

Having passed her youth very virtuously, she was seized with a violent sickness which lasted in all for seven years, after which it pleased God at two different times to restore her to her health and the perfect use of her limbs, in so very wonderful a manner that it seems to leave no doubt but that they were miraculous effects of His Divine power, obtained by the intercession of St. Francis Xaverius, to whom at both times she applied herself by particular devotions performed in his honour. In the first cure her side and arm, which had above a year been struck with a palsy and were almost rendered useless, were instantly after Communion perfectly restored in the sight of their own family, and I may say of all the town where she lived; every one of the neighbour-hood, who had been frequently witnesses of the sad condition to which she was reduced, proclaimed the power of God in the suddenness of the wonderful change. In the second, her disjointed hip, without the use of any human remedies, in an instant, immediately after Communion, became perfectly sound. (I must refer the reader, for several particulars, to the first part of her life, in which he will find an account of these passages.) St. Francis Xaverius, to whose intercession she attributes these great favours, seemed from this time to take her in a singular manner under his protection. He found means to facilitate her passing the sea some months after, and at last brought her to Antwerp, where she was admitted and professed among the English nuns of the holy Order of St. Teresa. These wonderful cures wrought upon her by Almighty God, together with the

*b*

singular and visible signs of His protection which appeared sensibly in her conduct, struck all that knew her with an esteem and veneration for her person, so highly favoured by heaven; but these were only exterior blessings, which are not always certain signs of interior sanctity. After this she found herself inspired to unfold the secret sentiments of her heart to her directors (till this time she thought it humility to conceal what passed in secret between her and Almighty God); they were then sensible of those treasures of Divine grace which God had so plentifully poured down upon this faithful soul. But because the councils of Almighty God were singular, leading her perpetually by manifesting His pleasure to her in frequent visions, revelations, and other supernatural favours, which, as we have seen, if not thoroughly examined, are subject to several illusions, they put her to those trials which they thought Almighty God required, both for securing her and themselves in her conduct. She was successively under five different directors, who were placed there by her Superiors, and charged with the direction of those religious, besides the ordinary confessors of the monastery. These were all of them so perfectly satisfied with her virtue that they thought themselves sufficiently authorized to approve of her conduct. I shall here set down some of the reasons which induced them to frame their judgment and some late passages which seem since to confirm it.

First, they observed that these spiritual favours were so far from raising in her the least motion of pride or vanity, that on the contrary they grounded her in a most profound humility, and inspired her at last with such admirable notions of the nothingness, as we may term it, of all created beings, that she became as it were insensible of everything which regarded her own private reputation, credit, or person. She was taught by them not to admire the gifts, but as much as they lead to the knowledge and love of their Author. She was so far from relying on them that in her instructions to her novices she constantly inculcated the practice of solid virtues, advising them never to seek nor to value themselves upon these extraordinary favours, and explaining at the same time the danger of them. And she was so industrious to hide everything in this kind which happened to herself from the eyes of others, that notwithstanding the numberless favours she received in this kind, several of the religious never knew she was led this way, but were surprised at her death when part of them came to light, which were then spoken by those who thought themselves no longer obliged to conceal them.

Secondly, these sentiments of humility were accompanied with an intimate sense of gratitude to Almighty God, the Author as she believed of these favours; and the sense she had of the wonderful tenderness and goodness of God in thus caressing His creature was so great that she could scarce ever mention these favours to her directors without putting herself into a kind of ecstasy. With most inflamed love to Almighty God it broke out in her countenance, and I have often found her unable to continue her discourse, but obliged to interrupt it to give way to these tender sentiments.

Thirdly, her exemplary life was a standing proof of the Spirit of God which acted in her. Her religious (it is the unanimous testimony of all that lived with her) found in her a most zealous Superior, who, without any regard to any human respects, made it her sole endeavour to bring everything up to the primitive spirit of their Order; a most tender Mother in her care of supplying every one, particularly those that were sick, with what was necessary for their body and soul; a pattern of religious observance, who the most of her time afflicted with grievous infirmities, led the Community through all their duties, confirming by her example what she taught in words, that their great perfection was necessarily annexed to an exact performance of religious discipline.

Fourthly, whosoever gives himself the trouble of reading over the first part of this life before her entrance into religion will find enough to convince him that nothing but the Spirit of God could have supported her in those sharp trials, by inspiring her with those sentiments which she then could learn from none but God Himself. He will there find a young woman, unlearned, without the help of any creature living (she never consulted anybody for her direction), passing through the sharpest trials, not only by suffering in her body to a degree almost incredible, but also engaged in the dark paths of that passive purgation by which God is accustomed to lead souls. He will find her in these circumstances directed by the Holy Ghost (we can atrribute it to nothing else) adhering by an inviolable fidelity to every motion of Divine grace, till she is advanced to a high degree of prayer and of union with God, practising the noblest acts of resignation, of the love of God, of a perfect conformity with the Divine will. And when we reflect on the Divine dispositions of her soul expressed in her writings at the time she experienced the power of Almighty God in the cure of her body, we shall certainly conclude that the finger of God was there. I refer the reader to the first part of her life.

Fifthly, this wonderful proceeding of Almighty God, Who, as I may say, Himself led by the hand this virtuous soul through most of these dangerous passages which occur in a spiritual life, which had already raised her to a high degree of prayer and settled her in a solid peace of mind before she had ever discovered her interior to any director, was a great security to those with whom she treated afterwards in the concerns of her soul, particularly since they could never remark any one false step she had made, unless they impute her long silence to a fault. Yet whereas she had no light to act otherwise, and was then persuaded it was humility to conceal all these extraordinary favours, I cannot doubt, as she says herself, but that this simplicity was then pleasing to Almighty God. As to her own part afterward, she had all the security which God is accustomed to give in this life, both from the testimony of her own conscience, if we can credit her, and from the approbation of those whom God had placed over her. She never met any director who, after the trials he thought fit to put her to, did not approve her conduct. And I must add one thing more which is certainly true to my own knowledge, that she scarce ever met a director who, besides the security he had drawn from her solid virtues (the true touchstone of sanctity), was not also confirmed in the opinion he had of her virtue by something particular which passed between God and himself, and by which Almighty God seemed to confirm the approbation her director gave of her spirit.

Sixthly, we must add to these that Almighty God, in several extraordinary cases, seemed to declare in her favour. She told several persons upon occasion what passed in their souls, and what they declared was only known to God and themselves; in the temporal necessities of the monastery they found themselves relieved in an extraordinary manner, and in circumstances which made them attribute these sweet effects of Providence to the merits and prayers of this holy woman. She foretold to several of her directors things that were to happen, and the event proved always the truth of her predictions. In particular, above ten years before the treasure was discovered of the incorrupt body of the venerable Mother Margaret Wake, she positively told her director that God had revealed to her that there was an incorrupt body in the dead cellar of the English monastery at Antwerp. She told the same to her last director some time before her own death, and she opened several graves and spoke several things which the religious found afterwards had relation to this revelation made to her by Almighty God. I might add several things obtained by her intercession and prayers, both before and after her death. I refer as before for all these particulars to the different parts of her written life.

Seventhly, a happy death was the crown of her virtuous life. Her manifold virtues manifested at that critical time will always serve as a standing proof of all that is said in her commendation; an invincible patience, a most heroic courage under the surgeon's hand, a most wonderful presence of mind even in the sight of death, an indefatigable zeal in commending to the religious the observance of their rules and constitutions till her last breath, an ardent desire of enjoying the Divine presence, were the happy dispositions which rendered her death, as we have reason to believe, precious in the sight of God, and the favours which several since that time are persuaded they have received by the power of her intercession seem to confirm this belief. I must refer you as before for particulars upon all these heads to those chapters of her life where they are minutely related. If what has been said in commendation of this holy woman, to prove that we have reason to believe she was led by the Spirit of God, be of any weight, the reader will be satisfied in reading those extraordinary visions and revelations when he is informed that they are not taken by hearsay, but penned down by herself. It is true that, speaking of the generality of men, it would be a thing very much out of the way to put every one upon penning down to posterity what is most commendable in his life and actions, yet there are circumstances in which this method is not unprecedented. St. Paul thought it was for the glory of God that he should declare to the world those wonderful ecstasies and raptures with which God had favoured him, and it would be blasphemy to question whether he was inspired by the Holy Ghost. This seemed a sufficient warrant for virtuous and learned men to put St. Teresa and other saints upon this method of declaring what God had wrought in them, and perhaps in these later cases the securing of directors to whom their whole soul was to be unfolded made it absolutely necessary.

The reader I hope will be satisfied with the directors who put this holy woman upon the same method, when he has read in the first sheet of her life the motives by which she and they were induced to act in this manner, and the sincerity, integrity, and candour of the person who relates what passed in her soul will add no small weight to the credibility of the relation.

St. Xaverius, if we can trust this holy woman, was pleased to promise her one day that he would not fail to procure blessings for those who should peruse what she writ by his orders and direction, and though these papers have not been communicated to many, yet I have reason to believe they have proved of very great edification and instruction to several who have seen them.

I wish, pious reader, with all my heart you may feel the same effects, and that you may learn both to admire the goodness of God Who, as you find here, deals mercifully with those who love and fear Him, and square your actions by those rules she points out to you, both by word and example.

I have thought fit to premise this in behalf of such as are disposed to reap some advantage from these sort of writings; at the same time I cannot but suppose they may fall into the hands of many who will even make it their business to turn into ridicule most of the passages they meet with in them; neither do I think this much to be wondered at in the age we live in, seeing there is nothing so sacred which is not made a subject of cavil. If I may be permitted to speak my opinion in this case, I would advise such persons if they happen to light on these sheets to lay them down quietly, without pretending to pass sentence in a case in which they are not altogether qualified to be competent judges; they may reflect that the vision of our Saviour's apparition to the holy women at the Resurrection appeared dotage (as the Scripture expresses it) to the Apostles, not yet sufficiently enlightened to understand this mystery. The apparent incredibility of the fact was more to be imputed to the indisposition of the Apostles than to any defect in the pious women or to the uncertainty of the apparition.

In following the advice here given they may possibly be deprived of some advantage which others better disposed may reap from these writings. In this case the loss will be their own, but the harm will end here, whereas their too great liberty of condemning what perhaps they are not worthy to experience in themselves may be attended with fatal consequences to others, and the spirit of irreligion and impiety, which reigns so much in the world, with the loss of innumerable souls, will prove one day a heavy charge on their heads who too freely decry whatever savours of extraordinary devotion and piety. Persons that are thus disposed should first bewail their own blindness and purge their peccant humours, which corrupt their hearts and affections; thus perhaps they may come to admire the gifts of God in others and experience them in themselves.

### *The protestation of the Collector of these writings.*

In obedience to the decree of our Holy Father, Urban VIII., of happy memory, March 13, 1625, and to the other confirmations and declarations of the same decree, I protest that I understand all that I have written in this life of Mother Mary Xaveria of the Angels to have no other force or credit than what is grounded upon human authority, without the Church's approbation. I also declare that by any title given to her or others in these writings (excepting those who are canonized by the Church), I had no intention to rank them among the beatified or canonized saints, which power only appertains to the See Apostolic.

T. H.

# CONTENTS.

# *Contents.*

# CHAPTER I.[1]

## Of the birth, parents, and infancy of Catharine Burton.

MRS. CATHARINE BURTON was born at Bayton, near St. Edmund's Bury in Suffolk, on the 4th day of November, in the year 1668. Her father, Mr. Thomas Burton, was descended from a very good family of that name in Yorkshire. Her mother was Mrs. Mary Suttler, only daughter of Mr. Christopher Suttler, of a gentleman's family in Norfolk. Her parents, considering the hardness of the times and their strait circumstances, provided very well for all their children : but their chief care was to bring them up in the fear of God, and leave them heirs of their virtues. They lived together twenty years in great peace and concord, and their whole family was always remarkable for their piety and virtue. Their children used to ascribe their happiness in the frequent blessings they received from God to the piety of their parents, and their father, who lived till his children were grown up, had the satisfaction to see them all (this daughter in particular) correspond perfectly to the care and pains he had taken in their education. Her mother left nine children behind her, four sons and five daughters. She died of her tenth child in the thirty-fifth year of her

[1 This and the following chapter, written apparently by the Collector, Father Thomas Hunter, are transferred from a later part of the manuscript in order to make the reader acquainted with Catharine Burton before he begins her autobiography.]—ED.

B

age, much lamented by her husband, children, and all
her neighbourhood, particularly by the poor, to whom
she was wonderfully charitable. She was of a sweet
agreeable temper, of a tender complexion, and wore
herself out with pains and cares of her family and
children, nursing them with her own milk. In a word,
her life and death were so exemplary, virtuous, and
pious, that her confessor was heard to say after her
death that he believed her soul went straight to heaven.

Mr. Thomas Burton, after his spouse's death, employed his whole care in bringing up his children
virtuously. He animated them not a little by his own
example. We find in Mother Xaveria's Life, written
by herself, several passages in which are expressed his
tenderness of devotion, his constant practices of piety in
gratitude to Almighty God and St. Xaverius for the cure
of his daughter, his great confidence in this Saint. He
was fully resolved, after he had settled his affairs, to pass
the seas, and enter as a lay-brother among the English
Fathers of the Society. He could not do this when his
two daughters became religious, because he had been
left executor to his son-in-law and trustee for his grand-
children. There was a suit in law commenced in their
concerns, and he was told he could neither in charity
nor conscience abandon them at that time. He told
his daughter Catharine before she went over, that
St. Matthew, following the call of our Lord, left the
custom-house money, and all things else, as uncertainties,
but that they would not permit him to do the same.

He was after this employed near two years and a
half in those concerns, writing often to his daughter
to recommend them to St. Xaverius, that he might be
at liberty to complete his pious designs. His affairs
were just finished, and she in daily expectation of seeing
him at Antwerp in his journey to his noviceship, when

it pleased God to call him to Himself. He died of a
fever, receiving all the rites of the Church, and was
upon his death-bed admitted into the Society, which,
though unknown to his daughter, was the reason why
she saw him ranked among the religious of the Society
in heaven. In her writings she seems to suppose he
died in great desolation, for his greater merit. We
cannot doubt but he died most happily, if we can give
any credit to those supernatural favours she received
from God, seeing she there declares that some few
months after his death she saw him living among the
blessed in heaven, where she could have more free
conversation with him and oftener than if he had been
in the world.

It may not seem proper to add much of her relations
who are yet alive. I shall content myself with saying
they do not degenerate from the virtuous examples given
by her father, mother, and herself. She has yet living
a brother, a priest of the Society of Jesus.[2] Her youngest sister is now Superior of the most worthy community
of the English Carmelites of Hoogstraet. Her eldest
sister has been many years professed in the English
monastery at Bruges of the holy Order of St. Augustine.
Her sister, Anne Burton, *alias* Woolmer, after several
years of widowhood, had the happiness of being professed by her own sister, whose life I write, in the
monastery of the English Carmelites at Antwerp. One
thing I cannot omit, which is much to their satisfaction
and comfort, to wit, that Almighty God promised to
Venerable Mary Xaveria that He would, in a particular
manner protect, favour, and advance her relations on

[2 This was Father Christopher Burton, born 1671. He made his
Humanities at the Jesuit College at St. Omers, and entered the novitiate
at Watten, September 7th, 1693. He served for many years the missions
of Formby, Lytham, and others in Lancashire, and died at Watten,
July 23rd, 1744.]—ED.

her account. But then we must observe that this
advancement, which she says began in her own time,
consisted in this, that she heard they were fallen under
several unforeseen crosses and afflictions, which they had
suffered with Christian patience and resignation. This,
in her language, was to be advanced to new dignities
by Almighty God.

Her grandfather Mr. Henry Burton, noted for his
grave and virtuous behaviour, who died afterwards in
prison, into which he was cast on account of his religion,
was always particularly fond of his granddaughter, and
used frequently several expressions in her commendation, as if he had foreseen what she would come to.
She was observed from her childhood to be of a mild
temper, tractable and obedient, without showing any
impatience or uneasiness, even when she was chidden
or found fault with, and this though she were otherwise
observed to have a pretty high spirit. She was remarkable for her piety and devotion from her tender years,
and I have had several instances from her brother and
sisters of her attention and fervour in her prayers, at an
age when children are scarce sensible of their duty.

I need add nothing more in this place, but refer the
reader to the many passages he will find in her life. He
will meet there examples of her consummate virtue, in
her long exercise of patience during the seven years of
her sickness, the heroical acts of resignation and patience
which she learned from God Himself, without the help
of any master or book to instruct her, which shows
sufficiently the spirit by which she was led; and though
according to the common course of Providence, Almighty
God would have us led and directed one by another, yet
He seemed designedly to have let her remain in this
mistake—that she was not even to acquaint her director
with the extraordinary favours wrought in her—that we

might see the sweet, efficacious, and secure conduct of Divine grace when God finds a soul which without reserve abandons herself to it, and by a faithful compliance with all that is demanded of her, puts no stop to its powerful attractions.

As to what she endured in her long sickness, I think it necessary to repeat what is said in the short remarks on her Life. These violent convulsions, the dislocation of her joints, the violent tortures she suffered by the forcible stretching out of her body, those other unusual symptoms of which mention is made in the relation she gives of her illness, may seem to some persons incredible and exaggerated, and I must own I have never seen and do not remember to have heard of anybody who suffered so much, and in so many different ways, in any natural distemper. When I first heard the account from her own mouth, above twenty years ago, it struck me as much as it can now strike or surprise the reader. To satisfy myself and others who may come to hear this, I took the pains to copy out all that ever she said of her sufferings during these seven years. I sent the relation of it into Suffolk, the place where she was so ill, and I had it back again, attested by several, both Catholics and Protestants, who had been eye-witnesses of what she there relates. I know moreover that she was told when she left England, by some who had been with her all the time of her illness, that she need never apprehend exaggerating in anything she could say of her sickness, nor have any scruple on that account, because she could never represent it worse than it was, nor ever express to the full what she endured.

## CHAPTER II.

### *Of her settling among the English Teresians at Antwerp.*

THE Monastery of the English Teresian nuns at Antwerp was founded under the protection of St. Joseph and St. Anne in the year of our Lord 1619, thirty-seven years after the death of St. Teresa. It was founded by the piety and liberality of the Lady Mary Lovel, daughter to the Right Honourable Lord Roper, Baron of Teynham.[1] In the writings of the foundation I find these following passages.

This virtuous lady understood by revelation that the Queen of Heaven required that she should found a monastery, of an order most devoted to her service, upon which her director, a priest of the Society of Jesus, advised her to address herself to the Rev. Father Thomas of Jesus, Provincial of the Carmes. At the beginning he was unwilling to give in to the lady's proposals, hence this affair seemed dropped for a whole year, till at last he was severely reprehended by our Blessed Lady in his morning prayer for opposing the designs of heaven, so much conducing to the glory of God. This he owned afterwards to the first Prioress of the convent, and withal assured her he had received several commissions from the Blessed Virgin relating to the concerns of that house.

[1 She was the widow of Sir Robert Lovel. Her sister was Elisabeth Vaux, the friend of Father Gerard.]—ED.

In effect, he immediately condescended to what the Lady Lovel had proposed, and was instrumental in obtaining a licence from the Infanta Clara Isabella Eugenia, to found a monastery in any part of her dominions. He pitched upon a place in the town of Antwerp, which very place had been before showed and marked out in a vision to the Venerable Mother Anne of the Ascension, who was chosen the first Prioress. His Holiness was observed to give more than usual marks of satisfaction. The Infanta favoured it much, and the city of Antwerp willingly concurred in it. In pulling down some walls for building the house, they found a large and beautiful image of our Blessed Lady, which is still exposed in their house, where several are persuaded they have received many favours through her intercession.

I give to the public these passages as I find them upon record in the authentic writings of this foundation. I am at the same time sensible, in the age in which we live, that these things will find little credit, particularly with those who give themselves the liberty of treating all as imaginations and dreams which does not suit with their own notions. As to my own part, the character of the persons here mentioned serves not a little to plead for the credibility of the facts. Father Thomas of Jesus was a man of known learning and sanctity ; he has distinguished himself by his admirable books of mystical divinity, and is mentioned with great commendation in several rules relating to the holy Order of which he was Provincial. Mother Anne of the Ascension lived and died in opinion of sanctity, and the Lady Lovel, much commended for her piety, was so convinced of the truth of the facts, that she not only gave all she had towards the foundation of the house, but spent the remainder of her days in embellishing several rich ornaments of their church, which are admired to this day, as monuments of her liberality and good will towards this family. Without pretending at present to refute what objections may be made, I shall only add, for the satisfaction and comfort of those whom God calls daily to succeed in this worthy community, and for the edification of others who may light on these papers, that the eminent virtues of persons, who since the first foundation have always flourished and do still flourish in this holy family, are a standing proof that this establishment was much to the honour and glory of Almighty God. I hope a short digression here will not appear foreign to my subject; it will verify the truth of what Mother Xaveria learned herself from our Blessed Lady, that she owed a great deal to this Queen of Heaven for having called her to her *own house.* It will further show that as God designed to raise her to a great degree of sanctity, He had prepared for her a place where she should find great encouragement from the heroical examples of those who had gone before her.

The five who first settled in this house had been trained up and instructed by the companions of St. Teresa. Among these the Venerable Mother Anne of the Ascension, *alias* Worsley, was chosen Prioress. Almighty God ordered the Venerable Mother Anne of St. Bartholomew, the most beloved disciple of St. Teresa, to bring her to Antwerp, where it was revealed she was to do Him great service. She lived and died in great opinion of sanctity; her life was truly wonderful, as appears by the supernatural favours and graces she received from heaven, and her death was precious in the sight of God, which the angels themselves solemnized even upon earth by repeating concerts of music, which were heard several times, particularly at the moment of her happy departure out of this life. She governed the family twenty-five years, and settled religious observance according to the primitive spirit of their holy Mother, St. Teresa, upon so solid a foundation that there is reason to hope it will never decay. I do not add this without grounds.

I have by me a catalogue of those who succeeded her, as well in the practice of her virtues, as in superiority, during the most part of one hundred years. I can safely affirm, according to the accounts I have, that they were all so eminent for piety, that a religious community might justly glory in any one of them, as their virtue was truly solid in the faithful discharge of the trust God had reposed in them; it was not confined to their own souls, and whilst they laboured by the duty of their charge to maintain the spirit of their Order in an exact compliance with religious discipline, they had the satisfaction to see as many imitators of their virtue as they had religious who obeyed their Order. The seventh in this rank of superiors was the Venerable Mother Margaret of the Angels, whose sanctity heaven itself seems to approve in the incorruption of her body. This treasure God has been pleased to discover in the close of the first century after this foundation, for His own glory and the commendation of this virtuous community, of which more shall be said in its proper place.

We have seen in our days, that the same spirit of piety with which this house was founded continues still in this happy family. The life I have written of the Venerable Mother Mary Xaveria of the Angels will be a standing proof of what I say. I have had an opportunity of inquiring into their conduct whilst I was employed in collecting these memories : this, with all the personal knowledge I had of that family when I resided at Antwerp, makes me with confidence assure them, in the Scripture praise, that they are the *children of saints;* and for their comfort I can justly add that they have not degenerated from the noble thoughts of their virtuous ancestors. There is reason to hope they will transmit to posterity the spirit of devotion and prayer (which is the spirit of their Order), the spirit of love and charity, of fervour and zeal, and the like, which they have received from their worthy founders.

I find a character of this virtuous community among the papers of their first Superior, who gave the habit to fifty English ladies, and what she said of them in her time, may justly be applied to them since her death. 'The regular observance of this monastery has been a powerful persuasion to several English ladies of distinction to leave parents and all things else, and to enter this land of Carmel, where they live in a rigorous observance of their rule, and so perfect charity, that they resemble the first Christians, having one heart and one soul, every one pursuing their duty with all possible application : so obedient, that they need but the least sign of the Superior to make them fly to the execution of the hardest matters : so exact to silence and recollection, that in many years not one word has been spoken by anybody in times appointed for silence ; so eager and emulous to out-do each other in virtue, that things most repugnant to sense, by continual self-denial, become easy and pleasant ; most addicted to prayer and duties of the choir,' and the rest.

Though they are not accustomed to train up young ladies, under their conduct, by which their number may be supplied, yet Providence has always taken care to provide them, and often times by extraordinary means. The call of Mother Xaveria seems to have been something very singular. In the year 1693, they lost one of their religious, a person of exemplary life, and a great client of St. Francis Xaverius. The community upon her death joined in the ten Fridays' devotion in honour of St. Xaverius, to beg, by his intercession, a novice who might worthily supply her place, and to this end they chose this great Saint Patron of the noviceship. Soon after this they received accidentally a letter giving an account of the wonderful cure of Mrs. Catharine Burton (her person and name were entirely unknown at Antwerp at this time) by the intercession of St. Francis Xaverius, and upon examination they found she was cured about the time they ended the ten Fridays' devotion. This gave them a great desire of having her in their house, and to this end they redoubled their devotions to St. Xaverius. After this a Protestant gentle-man who had a daughter in the Monastery of Hoogstraet (for which place Mr. Burton designed his youngest daughter) unknown to Mrs. Catharine Burton or her father, dealt with the Superior of Antwerp about her admission in that place. When she left England, as is related in her own writings, she designed to present herself in the Monastery of the Poor Clares at Gravelines, (having heard much of the austerity and regularity of those religious women), hoping she should be received there. But she was surprised the day before her arrival at Antwerp, when she understood by the nuns of Hoogstraet, whither she conducted her youngest sister, that the religious of Antwerp had notice of her coming and waited for her. She consulted her confessor who accompanied her, resolved at last to embrace the offer, and accordingly stopped at Antwerp. When she entered the monastery, the religious were surprised to see her go from place to place, as if she had been long an inhabitant of the house and no stranger. Upon which she told some of them that she had been led through every chamber in the house in her dreams in England, by which she became so acquainted with it that nothing was new or strange which she met with. It seems she had often in England, in her dreams (if they were nothing but dreams), seen the church and house, which

God had provided for her, which agreed perfectly with what she met at Antwerp. It was an accidental occasion which brought her to that town, to wit, because her confessor, who conducted her, could meet with no conveniency for continuing their journey without passing through the town of Antwerp.

At her first entrance in their refectory, she found a total alteration in her appetite, accommodating herself to their usual diet, which her stomach could never bear before. At her appearance at the gate with her sister, she was known from her sister and saluted by an ancient religious, a great servant of God, who knew, as she said, from heaven, that this was the person designed for their house. From these things which are partly mentioned in her own writings, and the like, it was manifested to her that she was conducted hither by Almighty God. She had nothing to do but to·say with the Psalmist: 'This is my rest for ever and ever, here will I remain, because I have chosen it,' and by her own free election to ratify the choice which heaven had made.

One of the religious, a person remarkable for her singular virtue and piety, and who was looked upon as singularly favoured by Almighty God, was used to say of her that if the community knew the treasure they possessed in this novice, they would not be able to contain their joy. They found afterwards the truth of this; for during the time of her Superiority they were not only supplied (I may say to a miracle) in temporals, which they thought they had reason to attribute to her prayers, as shall be mentioned more in particular afterwards, but Almighty God gave her also a wonderful foresight into all. their concerns, by which they received great light for the management of their affairs, both in her lifetime and since her happy death; and, which is the chief of her admirable instructions, her exemplary

life, singular industry and care in keeping up the spirit
of their Order, in settling everything according to the
strictest exactness of their rule, is a lasting blessing
which will make this community have a perpetual
veneration for her happy memory.

I shall only add here that she made her profession on
the 9th of December, 1694, and within three years after
her profession she was so remarkable for her exemplary
virtue, that she was chosen Sub-Prioress in 1697, and
soon after that Mistress of Novices. Though she was
both young in years and religion, yet, at the request of
the religious, by approbation of my Lord Bishop, she
was declared Superior in 1700, in which office she continued six years. In the election, 1706, another Superior
was chosen ; but she after three months being by sickness rendered incapable of complying with the duties of
that charge, the community was committed to the care
of Reverend Mother Xaveria, then Sub-Prioress, till she
was chosen Superior again in the year 1707, in which
employment she died in 1714, being twice re-elected.


[N.B.—The chapters which follow after this are written
by Mother Mary Xaveria herself.]—ED.

# CHAPTER III.

*The motives that induced Catharine Burton to write the relation of her own life, with a remarkable passage which happened to her when she was ordered by her director to leave off writing, and some short remarks upon her writings.*

WHEN I was first Sub-Prioress, I made the ten Fridays in honour of St. Xaverius for one of the Sisters who was dangerously ill and despaired of by the doctors. One of my intentions in this devotion was the recovery of her health, if it were for the good of her soul; and another intention was that St. Xaverius would obtain me light to know what I should do to make some return of gratitude to Almighty God for all the favours He had done me.

At the end of the ten Fridays, the sick person recovered, to the admiration of all, and St. Xaverius appeared to me as I was in our cell at work, and bade me write my life and the favours God had done me, giving me to understand that by doing this I should much advance the honour and glory of God, and that this would be the best return of gratitude which I could make. I cannot express the peace and joy I found in my soul. I remained an hour in a rapt; yet I found great repugnance in doing what the Saint required of me, having no talent in writing, nor time for it (I was then in the office of Sub-Prioress and had care of the novices), so that considering the little time I had, I concluded I must be years about it, and even then unable to bring it

to anything without supernatural help. I proposed to
the Saint the example I had heard of a virtuous woman
who, being bid by our Saviour to write her life, deferred
it for ten years. I desired to do the same, but the
Saint gave me a gentle reprehension for this, and asked
me how I knew I should live so long. He signified to
me that he would have me begin then, and that I should
not have so much time afterwards. Yet I found great
difficulty in resigning to this, thinking it would take up
all my thoughts. The Saint told me he would help me,
that he would indite it for me, and that there should be
nothing written but what was true. I was in fear, having
a bad memory, that I should write some things not so
exactly as I could wish.

Upon this I submitted, and resolved to acquaint
my director with what had ˙happened. The Saint had
ordered me to do so, and bade me do what he advised
me. When I proposed it to my director, he answered
if the Saint helped me as he had promised, all would go
well, otherwise, knowing what a writer I was, he thought
it could never be done. However, he bade me begin, at
which I was much troubled.

After this I fell into temptations, and was in great
affliction and anxiety about it. I begged my director
to recall his orders, telling him the many difficulties
which occurred. I apprehended it would disturb my
head and entirely take away my peace of mind, because
I found myself strangely distracted when I went to
consider anything of my life past. I believed I should
never put anything in order, and often thought that if I
wrote anything I should repent it. My director judged
these mere temptations. St. Xaverius had also told me
that the enemy would be very busy in hindering me, and
ordered me to begin to write. I still persuaded myself
that if I could, by representing new difficulties, bring my

director to condescend to me, and excuse me from writing, I should have nothing to answer for, because I was bid to advise with him and follow his directions. He, on the contrary, did what he could to frighten me, and ordered me to make no replies, but accuse myself in confession of my disobedience, and he enjoined me a greater penance than he had done before when I made a general confession of my whole life to him. I was troubled at this, and did not imagine there had been so much harm in it; but I perceived afterwards he only did it to try me. After this he appointed me a day to begin, and bid me write down my first year's sickness, which I did without alleging any further difficulties. I found still repugnance enough, not knowing what to say, yet as soon as I had set pen to paper, I found no more difficulty than if it had been all written before and that I had transcribed it. When I had ended my first year's sickness, my director was desirous to see what I had made of it, and when he had perused it he thought I had been helped by the Saint. He ordered me to continue till my coming to religion, but being soon after this called to Antwerp by his Superiors, he bade me leave off writing and follow the advice of my next director who should succeed him, which I did accordingly. After the manifestation of conscience which I made to him, before I said anything concerning my writing, he advised me to it, and ordered me to write down the favours God had done me. I then told him what I had done, showed him my papers, and was commanded to begin from my childhood, which I did purely in compliance with obedience.

I had now continued writing as far as my cure by St. Xaverius, when I received a letter from my director, who ordered me, without delay, to burn all the papers I had by me. At the same time he let me know that the reason why he permitted me to continue writing so long, was only to try my obedience, adding that if every nun were to write her fancies, we should have pleasant volumes. He also put some very slighting expressions in regard of the papers I had given him to transcribe. This letter gave me great comfort. I immediately burnt all the papers I had, without having a thought to the continuing, or the least repugnance in doing it; but rejoiced to think I had thus employed myself for Almighty God.

Two or three days after, when I had told him that, according to his orders, I had burnt the papers, he bade me again begin from my childhood, as if I had written nothing. Upon this I felt some repugnance at first, yet I began as soon as I could find an opportunity, and thanked God to see'myself employed in writing the same things over again. I had not written half a sheet of paper, when St. Xaverius appeared to me and said I should write no more the same thing over again, and that I had fulfilled my obedience. He seemed highly pleased with me for obeying so readily my director, and with what I had written : telling me he would do as he had promised, indite what I should write, assuring me there should be nothing in it but what was true and for the honour and glory of God. He ordered me to tell my director to go on transcribing without scruple.

I remained for about half an hour in a rapture, without being able to stir my right hand to make a letter, though I endeavoured never so much. The next morning my director called for me, and without knowing what had passed, asked me if I had begun to write again as he had ordered. I told him I had; and upon his demanding it, I showed him what I had written. I had by way of preamble put down the disposition I found myself in upon the fresh orders given me, of writing again; and

c

was just come to begin my life. My director asked me why I had left off there and had not continued it further. I told him St. Xaverius would not let me, and upon further inquiry, I let him know how the Saint had stopped my hand there, saying I had complied with obedience, and I should write no more the same thing.[1]

[1] 'Her director was very much surprised at this, because what the Saint had said was a direct answer to his own thoughts, which he had never made known to her or to anybody else.  He was resolved to try her obedience by bidding her burn what papers she had, and by using several expressions in his letter which showed a great slight of her papers (at the same time he had provided, unknown to her, to keep copies of what she had written).  He also supposed she would, when she began again, write something by way of preamble by which he would be able to judge better of her spirit, but was also resolved to stop her writing as soon as ever she should come to begin her life. And the Saint here, in answer to his thoughts, told her she had complied with obedience, as really she had, because all that he desired was to have her write this preamble.  The Saint also told her to write no more the same preamble again, which was also the design of her director, though he had never made it known to anybody, but had ordered her in general terms to begin her life again.  This made the director always believe that there was something here supernatural, and that Almighty God had revealed his designs to St. Xaverius, who gave these direct answers to his thoughts.  Though what she wrote seemed dictated by the Saint as to the substance, yet the orthography, expressions, and the rest were often very imperfect.  Hence her director took pains to transcribe what she wrote, and in this he was troubled even to a scruple for fear of altering the sense, and the Saint seemed to allude to these troubles of his in bidding him, by her, transcribe without scruple.  When she had ended the first part of her life she added what follows in regard of her writings.'—*Note by the Collector.* [The manuscript from which this volume is printed contains a considerable number of notes like that which has just been given, not all of which need be inserted in the text, many of them being merely reflections or admonitions to the reader, which do not convey any additional information concerning the subject of the *Memoir*.  Such of these notes, on the other hand, which seem to throw real light upon her life, will be either inserted as they stand, or condensed.  It may be added that the notes do not seem to be all by the same person.  There is a statement at the beginning of the first part of her life that they contain 'short remarks made upon her writings by some who had been sometime her directors ; but the reader if he pleases may entirely omit them without interrupting the course of her life.']  The Collector's notes are marked as quotations.  The Editor's are in brackets.

I have now ended what I designed to write, God be praised, and St. Xaverius, who has helped me in this, or, I may say, has done it for me; for though when I went to write I found great difficulty, not knowing what to say, yet when I had offered it to God, and implored the assistance of the Saint, though I was never so distracted and dull, all I was to write was presently laid before me, and I found myself as recollected as in prayer. I never asked leave to be dispensed from any of my spiritual duties on account of writing (only twice from half an hour of reading), neither did I exempt myself from any act of community, nor from the hour allotted for recreation, because I thought the Saint would not have this done. But I took such bye times as I could steal to myself in our cell. I am even amazed to see what I have written in four months time, what I thought would have cost me some years. And when I read over what I have written, it seems as if I had not done it, but as if some one had done it for me, and it gives me new lights to see that, because I undertook it for obedience, God hath helped me. I am ready to burn it all at this moment, if my director thinks fit to bid me, hoping Almighty God will nevertheless accept my poor endeavours in doing what I thought St. Xaverius required of me. If it should be thought fit, after my death, to publish what I have written down, I beg the reader to pray for my soul, for I shall have a much heavier purgatory than if I had died in my sickness, before I came to religion, having now greater cares and obligations upon me in this office of Prioress, in which I beg St. Xaverius to help me as he has done in other things; but I have found the cross very heavy as yet.[2]

---

[2] 'She had a lively sense of the many obligations of Superiors, and of the strict account they were to render to Almighty God for all those committed to their charge, which made her dread Superiority as the

heaviest Cross.  More shall be said of this in its proper place.  As to
her writings in general, whenever they are published, every one will take
the liberty to judge of them as he thinks fit.  Perhaps the following
remark will not be altogether useless to the reader in framing his
judgment.  She had not only the repeated orders of different directors
to authorize what she did in this kind, but they were moreover persuaded that God had sufficiently manifested both to her and to them
that it was His will she should mark down the favours He had done
her, and what confirmed them in this persuasion was the particular
assistance she found from heaven in complying with these orders.  She
declares in several places that as soon as she put pen to paper everything she was to say occurred without study, as if she had been
transcribing something that was laid before her ; and those who knew
the bad state of her health while Superior, and how much she was
taken up at the same time with different employments, cannot but see
it was impossible for anybody in these circumstances to have leisure to
study out such a series of transactions.  It is likewise to be observed
that her director was the only person who knew of her being employed
in writing her life : not one of the Community had any knowledge of
it.  As occasion served, she took bye times for this, in which she was
frequently interrupted, without exempting herself from any religious
duties on this account.  She gave from time to time what she had
written to her director, and so continued writing without having by her
for her direction what she had written.  The reader will find in her
writings such a variety of supernatural favours, such a variety of instructions adapted in these favours to the present state of her soul, that
it seems morally impossible after so many years, without supernatural
help, to retain a distinct knowledge of every particular, as notwithstanding it happened in her case.  She was near thirty years of age
before she put pen to paper ; and considering the multiplicity of favours
she had received before that time, as appears in her writings, what a
confusion it must naturally breed to think of bringing all these into
order with all their circumstances ! and yet I have several times on
purpose put her upon recounting some particular passage which had
happened many years before, and always found her as exact to every
minute circumstance as if she had seen it then transacted before her
eyes—a convincing proof to me that it was not a fiction of her own
head, made at random by the force of imagination and fancy.  This
would have altered sometimes, and by this have discovered itself.  She
was so far disengaged from any tie to herself in her own performance,
that she was perfectly indifferent whether her writings were kept or
not, liked or not liked.  It was this perfect disengagement from herself
which drew Almighty God and her Saint (as she called St. Xaverius) so
near to her, when she was employed by her director in this work.  She
seemed at those times as recollected as when she was actually employed
in prayer.  When, in trial of her obedience, she was ordered sometimes
to write, sometimes to burn what she had written, she received all

these orders with the same sedate calmness of mind, as unconcerned as if it had nothing belonged to her. Her director sometimes slighted what she had written, sometimes seemed to approve it. This pious soul was always the same, reducing to practice what she expressed in words. "Provided God be pleased with what I do, it matters not how I am employed." I observed sometimes that this holy woman had a great difficulty in mentioning the favours she had received from God, and more particularly to think of penning them down ; and nothing but the positive orders of those whom she thought herself bound to obey could ever have prevailed on her to do it. Yet I took notice that when she was obliged to mention or speak of them this had a very different effect in her from what might be expected from those who are less perfect. It was so far from occasioning any motion of pride that it appeared rather a continual subject of humiliation. This was manifest from that ingenuity and sincerity by which (professing herself an instrument of Almighty God, undeservedly favoured by Him) she was moved to continual acts of thanksgiving and praise ; and it was often observed by those to whom she was obliged to mention these favours, that by the repetition of them she was immediately inflamed with the love of God to that degree that she spread those flames of Divine love into the hearts of those who treated with her.'—*Collector.*

## CHAPTER IV.

*Of her infancy. Her inclination to virtue. She relents in the practice of it. She is sensibly moved by Almighty God to begin a new life. Her fidelity to this call. The many penances and practices of piety which she performed in her father's house from this time to her sickness.*

To the greater honour and glory of God, the sacred Virgin, St. Joseph, and St. Xaverius. With you, my God, I can do all things, and without you nothing! In this confidence in you, and distrust of myself, I begin this relation in obedience to my director, though my repugnance is very great and more than I will say.

God did me the favour to be born of virtuous and pious parents. My mother died when I was eight years of age. She left eight children behind her. I was the youngest but three. My father took care to have us brought up to virtue and kept to our prayers morning and evening, besides the time in which the family met at litanies, which were never omitted. To encourage us the more, he promised money to those who best learnt their catechism. I generally carried it, and was more pleased with the credit I gained than any other prize. In my tender years God was pleased to prevent me with His grace and to give me a sensible devotion in my vocal prayers; yet I loved my play, and remember once I had a great conflict in myself, when being at my prayers I heard my playfellows were come, yet God

moved me forcibly to stay and put an end to them.
I think they were some *Paters* and *Aves* in honour of
the Blessed Trinity. I was then about seven years of
age. I was counted wild and higher spirited than my
brothers and sisters, yet when alone I had very serious
thoughts.

My greatest difficulty till I was ten or eleven years
old, was to be obliged to go early to bed with the others.
I used to keep them awake sometimes by telling stories,
though I used to have a scruple of this, thinking it was
not so well done, and in place of it would relate some
passages of the Passion, saying it was a true story. I
was chiefly moved with the whipping at the pillar and
changing of His garments, which I used to explain by
some familiar comparisons. God did thus prevent me
with His grace; but as I grew up, in place of making a
due return, I neglected and slighted it, following too
much my own inclination. As for a mortal sin, I
remember I always had a great fear of it, and prayed
daily to God to deliver me from it; but for venial sin,
I sometimes thought it was no such great matter, and
that I should only be a little longer in Purgatory for it,
miserable and blind creature that I was, thus carried on
by servile fear without a due sense of the injury done to
Almighty God.

From ten or eleven till sixteen, I lived a more sensual
life, following too much the bent of my own passions.
Two or three times on occasion of some words of
humiliation said to me by servants, I found my blood
to rise and myself to tremble with passion, though it was
not my nature to be angry long.

My father, though times were troublesome, never used
to refuse the Fathers of the Society,[1] who resorted much

[1] [At that time there were ten 'Colleges' of the Society in England,
one of which was at Bury St. Edmund's. It was broken up at the
Revolution, 1688.]—ED.

to our house, and used to commend the family for virtue where they went. What I have said, and much more what I could say, in praise of my parents and relations, turns to my own confusion, seeing God gave me so many occasions and examples of virtue, and yet I remained so bad. What should I have done had I been in the frequent occasions of sinning, which many are? This I experienced, being two months absent from my father's house, in which I got much hurt, and this was the occasion of my many faults these five years. Here I lost that tenderness of conscience and devotion which I had, yet I continued for the most part constant in my accustomed prayers, though I performed them with much distraction, and chose places to say them in the window that I might see who passed. God used sometimes to touch my heart with thoughts of eternity; but I did not much regard them, thinking they served to make me sad and melancholy. I loved to be esteemed handsome, though I had a scruple to spend much time in dressing myself as, I thought, some did. I got much harm by conversing with a young gentlewoman of my own age, and committed many faults without knowing them to be faults. I hope God will not impute them to me on account of my ignorance. When she discovered her secrets to me I gave her sometimes good counsel; but I was not inclined to talk of good things as in my tender years.[2]

When I was sixteen years old, I caught the small-pox of my eldest brother. I chose to stay in the house where he lay sick, to accompany one of my sisters who would needs stay with him. I was in great danger

[2] 'She always bewailed her time misspent in these five years, and she understood afterwards that she should have had a severe purgatory had she died about this time. She observes also the great cause of all her failings, namely, her familiarity and conversation with a young woman of her own age of less virtuous principles.'—*Collector.*

of death, and prepared myself for it by confession,
though I was much afraid to die. I thought I saw on
one side of me a remote place of fire and full of confusion, and I thought if I died I should go to it. I
have had a particular light, since I came to religion,
that if I had died then I should have had a long and
tedious purgatory. I was in this sickness little sensible
of Almighty God, excepting two or three times, at which
I had a lively apprehension of another world; but I had
methought no friends or acquaintance to speak for me,
nor had I endeavoured to gain any. When I recovered
this sickness and a relapse into which I fell, I continued
a tepid life, though I do not remember I did any bad
thing. Some time after I took a liking to devotion and
to some little practices I found in a book in order to
preparation for death. I used to be serious when I
prepared for the sacraments, which was commonly once
a month, adding over-night some extraordinary prayers
to this effect; yet through ignorance, pride, or bashfulness,
I satisfied myself with a persuasion it was not necessary
to confess several things, which God gave me light of
about a year after the sickness I spoke of. I remember
I was one day in a chamber where the chapel was set up,
neither praying, reading, or thinking of God as I know
of, on a sudden I had a light of something of my life
past which I had never confessed. I thought our Blessed
Lord stood on my right hand in mean apparel like one
wearied out with seeking me. I found a great remorse
of conscience and an alteration over my whole body.
I went to the upper end of the room and cast myself
on my knees before the altar, bewailing my sins and
making a firm purpose to confess them at the first
opportunity. I shall only add that, by the grace of God,
I confessed them on the first occasion, as I had resolved,
and from that time began to change my life.

From this time I began to change my life, being
moved with a desire to do penance for what was past.
I was carried on to contradict my inclinations in all
things, and sought how to mortify myself in sitting,
walking, and the like. I loved to fast, and when I ate
I took what I liked worst. In Lent that year I passed
sometimes the whole day taking nothing but some
unsavoury pottage, which I made others believe I found
wholesome. At night, for collation, I used to take a
piece of dry household bread and seek out some dead
beer to drink. Sometimes I ate as the rest, but then
very sparingly. I took great delight once a week to
read the advices of our holy Mother St. Teresa, which
were commonly found in the manuals, without ever
reflecting whether there were any religious of that Order.
I endeavoured to follow her advice as near as I could,
yet I thought it very hard at first not to eat nor drink
but at the ordinary hours of dinner and supper, and to
forbear fruit, which was a great mortification. It often
came into my mind how Adam was overcome by eating
an apple, so I thought I was inspired by Almighty God
to mortify my appetite in these things, I endeavoured
not to let myself be overcome by temptation which
carried me to that which was less perfect.

I was thus carried on, as I may say, by a strong
impulse of Almighty God the year before my sickness,
yet I cannot say I found any sensible devotion that
year; but I had a great desire to please God, to follow
His inspiration, and not offend Him willingly in anything. I was so ignorant as not to consult my Confessor
in anything; but thought I might freely mortify myself
or do what I thought good, without further leave. Nay,
I believed it humility to let nobody know what I did
in that kind. This persuasion I always had till I came
to religion, and I think this simplicity was pleasing

to God because I knew no better. So I went on following the Divine inspirations, as I thought, and did often sit up all night, after the rest were in bed, in prayer, making adoration, and doing penances. It was then a greater mortification to kneel one hour than it is now to kneel five, because prayer was tedious to me, neither could I pray mentally, yet in my vocal prayers I had some sort of meditation. I would sometimes rise in the night as soon as I was awake and kneel down by my bedside, without putting on my clothes, though the weather was very cold. At other times I would go in the evening when it began to grow dark into an orchard and field nigh the house: there I would make stations, walking them so many times in honour of the Passion, so many in honour of the Blessed Trinity; sometimes without my shoes, prostrating myself upon the ground in imitation of our Blessed Saviour. Though the weather was cold and the ground covered with snow, this did not stop me when I thought myself moved by God. I followed the inspiration, first making my intention that I did it for the love of God.

My greatest difficulty was from the apprehension I had of being alone in the dark, and there was talk of the appearance of some evil spirit nigh one of the places I frequented. When I came to this place I used to be seized with great fear, and once I saw a light in the place before me, yet I went on with confidence in God, and resolution to recover myself. I was under great apprehensions, imagining still it was nigher me, yet the more I overcame myself the more help and courage I found. I came downstairs after the others were in bed, and stole out at the door to go to these my devotions; at first I found great repugnance when moved to these things, but as soon as I had resolved to go on for God's sake I found it easier than I expected. In the day I quitted company, and hid myself in some corner of the house, among the straw, there to pray. I received great grace and strength in my soul from these practices; I cannot say I found much sensible devotion. I took delight this year in reading the life of St. Catharine of Siena, though I read nowhere these practices I made use of. I used, in imitation of her, when I went up and down stairs, to say some *Ave Marias* and kiss the ground: I believe, some fifty times a day, without ever knowing that religious persons or others did this; it was a satisfaction when I came to religion to see it was the common custom at our kneeling and rising up. What I had practised in the world, made all things in religion easy to me. There I am animated by the example of others, whereas my great difficulty in the world was lest I should be seen.

I went often to pray in the garden, in imitation of our Saviour's prayer, to which mystery I much was devoted. As I was once kneeling down in an alley to make my adorations, I thought that some of the house were watching to see what I did. I was much confounded to think what they would say of me, and had some thoughts to give over for that time; but I seemed to hear a voice which said, 'They that will confess Me before men, I will confess them before My Father Who is in heaven.' This gave me courage to go through with what I had designed. After this I would choose to do things on purpose to be despised and contemned, and would make these adorations in the open field, in the daytime, where people passed, so that I wondered many times that I was not the talk of the town and country. Yet I never knew anybody speak of it except a Protestant neighbour: he had seen me as I walked often kneel down and kiss the ground, lifting up my hands and eyes to heaven. I had that day been visiting some poor sick body, for now I took great delight in serving the poor myself at the door, and privately carrying things to their houses.

I had more liberty in this than ordinary at that time, because my eldest sister, who since my mother's death had kept my father's house, and taken care of us who were younger, was for the most part absent, at which time my father left all to me, as being the eldest at home. Before this year I should have been glad to play the mistress; but now I employed myself in the meanest offices of the house, studying how to humble and mortify myself. I would sometimes dress myself in a contemptible manner to be laughed at; but in this dress had much difficulty to appear even among the servants, yet I used to consider how our Blessed Lord appeared in Herod's court and this gave me some courage to overcome my pride. Many times when I dressed myself as my other sisters did, I would lace myself so strait that my stays were more painful to me than any chain I have worn since I came to religion. I sometimes pulled off some of my own clothes to give them to the poor, and saved for them what I should have eaten myself; considering in them the person of Jesus Christ, I found joy to deprive myself of anything for them.

After I had practised these mortifications about a year, for want of a director, I fell into anxiety and disquiet, fancying it was a sin if I did not do whatever came into my mind which was against my inclination. I found after some time my head much disturbed and almost half turned. This did not continue long till notice was taken of it, and my father acquainted me with it: he called me one day alone and told me I must do nothing of mortification without leave of my con-

fessor. I was much out of countenance, yet answered
not a word. I thought but of obedience to him. I was
to acquaint my confessor with something, and after my
next confession, not without great difficulty, asked
whether I might not dress and do some other things
to be despised; but I believe he had been informed
by others of my proceedings, for he charged me to do
nothing which should be taken notice of, but conform
myself in my dress to my other sisters. As to the occasion of my scruple, he bade me omit things on purpose
when they occurred with anxiety as if I were obliged
to them. He counselled me to make half-an-hour of
prayer or meditation every day. For mortification he
bade me when others spoke peevishly to me suffer it
patiently and say nothing, and when I fell into any fault,
give myself a pinch in the arm, or some such penance;
when I desired to hear things out of curiosity, to deprive
myself of that satisfaction for the love of God, and the like.

I heard this counsel very patiently, and had practised
these things before, yet I would not tell him so, but
resolved to do so as near as I could, just as he bade me,
though as he told me, I believed him, it was no sin
not to curb my inclinations in everything, and to do
what occurred to me the most hard; yet I thought that
having the apprehension that it was a sin I was obliged
to follow it, and if I did not I should sin. This put
me into great anxiety and confusion, but by resolving to
obey I soon overcame the temptation, as now I see it
was one, though then I thought all were inspirations that
moved me to anything against myself.

After I recovered my peace of mind, which was about
Easter, before my sickness (this happened the August
following), I settled myself with some order. I read my
meditation every day or over night, fixed half an hour in
the morning or evening for it, and went into a little

closet or oratory, where I turned down my hour glass :
yet I was for most part very dry, and would often look
if the glass was out. I rather made it a study than a
prayer, and thought it a fault to make any colloquy
between or speak to our Lord till I had done, then
I said a prayer appointed by my confessor. I was glad
when the half hour was out, for then I thought I was at
liberty to say my vocal prayers. I had a devotion to
say every Saturday the Little Office of the Immaculate
Conception of our Blessed Lady, and the Litanies of
St. Joseph. I had a particular devotion to this saint.
I continued to give alms and was sparing in my diet.

I had now a vocation to be a religious, though I knew
not well what religion was, but I thought it much harder
than now I find it. I made my desire known to my
father. He, like a wise man would do nothing rashly,
but bade me consider of it. My greatest difficulty was to
leave my father, brothers, and sisters, whom I loved
passionately, but for any other love I thank God I never
knew what it was. I spoke of being religious by way of
discourse to my confessor. I never properly treated
with him of any spiritual things, excepting the first time
that my father bade me, neither did I give him any
account how I put in practice what he appointed. I
thought it sufficient to do what he ordered, though
without doubt he would have helped me much in my
way of prayer, but I think God would have me go on
in my ignorance till He taught me Himself, for if I had
thought it better to acquaint him, I should have done it.

I had a great desire this year and afterwards to correspond with the grace of God, and to do what I thought
He inspired me, though never so contrary to nature and
inclination. My confessor did not encourage me in
my desire of being a nun, so I laid aside all thoughts of
it till my cure, as I shall set down afterwards. He was a

virtuous man of the Society of Jesus. I have seen him
once since I came to religion; I spoke to him about
spiritual things, and was very free with him in declaring
the favours God had done me; he had the humility to
say afterwards he had not found himself so much moved
to the service of God in many years, either by his studies
or anything else as by talking with some innocent nuns
the short time he had been in these parts. Since I came
to religion God has given me a clear light that it was
more humility to declare to my director all that He has
done for me, and forced me to do by His grace, than to
conceal it, seeing all the good comes from Him, and
that I have nothing of my own but sin and imperfection,
and I can never enough admire how He drew me on by
His powerful grace in these my first beginnings, more
than by sweetness of devotion, for I knew not what
consolation in prayer was, but was carried on by a
vehement desire to please God and follow His inspirations. The devil did often disquiet me, and cast me
into anxiety, so that I count this year altogether much
harder than any year of my sickness following, and take
it as a preparation for what was to come, or else my
sickness would have been much harder to me, but then I
thought I had nothing to do but take patiently what
God sent me.

If anything I have said here be well, or what may give
your reverence a true light of me, I think my obligation
greater to my dear saint who has done all for me, in
whose name I begin and end this—'dear St. Xaverius.'

## CHAPTER V.

*Her first year's sickness and violent convulsions.*
*She is inspired for the love of God to offer it up*
*and obey all those about her. She animates herself*
*with the thoughts of the Passion. She is taught by*
*Almighty God that suffering is the road to heaven.*
*Our Saviour appears carrying His Cross to encou-*
*rage her. Her violent convulsions in her head. She*
*offers all to Almighty God. Strange symptoms of*
*her malady. She addresses herself to God in her*
*greatest extremity. She finds comfort in prayer.*

In the nineteenth year of my age, I was taken with a
violent sickness which held me in all seven years wanting
two months, but sometimes with much moderation or
else I could not have lived; nay, my confessor said, my
living so long was no less a miracle than my cure. I
was first taken suddenly with a giddiness in my head
and violent pains in my stomach. My aunt, an experienced woman, who took a tender care of us, put me
presently to bed, and gave me something to drive the
sickness from my heart, upon this my face and body
broke out into red spots, which they took to be measles.
A nurse was sent for who used to tend those in that
distemper. I kept my bed one day after, but being
desirous to rise, and those about me little apprehending
the consequence, I did, but the distemper striking immediately to my heart, I was put to bed again, and

D

had several cordials given me to drive out the spots, but all in vain, excepting only that four or five would by fits appear on my hands. I continued so fourteen days, in a high fever, very sick and faint, shut up in a separate room with a nurse, lest the distemper should communicate itself to my brothers and sisters.

My father, who was fond of us all, would not let me want for doctors, had not the nurse, desiring to try her own skill (as God would have it for my greater good), concealed from him and my aunt the danger I was in, making them both believe I should soon recover. She gave me many exercises of patience, her own house being in the same town she would go secretly away and leave me whole hours alone, which I thought very hard, not being accustomed to sickness. But God inspired me to make good use of this mortification, for I do not remember that I ever complained of her or showed any displeasure to her at her return ; I believe I mortified myself in this, being naturally very hot. When she saw I did not mend, she was resolved to try her skill further, and gave me remedies which struck the distemper (that had lain before in my blood), into the nerves, as the doctor said afterwards, and this was the beginning of all my sickness. If I offered to stand, I shook in that violent manner, as if every joint would have separated from each other. When my father heard and saw this he was amazed and affrighted. He sent for one of the best doctors of those parts, who affirmed that he never saw the like in all his life, and was of opinion that all proceeded from the wrong remedies the nurse had applied.

I was inspired in the beginning of my sickness to make a firm resolution to obey the doctor, nurses, and all about me for the love of God. Though the remedies were painful, and what I thought I had found by experience to do me harm, yet I did not positively refuse any the whole time of my sickness. This resolution, I think, was highly pleasing to God, and moved Him to heap blessings upon me. The doctor began with bitter potions, sweats, vomits, bleeding, and Spanish flies applied to my neck, arms, and legs. I fell into violent convulsions, which continued that whole year in great extremity, and was become so weak as not to be able to go, stand, or sit up in bed. Sometimes I shook in so violent a manner that it not only made the bed and room shake, but even the glass windows rattle, as I have been told by them that were about me. At other times my joints would turn out of their places, and snap so loud that the noise was heard all over the room, and in my father's closet at the further end of it. When they begged him at night, after his devotions, to go to bed, he used to say he would not go till my bones had done snapping. Thus I used to continue for hours together. Sometimes the bones in my shoulders would turn out of their place, and rise upon my breast, as they would say that assisted me and did endeavour to hold them. There was scarce any bone in my body remaining in its place. When these fits were over they used to swathe my wrists and ankles with fillets, for I found myself so weak as not to be able to lift a spoon to my mouth. Sometimes I was stretched out so violently as if somebody had stood at the feet of my bed, and endeavoured to pull me limb from limb. This pain was extreme, and would make me cry aloud, though I did not find myself more impatient by it.

God would often bring to my mind in those extremities something of His Passion and what He suffered when stretched upon the Cross. This moved me to great courage, and a desire to suffer much more, wishing I could have taken part of those pains and scourges inflicted on Him. Yet sometimes God was pleased to leave me to myself. Then I used to think my pains long and tedious, and be moved to impatience towards those about me. If they brought me anything ungrateful to my taste, I was moved to reject it in anger; but God gave me grace to overcome that by endeavouring not to show any dislike. My stomach was so weak in the beginning of my illness, and I had such a loathing of flesh, broth, and eggs, that the very naming of meat was almost enough to cast me into a swoon. I remember once my father entreated me to try if I could not eat some light meat, and to comply with him I was resolved to try; but as soon as it was set before me I swooned away, and they were obliged to carry it out of the room, that I might not so much as perceive the smell of it. My stomach remained so by fits all the time of my sickness, and when at the best it was very weak, and I could take little.

When I had been thus some months, one night, as I was in great recollection, I thought I saw a long lane, so full of thorns and bushes that there was no place or path to pass through. I thought those who had the courage to venture into it must be grievously torn with the thorns, and stopped by the way in a place where there was no comfort. It was at the same time made known to me that this was the road to heaven, and that I was in it, which was a great comfort to me, and it often comes into my mind. Another time, I think not long after, quite tired out with convulsions and desiring to lie still a little, I saw our Blessed Saviour, by my bed's foot, go across the chamber laden with a heavy cross. I cried out so loud that those who were by heard me and thought I raved, 'There is my Saviour: I will go help Him,' and I think I made some offer to rise up in my bed; but I was in great devotion, and found by this, great joy in

my sufferings. I kept this to myself and imparted it to
nobody, not even to my ghostly father. He was a
virtuous and learned man, and at that time Superior of
the Society in those parts. I loved him, and was free
with him in anything concerning my sins; but I thought
it was contrary to humility and not necessary to tell him
the favours God did me. I shall speak more of this
hereafter.

Finding no good from the present doctor, and my
father hearing of a famous one who dealt in chemistry,
made him be consulted, though he lived a hundred miles
off. Father Stafford,[1] my confessor, wrote him a relation
of my sickness, and he sent several spirits, but disap-
proved of any further blistering or bleeding. The first
thing he gave me drew the distemper from all parts of
my body into my head, which was his design. When
these convulsions seized my head, my aunt, who held it
with all her force, thought it would have split asunder.
I went out of myself, and used to rave, but all my discourse was of heaven and pious things. Father Stafford
told me I made them fervent exhortations, and that I
could not speak so well when out of these fits. I knew
very well what I said, and remember still I talked of
eternity and the contempt of this world, what a fine place
heaven was, and what a desire I had to be there. I
found my heart elevated with what I spoke of, and much
moved to devotion, neither did I feel any pain at those
times, but was all in cold sweats. When I came out of
these fits they often asked me where I had learned all
these fine things, saying they had sat down to hear me.
I was much confounded at this, to think I could have

---

[1 Father Nathanael Stafford, *alias* Phillips, was Superior of the
College of the Holy Apostles of the Society, which included the
district of Suffolk, in the time of James II. He died at St. Omers,
October 10th, 1697.]—ED.

nothing in my heart but what I spoke, so as to make it known to all, whilst I concealed it from my confessor. Upon this I made strong resolutions never to speak so any more, but I often broke my purposes. The shaking in my head was so violent that, as I have been told, it would continue eleven hours together, during which time they could not hold it still, so long as to give me anything to moisten my mouth, which used to be very dry with these pains. I felt my neck ache as if some bone had slipt out of its place. My head was very light, yet I could think of God and offer up to Him my sufferings, and I thought I lay in great solitude and recollection. They say I used to sing as they do in churches. I could never sing before or since.

After they had tried these remedies some weeks, and found I grew worse by them, they had recourse again to my first doctor. He, by the advice of another, began to bleed and blister me again ; but now no plasters would take place on my feet or legs, but put me to a great deal of pain, tore off the skin, and burnt up the flesh without drawing any blisters. They often took them off, renewed them, and rubbed the places with vinegar, which put me in mind of something the martyrs suffered. When they could fasten them nowhere else, they ordered the top of my head to be shaved, and a strong blister to be laid there, to draw out what the chemist had drawn into my head. After some hours this put me to intolerable pain. I did not ask to have it taken off; but my aunt and others seeing the torture I was in, removed it. I endeavoured to endure it with all the patience I could, and to think of the crown of thorns. It would be endless to name all the different remedies applied. I endeavoured to take all for the love of God, only this I remember, when they were to give me a certain quantity of something to take every two or three hours, I would make them believe I was asleep to avoid taking it. I cannot say I found relief from anything but bleeding in the arm, and the doctor seeing nothing else would do, was forced to try this. After, therefore, I had kept my bed six or seven months in this violent sickness, they bled me nine or ten times in the space of seven weeks, and never took less than eight or ten ounces at a time : only twice they could not draw so much from me. This bleeding eased me for the time, but weakened me much, and after a short time I felt as bad as ever.

It is endless to observe the different symptoms of my distemper. Sometimes my sinews were all drawn up on a heap, and then stretched out again, as if I had been upon the Cross. Sometimes I had such oppressions in my stomach that I was almost stifled, insomuch that they were obliged often at midnight to open the windows to give me air. My breast on these occasions seemed as if it would burst open, and I had violent beatings in my left side. I remained so several hours together without intermission, struggling for breath. I became an object of compassion to all that beheld me. I do not remember that I spoke any impatient word in these extremities, but complained to God aloud, when I was able to speak, in these and the like prayers, 'O my all-powerful Father, if I must needs drink of this bitter chalice, endure this long and tedious sickness, suffer these sharp torments, Your will be done.' Then with St. Paul I would say, when the fits were coming on, 'Lord, what would You have me to do? What is Your pleasure? Behold Your servant ready to accomplish it.' By these prayers I used to find myself raised to great courage, particularly when I found myself dejected, by this—

What dreadest thou, my fearful and faithless heart? Behold Christ, thy Captain and thy King, is gone before thee : take up thy Cross and follow Him. He leads to

a kingdom.  Heaven is worth thy pains.'  Sometimes I
was sunk so low after the violent shakings, and lay for
three hours, so that they could find no life in me, neither
by pulse, breath, or any other sign, that they often said
I was dead, and it was reported in the town.  But I
remember very well I heard them talk and pray about
me.  I seemed to myself to be closely united to God,
and lay in prayer and contemplation.  I found no pain,
only my hands lying upon my breast oppressed me, but
I could not remove them nor stir a finger.  When I
came out of these fits I found myself very much defeated,
but in great peace and tranquillity of mind.  Some said
I was bewitched, but all the doctors agreed there was
nothing but what proceeded from natural causes, though
they never saw any before come to that extremity.  The
prayers of the Church were often read over me, and
witch-water used ; but it pleased God that nothing should
do me any good.

# CHAPTER VI.

*Her pains augmented by new remedies. Her patience.*
*She lies for a month speechless. Her pains, patience,*
*resignation, and prayer during this time. Our*
*Saviour encourages her to suffer. She falls into*
*great anxieties. Resigning herself to God, her*
*pains are abated. She recovers in part, after a*
*year's sickness.*

My father, a man of great virtue and resignation to the
will of God, was much troubled to see me to continue
so without any relief. After I had lain nine months,
he was advised of a French doctoress lately come into
England, and who was famous for many cures. It was
said she had cured one of my distemper. All thought
this woman was sent by God for my health. My father
immediately sent for her. When she saw me, she said I
was very weak, yet she doubted not but she should do
me good. My father took her into the house for a
fortnight or three weeks. I cannot be precise as to the
time, yet it seemed to me very long. The very looks of
her at first affrighted me, yet I called to mind the
resolution made of obeying all for the love of God. She
put me into a course of physic, as if I had never taken
anything. She gave me strong vomits, and after that
endeavoured to keep me in continual sweats, the windows
shut and a fire in the room, and many clothes heaped
upon me, and this in very hot and faint weather in
the month of May. When my convulsions came upon

me and I began to shake, she chid me for having caught
cold : upon this, she would pin the bedclothes to my
pillow as high as my head. If my aunt and sister had
not relieved me, I think I should have been stifled.
I took all she gave me, though never so bitter and
ungrateful, but my stomach could not long retain anything, it being so weak, and all she gave me being
so unsavoury. I begged often they would send her
away, for I found she did not understand my disease,
but put me to much pain and torment, yet I resolved to
obey her as long as she stayed.

It was God's will she should still remain to exercise
my patience. One morning she gave me something, as
she said, to make me spit, for the doctor thought I was
too weak for vomits ; but two hours after I was so sick,
that I believe I shall not feel more in the agony of death,
than I felt that day with vomiting. Some called out to
me to pardon the woman, for they thought she had
killed me. So well as I could speak I answered, ' with
all my heart,' for I had no ill-will against her. This
vomiting continued twenty-four hours in great extremity.
Nobody knew what to do with me, because they knew
not what she had given me. As soon as I had taken it,
she went into the fields, and appeared no more till she
heard I was a little revived. I believe some had met
her before she came to me, for she was in a great passion,
and chid me for complaining so much, and making
people believe she had killed me. My spirits were too
low to feel any motion of anger or the least disquiet of
what she said. She was found after this to be a cheat,
who went about the country and knew nothing of physic.
God sent her for my exercise of patience, for I was never
so truly mortified, in all kinds, in my whole sickness,
but God gave me a great deal of patience to bear it,
and I cannot say I had ever any ill-will against her.

Father Stafford brought me a piece of the true Cross, which they say had wrought a miracle, for they thought I could not be cured other ways. When I saw it, I felt a great joy in my soul; but God had designed I should suffer more before I had a miracle wrought on me, for I found then no relief. Awhile after this woman left me, I lay a month and some days sleepless, without being able to speak one word or swallow anything but only once in twenty-four hours. After midnight I used to fall into a gentle slumber for less than a quarter of an hour, then if nothing interrupted me till I awoke of myself, I had power to swallow for above half a quarter of an hour. What I commonly took was either beer or ale syllabub, neither had I any other nourishment all that while, only once I think I tried to take part of a caudle. I cannot express what I suffered this month by reason of my great weakness, and the want I found of something to refresh me in the continual and excessive thirst I endured.

The convulsions were now more inward, with trembling and rattling in my throat, fainting, beating of my heart. They say I used to be many days without so much as opening of my eyes, so that they thought my eye-strings were broken. They who came to visit me (many came by reason of the novelty) would say, "certainly she is dead." All pitied me, and I became the talk of the town. I was perfectly sensible and understood all that was said and done, though I could neither speak nor move. It was one of my greatest troubles to see my father and friends concerned for me, for they saw what I suffered outwardly, but did not know the inward joy and comfort I had, which was beyond whatever I found in my life. I learnt by experience that the less of human comfort I had, the more I had of Divine.

The year before my sickness, I endeavoured to use

mental prayer, but found no gust in it; but now God gave me the gift of contemplation, for although my body was on earth, my thoughts and conversation were for the most part in heaven. I had a great light of the other world, and what this was is something more than I can express. Yet sometimes I had a feeling of what I suffered, but at the same time did rejoice in it. I remember two or three times I felt a raging hunger, which went beyond all my other pains, I thought I could have eaten anything, yet ,I remember I said this to our Lord in my heart: 'I give You thanks, O Lord, for making me so like Yourself, Who suffered hunger in the desert, and thirst upon the Cross; if I had before me all the dainties in the world and had passage to swallow them, I would not touch them if it was made known to me that it was not Your will.' I found such a joy in this resignation (methought our Lord was near me) that in a short time my stomach was as well as if I had eaten. I do not remember in this month's time that I found myself moved to impatience or that I had any trouble of mind. My confessor, Father Stafford, was now taken up in the Chapel of Bury, in King James' time, so that he could only come to me once or twice a week. He communicated me often, so great was his confidence, that although I could neither swallow before nor after, yet if I gave him some sign while he knelt by me with the Blessed Sacrament, he would always give It me, and I had no difficulty to swallow It. Once I remember I could not give the sign he desired, nor receive, which he told me was a trial sent by Almighty God. My communicating was looked upon as a great favour which God did me, and I was ordered to specify it, if ever I wrote anything which happened to me. After I communicated, I found a great desire to die, and what my confessor at those times used to say encouraged me.

He animated me to suffer with the hopes that I should go straight to heaven; and he told me, though I lived forty years, I should never be better prepared. I believed him, thinking, as he was a virtuous man, he knew more of the mercies of God than I did. I used to lie down and think what I would do first when I came to heaven, and methought I would cast myself at our Lord's feet and embrace them.

Once in this month's time, as I lay in great pain, I thought I saw our Blessed Saviour standing at my bed's feet, elevated as it were from the ground, but as He was conversing in the world. He spoke these words to me: 'Those that are My greatest friends, I send greatest sufferings to,' and He brought in for example His Blessed Mother, who He said though she never committed sin, yet had suffered most. This was a great comfort to me, and I remember it as perfectly as if it had happened yesterday. At this month's end, I fell into great desolation and anxiety, thinking how long I had been in this condition, and how long I might lie in it, for I had my senses perfectly well all that time. God had now withdrawn His hand, and left me to my own weakness. My life seemed insupportable. This lasted but a while, and God moved me to make strong resolutions to suffer as long as He pleased. As soon as I had made these acts of resignation, I thought my good angel spoke to me with an interior voice, making it known that God was satisfied and well pleased with the acts I made, and that I should soon find a change. I was well pleased with this, for I thought I should soon die, and within an hour I fell into a violent agony, every one imagined they saw in me the signs of death, and Father Stafford was sent for to give me the last absolution. After I had remained thus two or three hours, I began to revive, and found on a sudden I could both speak and swallow. My father and friends were all surprised, but thought me not out of danger. Father Stafford thought it was a lightening before death, and bade me not think of living. I told him I did not think I should die then; to which he replied smiling, if I lived and recovered it would be a miracle, and said I should be a religious, though I do not remember I had any such thoughts then. I fell sick in August, and on the 3rd of August following I revived, the violence of my pain abated, and I began to take some nourishment, but continued excessively weak, and it was a long time before I could be removed out of my bed to have it made.

### CHAPTER VII.

*She passes the four years following in a languishing condition as to her state of health, and with great desolation, yet a perfect resignation to the will of God. She is seized again with a violent sickness that she suffered by dangerous imposthumes for three months. Her resignation to them. She is reduced to death's door. The great difficulty she had in resigning herself to live longer.*

I HAVE little to add of these four years following. I was all that time as I may say continually rising and falling, and never without some pain and infirmity. I had frequent agues and fevers, and sometimes such extremity of pain in my head that I was not able to hold it up. The whole time I was not well enough to come down above ten or twelve times to the table, and seldom in a condition to take a little air in the garden, the least forcing myself in this kind would so defeat me that I was often obliged to cast myself upon my bed to recover my strength. When I consider all things, I think I suffered as much the time I was in this languishing condition as when I was in the greatest extremity, my pains these four years were increased by the state I found my soul in. It pleased Almighty God to subtract that abundance of sweetness I had felt in my great sickness. I was chiefly now led on in desolation, and great anxieties would sometimes seize me. I was then, I thought, without any sense of Almighty God, fearing He had abandoned me. These troubles, with a darkness of faith, would almost entirely oppress my mind, neither was I accustomed to discover these temptations to my ghostly father. My prayer was commonly without much consolation, yet I had for the most part a great resignation to the will of God, and great contempt of the world. I was moved to bear my sufferings in silence without complaint, and I found by mortifying myself in this point great quiet of mind and satisfaction. My sufferings were much augmented by the hardness of the times; for in the Revolution in which King James was cast out of his kingdom, the storm which threatened all Catholics fell very heavy upon us, and our house was pillaged to that degree they left us not so much as a chair or a bed, excepting one which escaped their knowledge. In the weak condition I was in I had much to suffer.

After this I fell into another grievous fit of sickness, which lasted a year and a half, in which I was altogether confined to my bed. As in the former it seemed much more strange and extraordinary I should hold out, because my natural constitution appeared to doctors and others entirely broken. I was not only reduced to skin and bone, but my entrails seemed by all apparent signs tainted and consumed. In November I began to fall into great extremity. Imposthumes in my head which

put me to great torment before they broke, that not
being able to lay my head upon the pillow, I spent the
night sitting in my bed and groaning through extremity
of pain. When I was in this torment I was often afraid
of losing patience for that I had scarce power to master
my thoughts, yet I used to be often saying, ' Lord, Your
will be done, grant me patience, and unite these pains to
Your suffering Passion.' But I said these words many
times with anxiety of soul and body, with little devotion,
having scarce sense of what I said. God prevented me
from speaking any impatient word the whole time of my
sickness as I remember.

The imposthumes continued all the winter, for as soon
as they healed up on one side by the remedies applied
they gathered on the other. Once in particular, when I
found myself at ease, I was taken out of bed to have
it made. I took great content to think I should lie that
night easily, but before I got to bed such violent pain
seized me as if one of my teeth were torn out of my
head, and from thence the humours gathering together
raged so furiously the whole night that I took no delight
in my soft bed, neither could I lay my head down. My
father and sisters sat by me the whole time, fearing I
should not live till morning. At midnight a priest was
sent for, though they thought I should die before he
arrived, for they said if the imposthume broke inwardly
it would immediately kill me, and it did little less, for it
broke before morning, and the blood and corruption fell
in such quantities down my throat that all thought it
would choke me, but yet a greater quantity discharged
itself by my ears. I think I was almost senseless,
though I had endeavoured before to prepare myself by
acts of contrition and resigning myself into the hands of
God, yet I desired very much to have a priest by me
when I died, and I prayed many years for that blessing.

The next day I came a little to myself, but my head was in such disorder and so weak, that I could not endure to hear anybody speak in the room, though in a low voice, yet I found myself very recollected and united to God in prayer. In this condition I lay with some interruption between, till the February following, when my fever increased to a high degree, and my body swelled half way up my stomach, insomuch that it was troublesome for me to bear the bedclothes. The doctor then thought I could not hold out long, and that I should no more deceive him, hence he ordered me the Last Sacraments out of hand. I received them with all the preparation I could make, rejoicing to think my end was so near. In this condition I lay twelve or fourteen days, my fever increasing, my strength decreasing, so as I could not turn myself in bed, nor lift up my head from the pillow, neither did I care to trouble others so often, though it was an excessive pain to keep always in the same posture.

As I lay one night in great solitude, particularly giving thanks to God for preserving me all this time from the convulsions I had felt in my former sickness, which were then most difficult for me, not only for the pain but also because I could not enjoy that solitude I desired, seeing several were to be about me to hold my joints in their places; as I was thinking upon this, it was made known to me by an interior voice as coming from my good angel, in these words which I cannot alter : ' What if you should have these fits return again ? you must resign yourself.' At first I was surprised, but soon offered myself to it if it were God's will. I understood by this that my fits would return, and I often prepared myself for them, but I said nothing of this to anybody. A fortnight or three weeks after, when I seemed quite

E

spent with the fever, Father Ireland,[1] who was then my
confessor, used to come often to prepare me for death
My father had disposed all things for my funeral, as I
understood afterwards, and bespoke a place for my
burial.    I dreamt, as I thought, about that time, that
I was in the churchyard looking about for a place where
I should be, but methought there was no place for me
there.    I suppose this must have been a dream, but I
could never imagine what made my head run upon any
such thing.    I lay after this manner two or three days,
like one drawing towards an end, every one expected
each day would be the last of my life.

The last of these three nights went beyond whatever I
felt before, being in such extremity in all parts of my
body and such anguish of mind that nothing can come
nigher the pangs of death.    My confessor stayed by me,
but I was not able to speak to him.    In the morning he
said Mass in the chamber, after which I fell into a strong
agony.    I could not draw my breath without excessive
pain, and that short, with rattling in my throat ; my senses
failed me by times, not knowing what they did about me,
but I soon returned to myself again, and with great
fervour of spirit rejoicing to find my soul expiring—I
expected every moment to be presented before Almighty
God.    I lay there hours, as I was told afterwards, in this
condition, among the prayers of my father and friends
who read the recommendation of the soul; my ghostly
father gave me several times absolution expecting every
time would.be the last.    I also by fits, moved with fervour,
prayed aloud with a love that moved the hearers.    I
remember perfectly this act from my heart : ' My God, I

---

[1] [Francis Ireland, born in 1656, entered the Society, 1675.  He was
serving in the College of the Holy Apostles, either at Ipswich or Bury
St. Edmunds, and was seized at the Revolution (1688) and confined in
Ipswich gaol.]—ED.

am sorry from my heart that I have ever offended You, not for fear of hell or hopes of heaven, but only and chiefly because You are my God.'

I desired my confessor to tell some whom I knew to have a great apprehension of death, that it was not so hard as they thought if they served God and lived well. I was moved to say this, though I found great difficulty and pain. Soon after this I lost my speech, my hands grew stiff and cold and quite without feeling, so that my confessor bade them go on with the recommendation of the soul, saying my hands were dead. I heard him, and found it true, which gave me new courage and joy in my soul; methought I was desirous to look death in the face, and would willingly have looked upon my hands to have seen them turned to clay, but I had not force to stir my eyes; thus my soul seemed forced out of my body by a strong agony, and they say my senses failed me. I cannot express in what a light all things of this world appeared to me at that time, how contemptible in themselves. I seemed presented to our Blessed Saviour, Who looked upon me as a meek and mild Judge, with a sweet and gracious countenance, as in His Humanity. He seemed coming towards me, even over my bed, which I believe is the place where every one is judged as soon as the breath is out of their body. My sisters say they thought once I was dead, yet I do not think my soul was separated from my body; it seems to me as present as what passed yesterday. I thought, I say, that I saw our Blessed Saviour stand like one considering whether He should take my soul out of my body or no, or like one who had designed a thing but was held back by the importunities of others, and after some consideration thought best to let that alone which He had designed. This disappeared, and I returned to myself again, to the admiration of all that saw me, and to my great affliction.

I had much ado to resign myself when I thought all would have been concluded and finished, and to see myself return again to the prison of my body with all its miseries seemed a sad thing, but yet I hope my impatience was not so great as to offend God much, neither was I come to that perfection to desire to die only to see and enjoy Almighty God and to be freed from the occasions of offending Him.

My ghostly father did all he could to comfort me, and he thought by reason of my weakness I could not hold out long; but I told him since I had escaped this bout I could not think I should die. My friends rejoiced at my recovery, but said I would willingly have gone from them. I could not dissemble the matter, for so I would. I felt not the trouble of leaving them, as in my first sickness. I resigned myself to suffer and live, though to this day I have a feeling of it, and cannot write this relation without some interruption of tears, seeing myself still in this banishment and exile, who so long ago saw myself so near enjoying God, all my good. I had not then anything in particular which troubled my conscience, but I had a great confidence in the goodness of God, to enjoy Him without any further purgatory; yet perhaps I might have been deceived, the judgments of God being secret. I am amazed now I am writing this, to think that I am still the same creature, and it gives me great light and subject of prayer, seeing the goodness of God that has used such wonderful means to preserve my life.

## CHAPTER VIII.

*Her former convulsions return. She is encouraged*
*in them by an angel, and prepared for new sufferings.*
*She passes three weeks in great extremity of pain,*
*not being able to take anything to refresh her. She*
*is comforted again by an angel, and passes most of*
*her time in high contemplation, though by fits.*
*Being left to herself she suffers great anguish and*
*interior pains. She is encouraged and taught by*
*angels to make a due use of her sufferings, and*
*forbid to ask they may be diminished. She feels*
*sensibly that her patience is a gift of God.*

Two or three days after I revived thus and began to take
some nourishment, I fell into convulsions again, like
those of the first year. They saw it was in vain to consult
other doctors besides him who had been acquainted with
me all the time of my sickness. He said I was too weak
to be blooded, though this was the only thing which
heretofore relieved me. They never durst bleed me after
this, finding my blood turned almost to water. Whatever the doctor prescribed to mitigate the convulsions
put me into a fever, and what he ordered for cooling the
fever advanced the convulsions to a high degree; so in
this dying condition I lay for a month, as I think, or six
weeks, without any human help, but with a great deal
from Almighty God; this gave me new courage and
patience, with supernatural recollection and solitude. I
saw an angel in the very place over my bed towards the

feet, where I saw our Blessed Saviour when I thought
He came to receive my soul. This angel looked very
beautiful and sweet, his countenance divine, he seemed
the bigness of a child four or five years old, he held in
his right hand a crown almost as big as himself, very
richly adorned; he held it, as it were, nearer to me that
I might delight myself with looking on it, giving me to
understand by a way very interior that it was my crown
which was so adorned by my sufferings and reserved for
me in heaven. I looked upon it more narrowly to see if
it were finished, or if I could see any place that was not
adorned, but to my great joy and comfort I could find
nothing wanting, which made me hope I should go soon
to enjoy it. After I had lain thus solacing myself, the
angel gently turned the crown (for it was round and not
like any in this world); on the other side there was
nothing but white sticks laid across, by which I understood I was to live and suffer much more yet.

I was now so fortified in soul and body as not to
be daunted; for the time I was thus taken up I think I
felt no pain or infirmity of body; when I came to myself
I was refreshed, as I may say, with these sweet dews
of Divine grace. This happened five or six days after
the agony I spoke of. It often returned to my mind and
encouraged me in great sufferings, thinking I added to
my crown; and the same thought does still encourage
me, so good was God to me to favour me in my greatest
pains, yet between times my sufferings were so great that
I could think of nothing else, and I was then in some
doubt whether these things came from God.

I had now convulsions or a fever continually upon me,
so that it was the admiration of all how I lived. In
these three weeks' time I never ate anything I know of
but once a piece of biscuit as big as my finger, and it lay
like a stone all night in my stomach. Some little thing

I drank between times, as barley-water or the like. God
was pleased in these extremities to increase my patience,
and I would be often confessing my sins in the day, for
though I had sometimes abundance of consolation, yet
sins of my past life would be often returning to my mind.
Once as I lay panting for want of breath and in great
desolation, those who stood about my bed to assist me
opened the curtains to give me air. Whilst I lay in this
condition I saw again an angel, who came to comfort me.
He was beautiful, like the former, yet not the same, but
of a higher choir. He spoke nothing as I remember, but
delighted and comforted my soul and body with his
presence. On a sudden I lay in great repose, and
seemed much changed to those about me. My ghostly
father asked me what had happened to me. I told him
in a low voice, I saw an angel, asking him if he saw it;
he told me no, adding he was not worthy, but said this
with a great tenderness of devotion, and asked where he
was. I pointed to the place, saying with a joyful and
earnest voice, There he is. One of my sisters, seeing
me much better, brought me something to take, but I
refused it, saying I had better comfort. She wondered
what I meant, but my ghostly father bade her let me
alone. What passed between my confessor and me was
in so low a voice that nobody heard us.

This angel did not stay long, yet I found myself much
strengthened and fortified. I asked my confessor awhile
after if he thought this was a true vision : he said he did
not doubt it, and since by faith we do believe the angels
do assist us, he thought Almighty God had given me
the sight of one to strengthen me in my great sufferings.
I replied nothing, but I think I repented myself for
having told him, and thought it best to keep such things
to myself. I said nothing, though he asked me afterwards many things, about what I had seen when I lay

in my fits. At those times many thought I was dead.
My body was stiff and cold, so that I could by no means
bend it, though they strove to raise me up in my bed
to give me air and convenience to breathe. I cannot
describe how I found myself as to my interior, but I
think I was in high contemplation united to God in
prayer, and I had some strange light of another world,
which I cannot now express. I remember the doctor
once asked me how I found myself in such fits, and
without reflection I answered that I seemed to myself
to be in another world.

What I have said concerning my seeing these angels
is not to be meant that I saw them with the eyes of my
body, for I never saw anything of this kind in that
manner, but with the eyes of my soul, and it appeared
much more clear to me, though these things happened
many years ago, than any other things I have seen with
the eyes of my body. I had never read nor heard that
there was any other way of seeing things (if I may say so)
than with our corporal eyes, till I came to religion and
heard our blessed Mother, St. Teresa, speak of it in the
favours God did her, which was a great joy and satisfaction to me, yet I remained as certain before that
I had seen them. It was a trouble to me when I knew
afterwards that I had to give my director an account of
all which had happened to me, and I thought he would
not understand me when I should say I had seen things
otherwise than with my eyes. God was pleased in the
time I lay in these extremities often to send His angels
to comfort me, otherwise I see not how I should have
been able to live.

I was glad when the convulsions went off and the fever
came on. I counted that a great relief, because I could
lie still a little. When I seemed quite spent, these
blessed spirits would often, in these five weeks' time,

visit me, so that I may truly say, 'according to the multitude of my sorrows, my consolations did abound.' They would sometimes bring with them posies of odoriferous flowers, the smell and sight did much delight and recreate me. They told me they came to take an account of my pains and sufferings, and to carry them up with them to be presented to Almighty God. I did not feel that suavity and joy in these apparitions as to be insensible of what I suffered, but I found myself much strengthened and instructed, and I took more care to make a due use of my sufferings, seeing the least of them was presented to the throne of God by the angels, who seemed to be employed in this as if they had no other duty. I thought they excused what was amiss and brought down an increase of God's grace to my soul, so great a love do these blessed spirits bear to mankind, as if their happiness depended on ours. The angel that performed that office seemed to be my good angel. One of them came to me and bade me offer up my sufferings for the public good of the nation and for the King who was banished, which I did often after this, begging God would help him as most to His honour and glory.

I seemed to have a great zeal for souls. Thus my thoughts were for the most part taken up with some good things, and well united to Almighty God. I could never pray, as I remember, to suffer less than I did, only once, when I had the imposthumes in my head, I found the pain so sharp, that I was afraid it would make me lose patience, not having then these favours from God to strengthen me. I began to cry aloud to God in my heart to mitigate the violence of the pain; and when I had proceeded, as it were, half way in my prayer, I was stopped by an angel, who seemed to be very near me, at my bed's head, but like one in the dark, though I knew

he was there, yet I saw him not. He gave me to understand I should by no means pray that these pains should
be taken from me, for that I should be thus deprived of
the crowns and favours which sufferings would draw
down upon me. This gave me great light for the time to
come, and made me afraid to ask to be delivered from
my cross. I presently gave over that prayer, and
resigned myself to suffer whatever God pleased to send
me. I must leave myself in the hands of God, He
knowing what is best for me, and He has never yet been
wanting to give me grace to bear what He sends me. I
saw clearly that the patience which others admired in me
came from God, and it was more evident to me that if
the knowledge of it had come by my senses, nay, I found
that when I had least to suffer I was moved sometimes
to impatience, which showed me that in my extremities of
pain it came from God.

## CHAPTER IX.

*The Devil appears to disquiet her, but her peace of mind soon returns. She is comforted by our Blessed Lady, and by this finds new strength. While she is one day deprived of Mass, through the violence of her convulsions, our Saviour appears to her to comfort her. The light she receives from this apparition. The disposition of her soul during the violent convulsions. She is struck with a palsy, first in her left arm and after some days in all her left side. She first resigns herself to this cross before she discovers it.*

ONCE in the time of these five weeks amidst my favours from God, the devil stepped in, as it were, seeking to disquiet me. He seemed to stand at my bed's feet, not raised up high as the angel was but low upon the ground, like one much troubled. He put these following thoughts of disgust into my mind, that I had, by doing my own will in fasting and penance before my sickness without leave, brought my illness upon me, and would be the means of my own death. At this I was frightened and very much disturbed. Sometimes I thought it might be a temptation, at other times I feared it might be true. I resolved to ask my confessor, though speaking in a third person, not to discover myself. He told me if one did penance without leave, thinking they did well, they would not sin; but he suspected I meant myself, and ordered me to do so no more. I acknowledged it no

further than he found it out, thinking it the best way
to keep it to myself.   It was not long ere my peace of
mind returned, and I received more plentiful favours
from Almighty God.   My convulsions being very violent
in the day and my fever high at night, my sleep was so
short and interrupted that I seldom knew that I slumbered,
but only by some good dream.   I told one of them once
to my confessor, but he said it was no dream.   For want
of rest I was almost out of myself and in such confusion,
I cannot express it.   I dreaded this most of all, because
then I should have lost all merit.

One night, my head being in that violent disorder
and the fever very high, I know not how, but I fell into
a gentle sleep, when I waked I found myself in great
repose, both in body and mind.   I thought our Blessed
Lady sat upon my bedside laying her hand upon my
head.   I lifted up my hand to feel it, but was not worthy,
though I felt her blessed hand lying on the top of my
head, and I cannot doubt of it by the effects, for I found
my head quite eased and my soul in joy and repose.
This gave me a tender devotion to our Blessed Lady,
though I had often called on her in my extremities with
great confidence.   I never found so tender an affection
as after this favour.   She had favoured me once, in my
first years of sickness, when she seemed to appear to me
with a crown upon her head and a sceptre in her hand in
great glory; but I thought this favour went beyond it,
because she did here not only perform towards me the
office of a mother, but also of a nurse.   This often doth
return to my mind.

After these favours, I was strengthened to suffer cheerfully.   Once I remember they thought I lay still, but my
ghostly father opening my curtains saw me in my convulsions, my bones snapping, and joints turning out of
their places, he asked me in a surprise what I was doing,

I answered, with a cheerful voice, I was working for
heaven, at which expression, seeing withal the courage
God gave me, he was much pleased.  I did not suffer
half so much as did outwardly appear, which I was many
times concerned at, thinking I deceived them, for they
saw what I suffered, but did not see the interior comfort
I had, though I imagined many guessed at it.  What they
said in this kind makes me acknowledge more my great
obligations to Almighty God in my sickness.

Mass was said every day in my room when the priest
was at home.  Only once the convulsions happened to
be violent all the morning, that I was forced to groan
much, and have many about me to assist me, hence it
was not judged fitting Mass should be said there ; this
troubled me exceedingly, for I had passed over many
inconveniences when I could possibly hide them to have
that comfort.  I always loved to see the Sacred Host
elevated, and had a lively faith, though not as I have
now.  This time I mention there was no hope, though
the altar was dressed in my chamber, and the priest stayed
as late as he could, hoping the convulsions would cease
and knowing what a trouble it would be to me not to
have Mass there ; but when he saw there was no hope,
he in a very compassionate manner comforted me, and
asked my consent that the altar might be undressed, and
that he might say Mass elsewhere, and I think he said he
would offer his Mass for me.  I gave my consent ; but
when I saw them undress the altar, my grief renewed,
and I thought it went to my heart to see our Lord leave
me in this extremity, and deprive me of my only comfort.
I was much afflicted, but not yet in any way to disturb
my peace of mind.

I made my complaints more to God, and was in great
desolation ; but I think this my concern was pleasing to
God and moved Him to comfort me in a high degree,

for about the time of the Elevation, as near as I could guess, I was suddenly recollected and transported as it were. How I was to the exterior, I know not : but I believe the convulsions ceased for a time. Methought I saw heaven's gate open with a great noise and mighty force. This gate seemed to me to be up on high in the air or clear sky, yet as present to me, and just by me. It seemed of great bigness and length, richly adorned on the inside, but I thought very hard to open by the great noise it made. Our Blessed Saviour stood in it in a very beautiful and majestic manner, but, as in His Humanity; He looked on me very sweetly, saying these words : 'Child, I am come Myself to comfort you.' I could neither say nor do anything but admire what I saw. I seemed to see also into the heavenly country some little glimpse ; but I cannot express how it was, only that many angels were there. This is as present to me as if it had lately happened, and I cannot write it without being moved extremely. I am moved to see in what haste our Saviour helps us when we are under afflictions, for methought in this favour if the gate had not opened when it did, He would have pierced through, the more to show the haste He made to come to me. I know it is not hard for a glorified body to pass anywhere, but I use this comparison of expression for want of a better, to express His preventing readiness to assist us.

This was the last favour God did me in a great while after ; and when this passed, the convulsions returned, but I was much fortified by it to suffer. I often had so violent fits of convulsions that they who were by me thought me dead, seeing my body stretched forth and cold, without breath or almost any sign of life. And though I think I was in prayer united with God (and yet I do not think these to have been altogether ecstasies or rapts, but caused by convulsions), when I came to myself again, I found great pain in recovering breath, it seemed as if my breast would burst open, the pains were so violent. The doctor seeing these extremities thought it impossible for me to recover; and upon this, applied a desperate remedy, which he thought might abate the violence of the convulsions, and at least hinder my death from being so violent. He gave me a powder to this effect : after this the convulsions were much lessened ; but I was presently struck with a palsy on my left arm, losing the use of it so far as not to be able to move it.

This happened on St. Joseph's eve. I had a particular devotion to this saint, and used to call aloud to him in my extremities, but it was not God's will he should obtain me health, nevertheless this did not lessen my confidence nor my devotion to him. About eight days after, my whole side was seized with a palsy. The doctor said this could not be attributed to his remedies. It was God's will that thus the height of my distemper should be abated, that I might live to suffer more. This cross was very sensible to me, seeing I was like to languish in this miserable condition all my life. I did not think now that I should die, the best I could expect was to live a cripple. Before I told my aunt, who was by my bedside, that I was so struck, I offered it up and resigned myself to the will of God. In this weak condition I lay, continuing lame with many other infirmities, which I shall after speak of, until my great doctor, St. Xaverius (so my father used to call him), cured me, which was a year and two months after this. I have been sometimes in fear lest I should make my sickness appear worse than it was, but I think I have taken care to say less rather than more, and I am fully satisfied in this by what one of my sisters used to say to me before I came over, that I need not fear in relating my sickness that I should make it appear worse, because nobody but those who saw me could believe it so ill as it was.

## CHAPTER X.

*Her deplorable state of health, at the same time the supernatural favours are withdrawn. She is persuaded to make the ten Fridays' devotion in honour of St. Francis Xaverius for obtaining her health. But she is ordered by an angel to change her intention. Great troubles of mind during this devotion. Little sensible comfort, very great pains. She makes a vow of chastity. She finds some ease at the end of the devotion, but soon relapses into her former pains of body and mind and continues in them six months.*

I AM come to relate my last year's sickness, the devotions I made to St. Xaverius and the miracle he by the power of God wrought upon me. I was quite given over by the doctors, professing they could no way relieve me, lying under so many contrary distempers. I seemed deep in a consumption, many times spat blood, with almost a continued fever, palsy, jaundice, the imposthumes I spoke of, extremity of pains, symptoms of my convulsions, with other infirmities. The doctor ordered me ass's milk, cordial drinks, and what I could take else, saying I should live as long as I had any substance left. I was dejected finding myself given over, but had a strong persuasion when all remedies failed, that God would find out some other means, if it were to His honour I should recover. I was so weak that when they lifted me out of bed to have it made, though they did this with all gentleness, I was ready to faint and could not remove it for some time. In the meantime the supernatural favours were withdrawn, I lay for the most time in great desolation, yet I cannot but say in the bottom of my heart, I was entirely resigned to the will of God.

The April following, Mr. Collins,[1] one of the Society, came to my father's house ; though he was a stranger he had heard of me, and after a short time he desired to see me. He was touched with compassion at my condition, and spoke very fervently to me, encouraging me to suffer, adding I should be walking above the stars when others, that did not suffer in this world, should be broiling in the fire of purgatory. These words, and his way of uttering them, gave me great comfort, remembering ever since I was a child, I had prayed to God to send me my purgatory in this world, with grace and patience to bear it; and even in the extremity of my suffering, I could never give over this prayer, but I neither told this to him nor anybody else. When this father had heard my sisters relate some particulars of my sickness, he was mighty earnest I should begin a devotion of ten Fridays to St. Xaverius, which I willingly consented to. He promised me a book of instructions for the performing this devotion, which he sent me with a pious letter promising to join with me. I found myself strongly moved with a more than ordinary devotion to this saint, though I had never prayed to him before more than to all the saints in general. I found a kind of endearing affection, more than I had experienced to any saint before, with a great confidence that he would help me. I was very willing to begin the devotion, which my

1 [William Collins, who entered the Society in 1669, and died 1704, at the age of fifty-four, was living in Suffolk from 1690 to 1698, and afterwards till he died.]—ED.

F

confessor approved of, thinking nothing but a miracle would cure me.

The night before I began the devotion, as I was making my intention to beg of the saint that he would obtain health for me if it were for the good of my soul, all my designs seemed suddenly changed by an angel who seemed to make haste towards me. He stood by me, but as it were in the dark, so that I saw him not, though I knew he was there. He gave me to understand I should do better to offer up that devotion for the good of the nation, for the King who was banished, than for my health. I was much surprised at this, and I remember my blood rose up to my face as on a sudden reprehension, but yet this angel was not like one angry, nor did this disturb my mind, though I resented it.[2] I thought it was not God's will I should obtain any help for myself, so I presently changed my intention and made it as the angel had advised me. I told my confessor I was inspired to make the devotion for quite another thing than health, and mentioned what it was, but let him not know who brought the message. He bid me do as I was inspired, and said it was not God's will I should obtain health, but withal added that I could not be in a more meritorious state than that of suffering. I resigned myself and went on with the devotion for the good of the nation and conversion of souls, frequently offering my pains for these ends.

I suffered during this devotion great darkness and anxieties and troubles of mind. The sins of my past life occurred so fresh that I got leave to make a general confession of my whole life, which had been denied me before. I think the saint helped me in this to give a clear account of myself, and my ghostly father, to satisfy

[2] [The writer uses the word resent in its old meaning—to take well or ill, to feel deeply.]—ED.

me, let me say much more than he said was necessary. I repeated the same confession since I came to religion in a quarter of the time, not having now those apprehensions and fears I had then. I cannot say positively whether I made this confession during this or after. I think my mind was not much quieter by it; my ghostly father said it was not necessary to make it, but I endeavoured to persuade him it was; if he had been so far against it as to forbid me, I should have obeyed him, for I do not know that I ever failed in this, though I could not help thoughts contrary to obedience. When he saw me in great desolation, anxiety, and trouble about my sins, with despairing thoughts (though I cannot remember I gave way to them, or that any particular sin occurred which occasioned my disquiet), he would bid me call to mind the angel that appeared to me, how fine he was, and how I found myself then. This gave me some comfort, yet sometimes I was insensible of all these past favours and thought I was deceived in them, hence I was so far from endeavouring to keep them in my mind that I strove to forget them. At other times when my peace of mind was restored, they would return sweetly to my thoughts without my endeavouring it, and particularly that favour in which an angel showed me a crown that was to be finished, and I hoped the more I suffered the sooner it would be perfected. In this devotion, or awhile after, I made a vow of chastity with leave of my confessor, but I had then no further thought of being a religious, or making any such promise. I often called upon St. Xaverius that he would obtain for me grace and patience to suffer as long as God pleased, and then a happy death, for I had no hopes of health, neither would I pray for it, but left myself in the hands of God. I passed these ten days' devotion with many troubles of mind and very little sensible devotion, but

I felt so much the force of divine grace as to suffer with patience and without complaint. I took care in the night to forbear groaning as much as possibly I could, that they who lay by me might not hear me. But when the pain was raging in my head and teeth I could not hide it. I found the greatest trials in these pains, they came on a sudden so fast and sharp. I had scarce time for a good thought. I dreaded those pains most, and would be sometimes so fainthearted as to tremble when I thought they were coming on, which happened many times when the fever went off. If these pains continued long, I think I had more courage at the end than at the beginning, though no supernatural favours.

At the end of the ten Fridays, I unexpectedly found the help of the blessed Saint, perceiving some life or agility in my lame side, and so much strength as to be able to make a step or two in the chamber with help, though still extremely weak. I found also great peace of mind, and my faith and devotion to this blessed Saint increased. Many judged the alteration I found in my health a favour obtained by his intercession, but God had designed to try me yet further before He would work a complete miracle, for soon after I relapsed into my former distempers, only some little strength and agility was left in my lame side. I found no relief in my arm in this first devotion, it continued withered, the sinews being drawn up into knots, my fingers shrunk so that the nails were like to grow into my hands, and so stiff that there was no possibility of opening them without breaking the joints. I ended my first devotion in August, and relapsing immediately, lay in a dying condition till the February following. I suffered this time great troubles of mind without any sensible favours from Almighty God, or even sense of those I had received. I often recommended myself to St. Xaverius, desiring earnestly some of his relics, which I got at last.

## CHAPTER XI.

*She is persuaded to begin again the ten Fridays'*
*devotion. She is much tempted to leave it off. She*
*suffers much in her soul. She is tempted to despair,*
*but comforted by a child of six years old, whom God*
*inspires to help her. She acknowledges the sweet*
*Providence of God. St. Xaverius appears to her in*
*her great anguish, and sweetly promises his protection.*
*Her frequent prayer. She is taken up with the*
*thoughts of a religious life. Her usual form of*
*prayer in begging favours.*

FATHER LEWIS SABRAN[1] of the Society was lately arrived
in England, and being in our neighbourhood, my father,
out of civility, went to meet him, and invited him to
our house. He had heard of my long sickness, and
desired to see me. He spoke very freely and confidently
to me, and offered to say Mass for me in my chamber,
which my father would not propose of himself; but I
was obliged to keep my bed. He asked afterwards why
I had not made the ten Fridays in honour of St. Xaverius,
and understanding what had passed, he advised my con-

---

[1] [Lewis Sabran, son of the Marquis de Sabran, French Ambassador
in England, was born in London in 1652, and entered the Society in
1670. He was one of James II.'s chaplains, and at the Revolution
escaped from England with great difficulty. For ten years he was
President of the Episcopal Seminary at Liége, and afterwards he was
Provincial, Rector of St. Omers, and lastly Spiritual Father of the
English College at Rome, where he died in his eightieth year, in
1732.]—ED.

fessor to make me begin them anew. In some private discourse I had with him he gave me courage and confidence, and bid me hope that at the end of the ten Fridays I should find a great change.

In this my sickness my youngest sister had a vocation to become a religious, though I could not but resent much her departure, yet I both encouraged her in it and gave full consent to it. She was to have passed the seas with Father Sabran ; but his affairs calling him away on a sudden, she lost the opportunity. This Father seemed sent from God, not to take her away, but to raise me that I might accompany her : for unless he had urged it, I should not have begun this second devotion, particularly seeing my confessor was not very forward in proposing it, and having care of many souls, found difficulty to be with us every Friday for ten weeks together. I made my intention conditionally for health, if it were to God's honour and glory, or else for patience and a happy death, and desired several who joined with me in this devotion to make the same intention.

The devil was very busy to hinder me from going on with this devotion, often tempting me to give it over, that I should find no benefit by it. When I applied the Saint's relics to the place that pained me most, the pain seemed to rage more, so that I was strongly tempted to throw the relics away, as it were in a passion. But God gave me grace to overcome these temptations, by resolving to persevere in this devotion, and to shew no signs of impatience in word or action. I used to embrace the relics the more, to have them laid under my pillow and dipped often in what I drank ; but all this seemed forced without any devotion. I was careful not to intermit a Friday, though I was ready to faint with fasting. God was pleased to try me, particularly the first five weeks, with many trials and great temptations. Sometimes I

was drawn almost into despair : the troubles of mind,
joined to the weakness of my body, made me like one in
an agony, and, as it seemed, just ready to sink into hell.
The devil would be representing these thoughts : that
God did not love my soul ; that He would take no care
of me ; that if He had designed to save my soul, He
would have taken me out of the world when I was so
well prepared.  At this, methought, I could say nothing,
but made this firm resolution that I would endeavour to
love and serve God as long as I lived, and trust the rest
to His mercy whatever should become of me.  Once,
when I lay thus a long while, the curtains being drawn
and those that tended me retired, imagining I took some
rest, a little child of six or seven years old, a niece of
mine, who was left in the room, inspired and guided by
Almighty God, Who alone knew the anguish in which I
lay, came running to my bedside, and, opening the
curtains, jumped upon the bed, saying to me in an
earnest and devout way : " Aunt, God Almighty loves
you and will take care of you, and will not let you be
lost, but will reward you."  At this I was greatly
astonished, revived, and comforted.  The temptation
instantly passed away.  My thoughts were taken up in
admiring the goodness of God to me, which thus inspired
the child to answer the temptation I lay under ; and it
seemed to me a greater comfort than if an angel had
descended and said these things, because then I might
have been afraid of an illusion, but I thought I could
not doubt of this, and it did very often come into my
mind.  Yet God was pleased to let me fall into troubles
afterwards to that degree that I lost the memory of this
and of everything that could comfort me.

Some time after, I called the child to me and asked
her what made her speak so to me.  She could give me
no account, nor even remember to repeat the words

over again, though I entreated her; so it seemed to me
that God put them into her mouth at that time for my
comfort. Such was the goodness of God to me that,
when He did not assist me in these troubles by spiritual
helps, He did by human means, and moved His creatures
to do it. Once in particular, I shall never forget. Being
in the night, as usual, oppressed with trouble and my
other infirmities, something of my life past occurred,
which I would willingly have confessed to ease myself,
but my confessor being abroad, there was no hopes of
this, so in this anguish I was like to remain. I knew not
what to, but as well as I was able I resigned myself to
suffer. Amidst these thoughts, I heard somebody knock
at my chamber window. It was my confessor who came
straight up to me, saying he knew he should find me
awake, though all the rest were asleep. He never used
to come home at that hour, but this happened by some
accident, and a particular providence of God to me. I
discovered my trouble, and he gave me much ease. I
cannot say positively whether all I have related happened
in this devotion or a little before it.[2]

---

[2] 'Whoever considers this wonderful proceeding of Almighty God
with this devout soul, will find admirable instructions both for himself
and the direction of others. He will see here, in the series of her life
and sufferings, those ways by which God leads souls to perfection. It
may seem strange that the high and supernatural favours, of which she
has already spoken, should be followed by such anxieties and troubles
as seem to reduce her to the greatest extremity of darkness, and even
thoughts of despair. We should be apt to imagine that a soul could
never forget those favours, as not to find immediate relief in all her
troubles by refreshing the memory of them. But as the Spirit of God
breathes where He will, by raising a soul above herself, so, by a strange
effect of divine Providence, He as wholly withdraws Himself, leaving
her in appearance in her own nothing, that we may experimentally learn
that all our good comes from Him. If you would try whether the spirit
comes from God, reflect whether you advance with her in patience,
resignation, and humility, the only marks by which you can distinguish
the spirit of truth.'—*Collector.*

The sixth or seventh Friday, after Mass and Communion, all being retired, and my curtains shut to try if
I could rest, I found myself recollected, yet in sadness
of soul, thinking how I grew rather worse in body and
mind, and that my prayers were not worthy to be heard.
I complained, but in a way that was, I know not how to
express, between love and despair, that the Saint would
not give ear to my prayer, and would not hear my petition.
Yet this was not in a way to discourage : but still I
thought I did resent it, though resigning myself to the will
of God. As I lay thus, Saint Xaverius, the blessed Saint,
appeared to me on a sudden, standing over my bed. He
looked upon me with great majesty, compassion, and
sweetness. He gave me to understand that he heard my
prayers, and said to me in a distinct voice, though in an
interior way, these words, which were so imprinted on my
mind that I can never forget them, being of so great
sweetness and expressing such care of me; they were :
" Child, I will be to you a father, physician, and friend,
and will obtain of God for you that which shall be most
for His honour and glory and the good of your soul."
I cannot express the ecstasy of joy, peace, and recollection my soul was in to see this blessed Saint, and to hear
these kind promises from him who I thought a little
before did not hear my prayers. This was an imaginary
vision, and he seemed, as he is commonly painted, in a
white surplice. He stayed by me but a little while, but
I believe I lay for two hours (my aunt thought I was
asleep and would let no noise be made) in prayer, taken
up with the favour that had been done me; but I said
nothing of it to anyone till I came to religion, yet I often
comforted myself with thinking of it, and found great
effects of it left in my soul, enjoying for a long time a
great peace of mind with a sure confidence that the Saint
would obtain for me what was most for the good of my

soul. The other temptations ·between times assaulted
me, yet I never remember any want of confidence in
the Saint.

I was after this much comforted as to my soul, but
the infirmities of my body continued. I often thought
the Saint would cure me, and used to dream I was a
religious, and beyond seas, conversing with nuns.
Whether they were only dreams or particular favours
from Almighty God I know not; but as soon as I came
afterwards to this place, though I was not designed for it,
I told my confessor that accompanied me this was the
church I saw in my dreams, and I find within the
monastery those places which were then represented to
me and in which I seemed conversing with the religious.
When I awaked I used to find myself in a great quiet
and disposed to pray, and I spent much time in conversing with God whilst others thought I was asleep.
I said once to my confessor, whilst I heard him discoursing in the room about nuns, that I dreamed I was
one already. He and others replied that perhaps St.
Xaverius would cure me and make me one. When I
added that must be almost a miracle, he said it must
be altogether a miracle, and that he would have it
recorded. Yet he went and gave himself a check, saying
it would be scarce a greater than my out-living so many
distempers for so many years, adding that a miracle in
curing me might be more for God's exterior glory, but as
for me I was happier in suffering as I did. Once
particularly I thought in my sleep I saw myself in my
journey to be religious with my youngest sister, and
several other particulars, which all happened afterwards
as I shall relate.

I went on with the devotion of the ten Fridays without
any inspiration to the contrary, as in the first: so I
begged the Saint heartily to obtain my petition, yet could

never beg health but conditionally, and if it were for the
honour and glory of God, and the good of my soul, which
gives me a great satisfaction when I think of it, otherwise
I should be afraid God gave me health for my importunity,
as He gave the Israelites quails in place of manna.  I
urged my petitions more pressingly in time of the
Elevation at Mass, begging them of the Eternal Father
in these words: "O Father of heaven and earth, and
Father of great mercies, grant my request for the merits,
death, and passion of your only beloved Son Jesus Christ."
This I repeated three times together with great confidence, knowing whatsoever we ask the Eternal Father
for His Son's sake will not be denied.  I have known
great effects of this prayer, and do always use it when
I beg any particular favour for myself or my friends, and
commonly when I prostrate before the Blessed Sacrament
in time of Mass.

# CHAPTER XII.

*The excess of her pains both in body and mind.*
*They increase towards the end of the devotion. She*
*confesses on the eve of the last Friday, and is inspired*
*to make several promises if she recover. After this,*
*she is blessed with a wonderful peace of mind bestowed*
*on her, though the violent pains of the body continue.*
*She is cured suddenly after Communion. The effects*
*she finds in her soul by this favour. Her cure is*
*divulged in the neighbourhood. The effects both in*
*herself and others. She has hopes of being received*
*amongst the nuns of Gravelines.*

As I drew near the end of this devotion, I began to
have again great troubles of mind and temptations, so
that as soon as I had confessed, I was obliged to call
again for my confessor. My ghostly father was strangely
surprised to see the troubles I had, which were, I think,
worse than ever. I remember the last Friday but one
having called for him the second or third time before
I could communicate. As he went from my bedside,
he turned back and said he thought God designed to try
me in all things, and he did what he could to comfort
me. I had now less hope of the Saint's curing me than
ever, because I had heard in the relation of the miracles
that towards the end of the devotion they used to grow
better, and I found myself worse in body and mind. Yet
I had some little spark of hope left, though very much

darkened, that the Saint would obtain for me what was most for the good of my soul. I was sometimes in such anguish that I had very little sense of this, and was often tempted not to go on with the devotion, nor to ask other prayers, thinking all would do me no good. But God gave me grace to overcome this, and to beg all the prayers I could. I procured some Masses to be said, and some alms to be given the last Friday, though I did all this with a kind of repugnance.

The eve of the last Friday they all began to lose confidence and seeing me so very ill, and even worse than I had been a great while. The fever and convulsions were so strong in my head, that I was almost out of myself. I took nothing the whole day. I am not able to express the weakness of my stomach during my sickness. I took so little nourishment, that all wondered how nature could support itself. Though I was very ill this last day, I was sometimes so present to myself as to have thoughts (I now think them inspirations, though then I knew not what to make of them), to make a promise to be religious and to perform some other things. In the evening, I called my confessor, resolving to confess over night. He wondered at this, it being very unusual, neither did I love to do it without necessity, fearing I should want to confess again before morning, and that my confessor would not permit me. But about this time I found myself very ill in the morning, and my head so much out of order, that I thought I should not be able to prepare myself. In the evening the distemper abated a little, and I took this time to confess. I think I performed it with less anxiety than ordinary. When I had done I found a great calm and peace of mind, with an entire resignation. My confessor told me he was sorry to see me so ill in the end of my devotion, and that there was no likelihood of my being cured, as he thought, and as I thought myself, being then much more like to die. I answered, however, that I was glad I had performed this devotion to St. Xaverius, and seeing so many good prayers offered and the Saint did not obtain me health, I was still the more satisfied it was not God's will. I added that I should love St. Xaverius never the less than if he had cured me, for I found a tender devotion to the Saint, with a great confidence that he would obtain for me what he had promised, and what was most for the honour and glory of God and the good of my own soul.

My confessor was glad to see me so well disposed, and said what he could to make me more in love with my present condition of suffering, telling me how meritorious it was. I heard him, but was all the while forcibly moved to ask him leave to make a promise of being religious. I had great difficulty to propose it, yet at last I told him. I was inspired to make a promise to be religious if the Saint cured me, as also to perform the devotion of the ten Fridays as soon as I came to the monastery where I was to be, and to make some short pilgrimages in honour of our Blessed Lady to a well dedicated to her about two miles off. He was surprised to hear me propose all this, and at first scarce knew what to answer, but at length gave me leave in part, for he could never persuade himself I should be able to go through with the rigorous observance of a religious life. Hence he would grant leave no further than to promise to dedicate myself in some religious family without being obliged to any duties. I thought if God wrought a miracle it would be completed, and that I should be able to go through with all, but I submitted myself quietly to do just what He would have.

All the family had lost hopes, excepting one of my sisters, who used still to say she would never lose con-

fidence till the last day was passed, and the others strove
to show how groundless it was, seeing I grew worse, yet
she remained still in the same mind.  My father, who
was absent, had procured several Masses for me, and had
a lively faith.  After I had made the promises I spoke of
on the eve of the last Friday, I found such an entire
resignation to the sickness or health, to life or death,
that methought if it was in my own power I knew not
what to choose, yet I desired health upon no other
account than to be religious, and had rather have continued sick in my bed than have lived in the world again.
I found so great a peace infused into my soul that I
cannot express it; but I think I never felt the like before
nor after, having neither rapt or vision, nor any interior
voice.  And blessed be God and St. Xaverius, this peace
has continued in some measure till this day, there being
now seven years passed since it happened : never any of
my former troubles returning, nor any new ones worth
speaking of.  This peace descended on me, methinks,
like a sweet dew from heaven.

I said I had no vision at this time, yet the Saint I
think was very near me, and made an union with my
soul, but I saw him not in any exterior or imaginary
form as I did the first time, and two or three others,
when I thought he stood on one side of my bed in an
old black cassock, and I found great comfort to lie near
that side of the bed.  I found greater effects of this
last favour than of the former, and had a tender love
and affection to the Saint, with a sweet confidence that
he would obtain what was most for the honour and
glory of God and the good of my soul.  I enjoyed that
night great peace of mind though I was very ill in body,
and in the morning worse, so that it would have been
impossible for me to have made my confession.

The hour of Mass being come, the altar was dressed

as ordinary, and for more decency and respect I was
raised up a little in my bed with pillows, and prepared
myself to communicate with a lively faith.   I had a
particular devotion on these Fridays to come to our
Lord as to a physician, and loved to read a point of
those meditations where our Lord cured the bed-ridden
man that was sick of the palsy, St. Peter's wife's mother
of a fever, the woman who had been twelve years in
her infirmity with the only touching the hem of His
garment.   I had a great confidence our Blessed Saviour
could do as much or more for me, having Him really
present in my breast in the Blessed Sacrament.   This
I experienced the last Friday after Communion.   So
great a joy seized my soul that it diffused itself all over
my body, as if new life and blood were infused into
me, and such an alteration all over me as gave me an
extraordinary agility, something methinks like one going
to be elevated.   My side had been struck with a palsy
for a year, and some months my arm was quite withered,
the sinews being drawn into great knots in the joints
of my fingers, which made each finger as big as two of
my other hand.   The fingers at the same time were
become so stiff they could not be opened without
breaking, and they were so bent that the nails were in
danger of growing into my hands.   All these became
on a sudden pliable, and I found as much strength
on that side as on the other.   I was amazed to find
this sudden change and myself so well.   I knew not
what to think of it, whether it would continue or
whether it were not, perhaps, some hidden transport
which wrought on my imagination.

   I designed to conceal it for a while but could not,
my countenance and voice betrayed me; for when Mass
was done, reflection ended, and all retired besides my
sister the widow, she came according to her custom,

opened the curtains, and asked me how I did (till then
I had concealed it, being taken up in prayer). I
endeavoured to speak as usual, and answered, I think,
'indifferent,' but she, surprised to see the change
of my countenance and voice, said she thought St.
Xaverius had cured me, and withal importuned me to
tell her how I found myself. I told her, being pressed,
that it seemed as if new life and blood were infused
into me, but bid her say nothing as yet. But I think
she told the first she met. My aunt came and wondered
to see the sudden change, but feared it might only be
some lightening before death, and was not willing I
should try to rise. But when she and the others were
gone to dinner, my youngest sister, who stayed by me,
brought me some clothes. I rose, and when my aunt
came back, she met me walking about the room, to
her great surprise. She admired the works of Almighty
God and called others to admire them, but would not
let me stir out of my room saying that though God did
miracles we must use discretion.

None would believe the report till they saw me, and
they were in an ecstasy of joy, giving thanks to God
and St. Xaverius. My confessor bade me be grateful
to God for these miraculous favours, telling me this
was not done for myself alone, but for the good of some
others, for it was his opinion I never could be in a
better condition for my own soul than I was in that
sickness. The same had been told me by my former
confessor in my first sickness. This gave me trouble
sometimes, but now I am confident the Saint had
obtained for me what was most for the honour of God
and the good of my own soul. This quieted all my
troubles.

They made me keep my chamber three or four days
for fear of catching cold, for though this happened the

G

12th of May, the weather was very sharp.  I was willing
to stay in solitude, knowing how to spend my time.
When I heard or read of those who were cured by
miracles, I thought that, if I should find myself well
on a sudden, I should be strangely transported with a
natural joy, but now I found nothing of this, but so
great a joy in my soul to think what sensible favour
the Saint had obtained for me, that it much increased
my faith and confidence.

I found, when I went out of my chamber, the more
I tried for strength the more I had it.  This was a
continual subject of prayer to me and of admiration to
all that saw me.  In a short time I was stronger than
ever in my life before, and in journeys, in walking and
riding, and the like, I tired out the strength of the
strongest without being wearied myself.  For many
months I ate very little and found no appetite till I
left England.  I had a great contempt for all things in
this world, and for many days was almost in continual
prayer, whether in private or in my oratory or in public.
I cannot say I found many distractions.  All glory be
to God and His saints, Who has been pleased to show
His power in so poor and unworthy a sinner, which
I attributed to the many good prayers that were offered
for me and to the lively faith of my sister and other
friends.

The noise of my sudden recovery being spread abroad,
few would believe it but those that saw and conversed
with me.  Hence I was advised by my confessor to
return the many visits which had been made me in my
sickness, both by the rich and poor.  The first time I
came into the air I found no alteration nor giddiness
in my head, and refused to be led by my sister, who
apprehended some change, seeing I had not been
so long a time in the air.  As we walked along

we said the *Te Deum* and other prayers in thanksgiving.

My father, after some days, returning, I went to meet him, he being surprised to see me come so fast, made haste to take hold of me and bid me take care of falling. He had heard something of my recovery, but did not think to find me so well. When he heard the manner of my cure his joy and gratitude to the Saint was increased, and, from that time, he said every day with the family the *Te Deum* and the Litanies of St. Xaverius, which custom he never omitted till I came away, and I believe he continued it till his dying day. I am sure he did much more in his own particular, and he became so devoted to St. Xaverius that upon all occasions of difficulty he would bid me make a devotion to the Saint, which I did willingly, and he used to tell me he found himself very much helped even in temporal concerns.

I told all my friends that I had made a promise to be a nun. They were all pleased with it, and my father told me he also designed, after he had settled his affairs, to be religious, which was no small comfort to me. He had designed this long before, but judging reasonably that I should be dead before he could accomplish it, had not acquainted me with it, knowing what a cross it would be to me to think of leaving him. Yet I believe I should not have hindered him though it had cost me my life. The truth is I loved him extremely, and the greatest sacrifice I had to make was to part with him and my other friends. But now to think of his coming over with me was too great a satisfaction. He wrote to Father Sabran to acquaint this Father with my cure and to desire him to provide a place for me. I wrote also myself telling him I did not fear the rigours of any religious order. I thought all I could do for God too little.

I was not inspired to pitch upon any order or particular place, but had thought of being a Poor Clare, thinking that the hardest rule. Some months passed before I had any answer from Father Sabran. My friends said they were glad of this, that they might enjoy my company longer in good health, who had caused them so much trouble in my sickness. I think God permitted this delay that the miracle might be spread about. The longer I stayed the more came to visit me, and though the parson of the place had declared from the pulpit, not long before, that miracles were ceased, yet the Protestants themselves looked on my cure as miraculous. Not long after my cure, going out one day to seek some solitary walk, I was followed by one of my sister's children. I found myself moved to go with her and visit one of our neighbours, who had always been kind to us and ready to help us in the hardest times. There were many high gates and stiles to pass, and I know not whether I was ever able before my sickness to make this way without help, but at present I found so little difficulty that I easily helped the child over the passage. The woman herself was the first that appeared when I knocked at the door, but she was so amazed to see me that she could not recover herself the time I stayed, but said if I was the same person (calling me by my name) it was the greatest miracle the Lord ever wrought, and unless my niece had been with me, she said, she never would have believed I was the same.

When my father knew where I had been, he was astonished to see I could go thither without help. I understood since I came to religion that this woman was converted, which was a great joy to me. This was not the only person thus surprised, but it is too long to relate all here. They used to follow me and invite

me to their houses. I went to see a lady of quality
about a mile off. She was so frightened that she was
obliged to call for cordials to recover herself, and asked
my sister that accompanied me if I were the same. She
met me afterwards at the parson's house, and knowing
I had made a long pilgrimage on foot, inquired of him
whether he thought miracles were ceased (as he had
affirmed in his sermon some months before).

The pilgrimage I mention was that I had promised
to make to a Well of our Lady two miles off. My
brother seeing me walk so well, told me if I would go
on two miles further we should come to a place to hear
Mass. I did it with so little difficulty, that though my
sister who accompanied me was forced to rest, I went
about conducted by the lady to see the house and park.
My inquiry in the houses I came to was to find their
chapels, where I willingly entertained myself.

I do not remember that any of the supernatural
favours was even any occasion of pride or vanity (though
some feared they might), on the contrary, I found they
gave me a true knowledge of my weakness, and were
a continual subject to me to praise and glorify God for
what I continually found in myself. Two or three
months after, my father received a letter from Father
Sabran by which he understood there was hopes of my
being received among the Poor Clares of Gravelines.
I was very glad of it, and pleased myself with thinking
how I should hide all the favours done me for ever
from Superiors and Directors, how I should live
unknown to all, attending only to Almighty God, and
I desired to be employed in the meanest offices of the
Community. But it was the Divine Will to try me yet
further before I attained that happiness.

# CHAPTER XIII.

*She puts her hip out of joint. She tries several remedies in vain, and is advised by a Protestant to consult her former doctor. She begins ten days' devotion in honour of St. Xaverius, persuading her friends to forbear further remedies for that time. Her dispositions during this devotion. She is instantly cured after Communion. The effects of this favour in her soul. A small contraction left in her hand after the former cure, which was looked upon as a mark to remind her of the favour.*

On the Assumption I made the second or third pilgrimage to the above-mentioned well, in company of my father and several others. On our return in the evening I was like to fall into a ditch by the path-side. I saved myself from falling, but with the great violence of the motion put my hip-bone out of joint. I did not think then I had hurt myself so much, and perceiving the company, which was a little advanced, did not see me, I was resolved if possible to take no notice of it. I desired my brother to give me his hand (though I always used to refuse any help), pretending it began to grow dark. I was in great pain all that night, and in the morning found I was not able to walk. My father and friends were much troubled at the accident, and he immediately sent for a woman very expert in surgery. As soon as she examined it she said it would be a hard cure, and

made me keep my bed for ten days, applying all sorts of
remedies but without any effect, nothing did me good
nor helped to settle the bone, which remained quite out
of its place. After this, despairing of my cure, she bid
me apply myself to my doctor that had cured me before,
meaning St. Xaverius. This she seemed to say with
great confidence, though she was a rigid Protestant. I
followed her advice, and was often much confounded to
think that she should be the first that proposed this to
me, and that I had not thought of it more myself; but
I think it was not want of confidence in the Saint, but
because I thought I was first to use all human means.

I was willing to begin a devotion to St. Xaverius. One
thought if I made the ten Fridays I should not have
time enough to pass over that year, the winter coming
on. I was then inspired to reduce the ten weeks to ten
days, a devotion I had never heard of before, though
since I came to these parts I find devotions of seven
and nine days very usual. I proposed this to my confessor, who allowed of it, but told me he could not be
at home above three in the ten days. I told him I would
communicate three times, in honour of the Blessed
Trinity. I was now very full of pain, and grew worse,
so that my father resolved the next morning to send for
a man surgeon, a mortification I could not away with,
and which I had begged off till then. I overheard him
tell his design to my aunt, though he resolved I should
know nothing of it till the surgeon was come. I called
him to my bedside, acquainted him that I was beginning
a devotion to St. Xaverius, and begged that no other
remedy might be applied, promising if I were not cured
at the end of ten days, I would undergo whatever should
be thought fit. Moved with tenderness he condescended
to my petition, and with leave of my confessor I began
my devotion, importuning my Saint more than ever, and

that in a familiar way and simple style. Thinking him
sometimes very near me I would beg him with tears:
'Dear Saint, cure me but this time and I will never
importune you so any more; make me but a nun, then
send what you please.' I thought if I were but religious
I should be glad to see myself sick; but to see myself
cast down, and not without fear of remaining for ever
lame, just when I was upon the point of coming over,
was a cross beyond all my sickness before, and I felt
it heavily, yet I think I was entirely resigned to the will
of God. I often examined what my intention was when
I made this pilgrimage, fearing I had some less right
intention, but I found nothing I could accuse myself of,
and I had particularly recommended myself to God that
time, which was a satisfaction to me. I spent most of
my time in praying and reading the life of St. Xaverius,
for though I felt pain it was nothing in comparison with
what I had suffered.

Though my brother and sister used to say it was God's
will I should not leave them, at least at this time, yet I
was comforted with the story they told me of a woman
cured of a sore breast by miracle because out of modesty
she would not let the surgeon touch her. Many blamed
my father and confessor for condescending to me, saying
when the bone was so long out of its place it would
never settle again. I was in desolation most of these
ten days, and felt not so lively a faith, knowing myself
unworthy of such a favour. Yet two days before my
cure I perceived an angel suddenly by me, as it were,
half in the dark. He bade me promise to go the same
pilgrimage the next week in honour of our Blessed Lady.
I was surprised, and thought I must again be cured by
miracle. On this account I made some promises, but
said nothing of them to my confessor.

The evening before the last day, the family met in the

room to say the litanies, and I was placed in a chair
with pillows.  They all saw what difficulty I had to stir,
and my eldest sister bid them take notice of it, saying
withal, she had received great confidence in time of
prayer that I should be cured on the morrow and able to
walk about the house, which they all concluded would
be a miracle.  Excepting her, none did much expect it
would happen.  The last day being come—it happened
to be a Friday, and the feast of the Nativity of our
Blessed Lady—I was in some desolation, knowing if I
was not cured I must submit to all, which made me
importune my Saint, though with resignation to the worst.
I confessed and heard Mass sitting upon my bed. (When
they found confinement to my bed did not help me, they
gave me leave to put on my clothes and sit or lie on my
bed).  I durst not venture to kneel, finding myself too
weak for that.  As soon as I had received I found myself
entirely cured and the bone set fast.  In my interior
I felt great devotion, gratitude, recollection, and contempt of all things, and much as I found myself after my
first cure.  Mass and reflection being ended, and most
of the company retired, my aunt and sisters came to me
one after another, asking if St. Xaverius had cured me.
I would give them no assurance, being taken up with my
devotions ; but they importuned me till at last I told
them they distracted me, and rising up I went suddenly
from them out of the room into a little closet where I
used to pray.  They were surprised at this, and cried
out St. Xaverius had cured me again.  One of my sisters
ran down stairs to tell Father Ireland, my confessor (he
was just going away to say a second Mass, as he was
sometimes obliged to do on festivals).  My sister stopped
him before he got out of the gate, and told him with
great joy that St. Xaverius had cured me again.  He was
much struck, and replied that he thought the Saint would

do more than remove mountains for me, and though he were in haste—I knew Lady Audley[1] waited for him—yet he came back into the house and bade my sister tell me to come to him if I were cured, which I presently did without difficulty. We said the *Te Deum* to thank God, Who by the intercession of St. Xaverius had bestowed such a favour on me so unworthy.

My aunt asked the Father, before his departure, whether she should give me a chicken which was killed and dressed for my dinner. He told her No, though that morning when it was killed he would have had no scruple to give me leave, and I was glad not to break my fast, being Friday.[2] After some time I was left to myself, and retired to pray, being much moved to prayer and solitude. My friends had been so solicitous and pressing as to make my father consent that if I were not cured, as they supposed I should not, without further delay I should follow the surgeon's prescriptions. And to this purpose there came a messenger that afternoon with orders from the surgeon, who had been consulted. When I heard what had been ordered I was overjoyed to have escaped their

[1] [The family of Touchet, Barons Audley and Earls of Castlehaven, was Catholic. The father-in-law of the Lady Audley here mentioned, however, apostatized in 1624 at Salisbury Assizes, but was attainted and executed for atrocious crimes on Tower Hill, May, 1631 (Dodd's *Church History*, vol. iii. p. 167). His eldest son was restored to blood, June 3, 1643, by Charles the First. He had already been reported to the House of Commons (in 1641) as 'a recusant whose person ought to be secured. He ended a life of persecution at Kilrusk, in October, 1684. He was succeeded by his brother, Mervyn Touchet, who married Mary, youngest daughter of John Talbot, ninth Earl of Shrewsbury, and widow of John Arundell, Esq. This may be the Lady Audley mentioned in the text. There was also a George Touchet, brother of the two lords just mentioned, who was a Benedictine monk and missioner in England, much esteemed for a work which he published called *Historical Collections concerning the Reformation*, 1674.] —ED.

[2] [All the Fridays of the year, except in Paschal time, were fast days in England, till Pius VI. dispensed English Catholics from the custom in 1781.]—ED.

hands, and this increased my sense of gratitude to my dear Saint. My father had been much in pain, being blamed by many for his condescension to me and for neglecting the surgeon's skill. I believe his gratitude to St. Xaverius for the former favour moved the Saint to do more for me. These three weeks I lay lame he was constant with the family in saying daily the *Te Deum* for my former cure.

It was remarkable that the side on which I had got the hurt was not my left side, which had been heretofore struck with the palsy, which many took notice of with admiration. After my cure they would not let me pull off the plaster which had been applied to my hip, for fear they should seem to tempt God, but in a little while it fell off of itself. This puts me in mind of something forgotten in the relation of my former cure. Though I was perfectly well, yet the fingers of my left hand, which had been lame, remained somewhat contracted, so that I could not stretch them out at full length ; the shrinking, nevertheless, which remained was no hindrance to me in anything I wanted to do. I was now advised to try an ointment which I had often made use of in my sickness : the nature of it was to stretch out the sinews ; and though in time of my great sickness the sinews were so much shrunk that nothing took effect, they were now pliable and almost well. It was thought this might help me, but when I now made use of it I found a contrary effect, for the sinews began to shrink again and I was in fear of losing the use of my hand. Hence my confessor and others judged it was God's will this should be left as a token to put me in mind what God had done for me, and I was forbid to apply anything else. Then my fingers, shrunk by the application of the ointment, stretched out as after my cure.

# CHAPTER XIV.

*Her desire of passing the seas that winter is diversly crossed. Our Blessed Saviour reveals to her He would have her go immediately; and promises to facilitate her passage. She finds visibly His assistance. Her dispositions in leaving her friends. New difficulties are raised at the sea-side. She persists in God's call, and at last embarks. A tempest arises; her sentiments at that time. She is obliged by accident to pass through Antwerp. Several things determine her to settle there. She quits the thoughts of accompanying her sister to Bruges and immediately takes the habit.*

BEING now recovered of my second illness, I was desirous to make all the haste I could to pass the seas and become religious, thinking God required it of me, as some return of gratitude, but I found many strong oppositions. My father consulted many Fathers of the Society, virtuous and prudent men, and all concluded it was a rashness in me to undertake such a journey at that time, that the year being far advanced and the weather cold, I might get a sickness and be sent back again. Father Sabran sent word I should not be in so much haste for fear of casting myself down, and my sister, a religious, represented the hardships they suffered in winter for want of fire. All this did not satisfy me. I importuned my father to get a pass, telling him I was sure it was God's

will, and that St. Xaverius would take care of me, at
which I remember he smiled and said, if he were sure
the Saint had told me so he would give me leave without
further delay. I answered nothing then, but remembered
what our Lord had said to me in prayer, which carried
me through all these difficulties. Being sometimes
oppressed with what people said, I had some fear and
mistrust whether it were God's will or no that I should
go that winter. I made my prayer and begged light to
know what I should do in this case. Our Blessed
Saviour appeared to me as in His Humanity, and gave
me, as it were, a gentle reprehension for my want of
confidence, saying : " Look back and see what I have
done for you, how I was pleased by miracles to cure
you." These words were spoken interiorly to me. He
added : " Child, it is My will you should go," and He
said I should get through all in time, which seemed
almost impossible to my friends, that my journey should
be beyond all expectation, and that where I went (by
this I understood the monastery where I remained), His
works should be perfected in me. But I replied : " Lord,
I have but a small portion, and no place provided
whither to go " (for as then I had certainly not heard of
any, and was in doubt whether any house would take
me). Our Blessed Saviour gave me to understand there
was a place provided for me, and that He would bestow
blessings upon the house for taking me, which should be
more than a portion. I replied again that I could not
tell them this. He answered : " I will make it known to
those that have care of the house." Which He did to
my Superior in my noviceship, as I shall hereafter relate
if I am ordered to continue writing. All this happened
in a short time. I have seen it all come to pass which
makes me have no doubt of it.

After this time I had so great a confidence in God,

and trusted so much that St. Xaverius would take care of
me, that I could have been content to pass the sea alone
if my father would have permitted me, though I had not
a word of the language.  God permitted my journey to
be put off several times when I was just on the point of
setting out, and then when I thought that things were
ordered so that nothing would hinder it, some virtuous
man would dissuade my father, by which all was over-
turned again.  My friends upon these disappointments
would have persuaded me to lay aside all such thoughts
that winter, that in the spring my father and aunt would
accompany me (they both desired to be religious), and
this I must confess was much according to my natural
inclinations, but I knew the other was more pleasing to
God, and besides my youngest sister desired to go along
with me.  I never left importuning my father, till one
day he bade me in a cheerful manner pray to my Saint to
send him money to provide for and supply my journey
if he would have me go soon, or else he did not know
how to assist me, tenants being very backward in their
payments.  I took my recourse to the Saint, for this as
well as other things, and within a few days I heard my
father tell one of my sisters that he never saw the like,
that people would force money upon him, and that he
thought the Saint would admit of no delays.  I being in
the room overheard him, though he endeavoured to
speak softly and to conceal this from me.  I told him
what I had overheard, and he confessed it was true, and
after this left me to myself to do what I would.  I had
no sooner heard this but I concluded to go over without
further delay.  A pass was soon procured, and thus,
about the end of November, I left my father's house and
my friends in tears.  God gave me so great courage that
I could not shed one myself.  When I had first a vocation, I could scarce think of leaving them without fainting,

but now I desired nothing so much as to make haste in taking leave that I might the sooner get away for fear any other thing should happen to hinder us. My youngest sister came over with me to be a nun of the order of St. Teresa, and I came with a desire to be a Poor Clare at Gravelines.[1]  I was very glad when I got into the coach and out of the town where I had lived all my life, excepting three months, rejoicing to leave my friends and country and all natural satisfaction for the love of God. Our confessor accompanied us over as he had promised, he was the only friend I had to assist me in effecting this, and he stood by me, knowing something I had told him of what our Lord said to me.  He bade me follow the directions God gave me in prayer, and would give me no other advice.  He was equally concerned with me when he saw my journey so often put off.

My father and brothers accompanied us to the seaport town and I supposed all ended, but here I found no less difficulty than I had met with before.  My sister fell sick of a fever and was obliged to keep her bed.  My father and confessor seeing things happen so cross till the end, resolved we should not go till spring, but return as soon as my sister was able.  This moved me more to importune my Saint, and my father when I found him alone. My sister suspecting my design begged me sometimes not to leave her, and I had a great difficulty to do this, yet was resolved nothing should hinder me from giving myself to God as soon as possible.  I therefore importuned my

---

[1] [The Convent at Gravelines was founded in 1609 by the efforts of Mrs. Mary Ward and Father John Genings, O.S.F.  In 1793, at the French Revolution, the nuns were imprisoned in their convent with the Benedictinesses and Poor Clares from Dunkirk, and it was not till April, 1795, that they were able to escape to England.  Their first home was at Gosfield in Essex, then at Coxride, Plymouth.  Afterwards they joined the community at Clare Lodge, Catterick, Yorkshire, which has since moved to St. Clare's Abbey, Darlington.]—ED.

father (seeing my confessor thought it not proper in these circumstances to accompany me) to let me go alone, being confident St. Xaverius would conduct me, and though I had no language I thought I could go with all security. My God gave me so great confidence in the Saint that I think had there been no ship I could have gone upon the water. My father would not hear of my going alone, but at last consented I should go, though my sister was not able to accompany me. I never refused my confessor's advice in anything but this, and in this I thought myself not obliged to follow it. He had a tender care of us and did what he thought best, and if I had been in a way of making my interior known to him, I believe he would not have said a word to defer my journey, but I had not that light at this time, neither did I discover to him the agreement I had made with my father of going by London with another father, who was coming over (for we were now at Harwich), and this I did for fear he should dissuade my father from it. I told him I would make a devotion to St. Xaverius to cure my sister, and said I hoped she would be well enough to undertake the journey by the time the packet-boat arrived. He liked this well and encouraged me in it. I made several promises to the Saint if he would obtain my sister's health, and a successful journey to us. Father Ireland and my sister made the same promises, and I importuned the Saint day and night to obtain my petition. I encouraged my sister, who had also great confidence in the Saint, and not in vain, for that night the packet came in, her fever left her, and the next morning I got her up, and though she was so weak she was scarce able to walk alone, yet I persuaded my father and Father Ireland to let us embark that morning, and begin our much-desired voyage. They consented to it, relying on the Providence of God and the protection of St. Xaverius.

We set to sea in the worst of seasons, the 23rd of November. Father Ireland accompanied us; our voyage was prosperous beyond expectation; we were only twenty-four hours at sea. A tempest arose at midnight, which put most into apprehension. Though I naturally fear the water, yet now I apprehended nothing, seeing St. Xaverius standing by in a black cassock protecting me. I thought he had not cured me to let me be drowned then; and seeing he was called by the infidels god of the sea, I knew Almighty God had manifested the powerfulness of his intercession in sea voyages.

We landed at Helvoetsluys the next morning at nine o'clock, and, it being a Friday, gave thanks to God and St. Xaverius for our speedy passage, and for that my sister continued so well. The rest of our journey was performed partly in waggons, partly in boats, as we found convenience. I was never the least defeated or tired, and performed my journey with much ease and without the least illness, though sometimes exposed to snow and rain. When we were within some leagues of Hooghstraet, Father Ireland resolved to make the best of our way for Gravelines. In order to do this he sought out for some convenience to carry us directly to Bruges without passing through Antwerp, at which I was much concerned; for though I had no mind to be a nun here, yet I had a desire to see these nuns. Father Ireland thought my desire unreasonable, seeing I could give no grounds for it, and persisted in his design. I took my recourse to St. Xaverius, and was glad to hear, after all inquiry made, that he could find no other convenience for continuing our journey as he designed, but was obliged to pass through Antwerp.

We arrived at Hooghstraet[2] on the eve of St. Xaverius.

---

[2] [We follow the orthography of the manuscript before us as to the name of the place, which is more commonly written Hoogstraet. The

H

I returned hearty thanks to the Saint for all his favours,
and in time of Mass found myself moved with affections
of tenderness and gratitude. At our first appearing at
the gate the Reverend Mother bade my sister welcome.
She was designed for that place, and told me I should
be welcome at Antwerp. I had no such design, but
told her I was going to Gravelines, upon which she was
surprised, but she said I had been expected there as
long as my sister had been expected at Hooghstraet. I
knew no letter had ever passed from my father about
that business, which made all wonder; but it seems all
was effected by a Protestant gentleman living in England,
a stranger, who had a daughter at Hooghstraet, upon
which one of my brothers was sent to him to know how
my father might direct his letter thither, when he wrote
about sending my sister to that place. I was then just
recovered, and my brother in discourse related to him
my cure, and he said he believed I should likewise be
a nun. This gentleman had a great aversion to the
Jesuits; and understanding that the house at Hooghstraet was directed by them, he begged my father that
his daughter, who was cured by St. Xaverius, might not
be sent to the house where his daughter was. Hence
it seems he dealt with the nuns of Antwerp (he probably
did not know by whom these nuns were directed, being

Teresian convent there was founded from Antwerp, August 18, 1678,
by the Countess of Hoogstraet, whose daughter, Mary Margaret, was
afterwards Superior. The convent left in consequence of the French
Revolution in 1794, and moved first to Fryers Place, near Acton,
Middlesex, then in 1800 to Great Canford near Wimborn, and in 1828
to Valognes in France. We are glad to add that this Community has
now returned to England and settled at Chichester, where they have a
beautiful convent, built after the model of St. Teresa's own foundations
in Spain. The sister of the writer mentioned in the text was Agnes
Frances. She was professed in 1695, elected Prioress in 1727, and continued in that office till 1733. She died in 1742, a bright model of every
religious virtue, and held in great veneration in the Community.]—ED.

much a stranger to them) about my coming hither. I
had a great contest within myself, and was very loath to
change my determination of being a Poor Clare. Though
my inclinations carried me to be a Teresian, I thought
the other Order was harder, and chose it on that account.
I proposed my difficulties to Father Ireland, who assured
me, if I would believe him, my vocation was to be a
Teresian. He told me also I was not always to strive
against the stream, and choose the hardest things.
Whereas he spoke positively, I was inclined to submit,
and took my resolution of staying here just before I
came into the gates of the town.

We arrived here late in the evening the day after the
feast of St. Xaverius. The Reverend Mother and Sub-
Prioress bade me welcome at the speak-house gate.[3]
They told me afterwards I looked very sad and pensive.
The truth is, I was in concern, doubting whether this
was the place our Saviour, as He had promised, had
prepared for me. But when the Reverend Mother
narrated to me what a Providence it was I was brought
hither, and that the Community had made the ten
Fridays to St. Xaverius, to beg by his intercession for
a novice, the same time I made them for my cure, I was
much comforted. When I went afterwards to the Church
to adore the Blessed Sacrament, I found a great joy, and
the Church was perfectly like that I had seen in my
dream at the time of my sickness. The Sub-Prioress,
also a holy woman, as soon as my sister and I appeared,
knew that I was the person of the two designed for the
house, saying she had seen me before in a dream. I had
an excessive joy when I embraced the religious that night
at the gate.

This happened upon Saturday, and they desired I

[3] [The English nuns in Flanders adopted many Flemish terms. Thus
the parlour they called 'speak-house,' and the cloisters 'pants.']—ED.

should enter the Tuesday following, being the Conception of our Lady, but I was not sufficiently disengaged from myself. I designed first to go and see my sister[4] at Bruges, and she that was to be religious at Hooghstraet was come so far with me on the same design. The Reverend Mother here was against it, and I was moved to make that little sacrifice in imitation of St. Xaverius, who had done so much for me. I told this to Father Ireland and Father Wright,[5] the director of this house, and they, condescending to my desire of going to Bruges, bade me do something else in honour of St. Xaverius afterwards. I had no sooner resolved this, liking their advice according to nature, but Father Wright asked me what I would do in this case if I had nobody to consult but St. Xaverius. I answered readily I was sure I should stay, upon which he bade me do so now, and I presently laid aside all thoughts of going to Bruges, and never mentioned it afterwards. My sister took it ill of me, but I found great satisfaction in this small victory, and I am confident God has done me many favours since on that account. I took the habit without further delay on our Lady's Conception, and found no difficulty then to part with my sister. I passed my noviceship with great alacrity, without finding any trouble. I used to complain to my director that I had nothing to suffer. The first year I had few visions or supernatural favours of that kind. I thought God would now deprive me of them, and I was content, knowing my own unworthiness ;

----

[4] [This was her eldest sister, mentioned above as an Augustinian nun at Bruges. See p. 3.]—ED.

[5] [Father Wright' was probably Thomas or Edward Green, who entered the Society in 1668, and was appointed Minister of the Jesuit College in the Savoy, Strand, opened in 1687, and highly favoured by James the Second. At the break-up in 1688, Father ' Wright ' escaped with some others with great difficulty to Belgium. He was afterwards Rector at Watten (1694), and at a later period returned to England, where he died in 1727 at the age of eighty-three.]—ED.

but since that time I have received them frequently, and once in my noviceship St. Xaverius told me I should be Superior, which I told my director with tears in my eyes, because I desired nothing so much as to live privately and unknown. These favours have increased every year, and have advanced me in prayer and mortification. To my confusion I was chosen Sub-Prioress soon after I came out of my noviceship, and now as I have done so much of this relation, the heavy cross of Superior is fallen upon me very early, having been but six years and a half in religion. I have passed my time since I came here in perfect health, and have gone through all the rigours of the Order without any dispensation, and am able to do much more than my Order requires. All praise to God and St. Xaverius, in whose name I began this rela-tion and end it.

[Here ends, in the manuscript from which this volume is printed, the first part of the Life. Father Hunter prefaces the chapters which follow with the following observations. ' The reader who has perused the first part of this Life cannot but admire the great example of patience and virtue which she showed in her father's house during her long and tedious illness, as well as the sweet Providence of Almighty God, Who was pleased in a wonderful manner to support her in her sufferings. He may perhaps be apt to imagine upon what he meets there that, when she is once settled in a religious life, he shall read nothing but what is extraordinary and sublime. And no doubt we have reason to suppose that, if these favours were from God, and her action as sincere as it appears to be, we have reason, I say, to suppose that the sequel of her life was answerable to these great beginnings, and that there was a stately structure to be raised upon these solid foundations. But then we must not deceive ourselves in the notion of solid virtues. An unwearied patience and undaunted courage in a long series of uncommon misfortunes is the crown of the patient Christian, who supports all for the love of God. It is a virtue which is not only pleasing to Heaven, but which shines with admiration in the eyes of the world. But if, by an alteration of state, we remove these exterior trials of patience, her virtue must be measured by another rule, and though it be not now so visibly placed upon the stage nor so much in the view of men, it may not be less solid nor less agreeable to Heaven in the private practice of an obscure life. The contemplative finds the conduct of Heaven and the Divine virtue of a God-Man no less admirable in the many years of His Hidden Life, than in the three last, in which He manifested Himself to the world in prodigies and miracles. And those few words, "He was subject to them" (to wit, to His parents), which is all the account we have in Holy Writ of our Saviour's Life from the twelfth year of His age to the thirtieth, speak aloud the infinite greatness and goodness of a Man-God buried, as we may say, in this obscurity Hence the masters of spirit judge of virtue, not by what appears most conspicuous to the exterior, but by the solid principles and practices by which it suits itself to that station in which God thinks fit to place us.

Whosoever admires in the person of whom we treat the great things which Almighty God wrought for her, and the supernatural helps which she received from Him, will not so much wonder at her high prayer and contemplation, in which she lay for days and weeks together in her sickness, as he will upon reflection admire her simplicity and humility, after all these favours, in her noviceship. She found herself now placed by Almighty God in a state in which she hopes to live unknown. She is so satisfied with being in a way to become the Spouse of

Jesus Christ, in consecrating herself to Him by religious
vows, that she willingly bids adieu, as we may say, to
those supernatural favours which are only the gifts of
God, hoping by this to embrace more closely God Himself and Him alone. She makes the virtues of her state
her only study. There appears in her whole carriage an
exemplary regularity, which made her to be admired as a
pattern of religious discipline and virtue. She was far
advanced in prayer, the great science of the saints, and
had been often rapt into high contemplation. But, concealing all this, which was then only known to God and
herself, she makes herself to be instructed in the first
principles of prayer and piety, as an ignorant novice.
She had privately practised such mortification in her
father's house, that she found nothing hard in a religious
course. She could be taught no interior mortification
which she had not practised, as appears by her writings,
and yet, without the least affectation of singularity, without discovering in any occasion that she had had any
previous knowledge of these things, she submits herself
to be taught by everybody, she is ready to receive lessons
from everybody, never contends for anything which seems
to be her right, but willingly yields to everybody. As to
myself, I cannot but own that this spirit of submission
and humility, even in the smallest matters, this ingenu-
ousness and simplicity and sincerity which appears in
this year of her noviceship, and which is still more
manifest in her manner of penning it down, at a time
when she was still more advanced in the way of God,
would, if other things failed, be no small proof that all
the favours mentioned before were from Almighty God.
For, according to the rule laid down by Truth itself, you
shall know them by their fruits. Nothing but the Spirit
of God could produce those solid fruits of submission,
humility, and piety, and I doubt not that there are some

who will admire her less when they see her caressed by
the saints and angels, in the midst of her sufferings, than
when they see her giving up her little rights to her fellow-
novices younger than her in religion, letting herself be
instructed like an ignorant novice in things of which she
was perfectly mistress, or when they see her checking
herself from giving an answer, when she saw by her
silence she should be brought into some disrepute, as if
she wanted wit to make a reply, particularly when these
do not seem only passing acts of virtue, but when they
argue a settled foundation, and a well-founded humility.
I thought proper to add this short remark, because we
enter now into a very different part of her life. And I
shall now continue to give the remaining parts of her
noviceship out of her own writings.']

## CHAPTER XV.

*She takes the habit. Almighty God grants the peti-
tions she makes at her clothing. She applies herself
to the constant practice of virtue without expecting
any more supernatural favours. She sees one of the
deceased religious, and learns several things from
her, though she supposes this to have passed in a
dream. Her prayers without distractions. She is
encouraged to pray for others. She takes her recourse
to St. Xaverius in all her wants, and finds sensibly
his help. Her self-abnegation. Her longing desire
to see herself spouse of Christ. St. Xaverius appears
to her. She has light to discover her interior to her
director. She makes her vows with great devotion.*

### JESUS, MARY, JOSEPH, XAVERIUS.

In obedience to my new director I go on relating my life,
though it may well be harder to me to find time, in regard
that I am in the office of Prioress, which is the reason I
have deferred writing these twelve months; but being
now ordered to continue writing, I begin again in confidence that I shall have the same help I had before, if it
be God's will I should go on, and I think this help was
supernatural, otherwise I could not have written what I
have. I hope Almighty God will accept it in part of
penance of my sins.

I think I am come as far as my entrance in religion,
but it is no wonder if I should repeat things sometimes,
not having the other papers in my keeping. I came to

the monastery on the 5th of December in the year 1693, and took the habit on Tuesday following, being the feast of the Immaculate Conception of our Blessed Lady. My sister, who was with me and saw me enter, was going to be a religious of the same Order, but in another monastery. We had some feeling to part with each other, having always lived together except one half-year, and we loved so much. But we resolved to follow the advice of our confessor, who brought us over and advised us not to be in the same house, saying we should meet many hindrances in the way of perfection. My joy was so great to see myself in a religious habit, and enclosed in a monastery, that I soon forgot all other things.

The Reverend Mother told me that when I prostrated at clothing, as is our custom, I should obtain whatever I asked. I had great confidence in this, so I begged of Almighty God the conversion of that Protestant gentleman, who, unknown to me, had procured me this place, as also of the woman I have mentioned before, who was so surprised at my cure. Not long after this I heard they were both converted, which increased my confidence in God. I begged also very earnestly my perseverance in religion, for I apprehended lest my want of fortune and parts might be a hindrance to the Community from admitting me to my profession. Yet I had a great confidence in God, and began my noviceship with great joy and alacrity. I found no difficulty in the rigour of our observances, in lying upon straw, in wearing woollen— difficulties which are commonly great to novices in the beginning. In these I had none at all. My greatest trouble was to learn my Breviary, having never learnt Latin. In this I was dull, and was often chid for it by my mistress. Another difficulty which I had was to do public penances in the refectory. In this I endeavoured to overcome myself by asking leave to do those first which I had the greatest mortification in ; but yet I did not tell my mistress so, for I was still of opinion that it was most humility to conceal from my Superior and director anything which was good, and I resolved never to discover to them any favour God had done me, though they would often be importuning me and asking me if I had never seen St. Xaverius, and what he said to me. At this I would blush, and be very much out of countenance, and make some excuse. I remember my director said to me one day that I was the strangest creature he had ever met in concealing things from my director, and he asked me if St. Xaverius had bid me say nothing. Sometimes my patience would be tried by these and the like questions. One day in particular my under mistress, who taught me to read Latin (she was one who would mortify me much in this kind), told me I ought to acquaint my director if God had done me any favour, as to let St. Xaverius appear to me, or the like, at which I was so troubled, I wept. I did not let my mistress know that I understood anything about prayer or meditation, but would be taught in all things as the other novices. I went one day to my director and desired him to teach me to pray : he bade me go and ask St. Xaverius, which I did most willingly.

My mistress being Superior, was often hindered from explaining unto us the subject of our prayer at night. In her absence it belonged to me to read the meditation to my companions, who were both younger in religion, yet they used to do it, and I was well pleased at it. I do not remember that I ever strove with them in anything, except it were for the first place in the choir, when the bell rang for morning prayer. In my first year of noviceship, as I said before, I had very few supernatural favours, neither did I expect them any more, as I had had them in my sickness. I thought Almighty God sent

me those favours at that time to enable me to support
my sufferings with patience; but now He had brought
me to religion to be a spouse of His, this was happiness
enough, being placed here where I had my health and
had nothing to suffer in any kind, for I enjoyed peace
of mind.[1]

About four months after my admittance one of the
most ancient of the religious died. She had made her
jubilee in religion, and was always looked upon as a
most virtuous person. Seeing her very old, and by consequence not likely to live long, I often begged of her,
but most particularly a month before her death, that
when she came to heaven she would recommend me
earnestly to St. Xaverius, and pray him to take care of
me. She promised she would. About six weeks after
this, as I remember, she appeared to me in my sleep,
and I cannot doubt of it by what followed, otherwise I
am not apt to believe in dreams. I think it was about
one in the morning that I thought this religious was
represented to me in my cell. At first I was affrighted,
knowing she was a spirit, but at length I resolved to

[1] 'In what she says of her being very dull and of mean parts, she
expresses the humble sentiments of her own heart. But she appeared
to others and was of a solid judgment and very capable of business, of
an easy, quiet, sedate temper, being mistress of her own thoughts and
always recollected with God in prayer, never disturbed with any
motions of passion. This made her act with a great deal of calmness
and prudence, even in the most difficult and unforeseen circumstances.
Though she was very sensible of the uncommon favours which God
bestowed upon her, yet there appeared in her whole life a spirit of
simplicity, which made her always tractable and submissive to those
who were over her, and nourished her in a strange tenderness of devotion to Almighty God. She dealt with God and her Saint, as she
called him, as a loving child with the best of parents, and in a way
which may appear too familiar to those who have not experienced the
tenderness of Almighty God to a faithful soul. She had found such
sensible marks of God's goodness, that it is no wonder she should run
after Him, carried on with the odour of His fragrant sweetness.'—
*Collector.*

take so much courage as to speak to her. Then calling upon her 'Sister Clare,' so she was named, I asked her if she were in heaven. She then seemed to come nigher me, and appeared extremely beautiful, and answered 'Yes.' I asked her then if she had been in purgatory: she said she had been there sometime. I demanded on what account she had been there, likewise what sort of a place it was. To the first she replied it was for some negligence in point of obedience, and at the same time she seemed to give me some caution to be very punctual and careful in the observance of that virtue; and as to the second, she told me purgatory was a sad place, and that one of the greatest torments was the sight of the devils.

It is impossible to express the change I found in myself, and in how great fear and anguish I was during all this time; but at last, to my great comfort, I remembered what I had requested of her concerning St. Xaverius, and asked her if she had told the Saint. She said she had, and added that St. Xaverius had a great love for me, and would take care of me and of the place where I was, and would have me a great saint, and would not have me a moment deprived of the sight of God after this life. Then I asked her how St. Xaverius looked in heaven and what a fine place heaven was. With that, I thought I saw St. Xaverius there, as it were, on high over me and protecting me. He looked very sweet, amiable, and beautiful beyond what I am able to express, he seemed like one in a rapture, and inflamed with the love of God. I cannot express the excessive joy I felt in my soul at that time, but this contemplation soon passed, and the spirit, in a low voice telling me two and three times of a novice, vanished away.

I awoke, and found myself much defeated, but in

great devotion, and methinks like one come out of another world. I rose to pray at the accustomed hour, yet could think of nothing but what I had seemed to dream that night. After the Divine Office and duties of the choir were ended, and that I came to employ myself in exterior actions, as sweeping and brushing in the choir, my thoughts were so taken up and my mind so transported, that my mistress of novices chid me and importuned me to tell her what was the matter with me, saying she was sure there was something more than ordinary. At last I told her what I dreamt, at which she seemed strangely moved to devotion, particularly a day or two after (as I remember it was no more), when she heard unexpectedly of a novice who offered herself. She is a fine young woman and very virtuous, but has been led by great interior suffering. When the Reverend Mother and Sub-Prioress, who were both my mistresses, heard of this novice they with great joy told me it was the novice of which Sister Clare told me, and that they did not doubt but that all the rest was true. I was much out of countenance, for I did not care they should think it anything but a dream.

When I had been there about eight months, I went into the Spiritual Exercises, at which I made a general confession of my whole life, though I did not think myself obliged to it, not finding anything in particular which troubled me, but I thought it more perfect. I made it with good peace of mind. My mistress wondered to see me return so soon, knowing what I had been about. I was very short, my confessor not asking me above two questions, nor did anything occur to my mind afterwards, but I remained in great peace. As to my prayer in that Exercise,[2] I remember not any particular

[2] The writer frequently uses the word Exercise, in the singular number, where we should now use the plural.]—ED.

favours I had, only I did not find many distractions nor
temptations. It put me in mind of my first year's
sickness, when I lay a month speechless. Yet there was
one great favour which I very much esteemed, and which
I forgot to mention. It was this, as I was praying in
our cell, I think I kept my mind too much bent in
praying for myself and others, and methought our
Blessed Saviour appeared to me on my right side and
said sweetly to me : 'Whatsoever you ask me, child,
for yourself or others, as the Saint has told you, you shall
obtain.' He soon disappeared, but left me in great
consolation. This often returns to my mind, and I
claim of our Lord His promise. My mistress told me
I was to give my director an account of my Exercise. I
showed him some of my good purposes, and said nothing
of this. I rejoiced to keep it to myself; yet when any
asked me to pray for them, which they did very frequently,
I thought it was something very extraordinary, as if they
had known what our Lord had promised me.

Though St. Xaverius did not appear to me often
this first year, yet I had great confidence in him, and I
performed several little practices of devotion, which I
hoped would be acceptable to him. I was moved by
some pious stories I had heard to address myself to
him when I wanted some little conveniences which I
thought necessary, and I often found my Superiors grant
them of themselves, without any application made to
them, which increased my confidence in the Saint.
There was something of this kind that happened when
I took the habit. The Reverend Mother understood
the day before my entrance that I had aversion to eggs,
and upon demand I told her I had not eaten one in
seven years. She was much surprised, and thought it
impossible for me to comply with our constant rule of
abstinence from flesh, eggs being the chief part of our

diet. She bade me go to pray to St. Xaverius, and said he could help me as well in this as he had done in all the rest.

I perceived she was concerned about this, as she told me afterwards. Some of the Community wondered she durst venture to admit me, seeing I looked pale and thin, and could not eat what is the best part of our nourishment. Perceiving this, I took my recourse to the Saint as she bid me. I was ordered to eat an egg at dinner the day before I entered. I took one into my hand, but my stomach immediately turned to that degree that my confessor who came over with me made me lay it down. Notwithstanding this, the Reverend Mother had so great a confidence that she let me take the habit; and the first day I came together with the Community my stomach was so much altered that I longed till they gave me some eggs, which they did that day and I eat them heartily. Reverend Mother was transported with joy, saying St. Xaverius had done this for me, which I have great reason to believe he did, and I continued after this to eat them with as good an appetite as ever I did anything in my life. My mistress asked me how I liked the other fare, as salads and the like. I could not but own I had never been accustomed to eat them; but I thought all that came to the refectory savoured to me like the manna that fell from heaven.

I thought I was well before I entered, yet I had a very little appetite, but now I could eat heartily of every-thing that was set before me; and when I had been here three or four months, I grew so fat that those of the house and others who saw me enter were amazed at it. My very clothes, which before were too big for me, grew too strait for me. I had some scruple at first to ask for much extraordinary penance, because my confessor who brought me over had forbidden me. I understood afterwards I had no obligation to observe these orders. He advised me to do this out of his too great care for me, imagining I should be indiscreetly fervorous if not restrained. I cannot say I was taught any interior mortification which I had not in some sort practised before, and when I came to be religious, I thought I was to do nothing I had inclination to, and that I was to be mortified by others. This I think carried me on not to make any replies or show any anger when some occasions were given me. I remember once I was told by one, speaking as if she thought I had little in me, such a one, meaning one of my companions, would have known what to say. I made no reply, not caring much what they thought of me, yet I was moved then to make a reply, very proper as I thought, but I have always found it much easier to refrain speaking at first than to break off when once begun, and in this practice I have found a solid joy and increase of grace. It has prevented all grudging at others, so that I do not remember to have had anything to accuse myself of in confession, not so much as an uncharitable thought. I always counted from my first entrance how many months, weeks, and as time drew near, how many days there were to my profession. I had that thirsting and languishing for that most desired day that I cannot express it. When the time was near, it was my first thought in the morning, and I found joy to think that there was one day and night passed, and that there remained now only such a determinate number till that most desired day would arrive in which I should be made a spouse of Jesus Christ. The nearer the time grew the more my desire increased, in such sort that if my profession had been deferred as it happens upon different occasions, I think I could not have lived.

I was sometimes in fear lest I should not have the

I

voices of the Community, yet the confidence I had in
God went beyond it, though I knew my own unworthiness. When the Community met to take votes for me
I knelt all the time before an image of our Blessed
Lady and St. Xaverius praying that I might be received
to my profession, being still in great fear and anguish
till the Sub-Prioress was sent as the custom is to call
me to the Community. Then the Superior told me
I was received, at which I was not a little transported
with joy. I never inquired whether I had all the voices
or no, being contented to hear there was a sufficient
number for my reception.

My chief fear and concern was lest I should not be
able to recite my office against the time so as to satisfy
my obligation. I begged St. Xaverius to teach me what
was sufficient for that end, that I might have no scruple
concerning it after my profession. I confided he would,
but I was left to myself awhile to give me some exercise
of humiliation, for I met with many mortifications by
that means, both from my mistress and others, but after
my profession I had no scruple at all concerning it.
About a month before my profession I went again into
the Spiritual Exercise, to prepare myself for that most
desired time. I do not remember any particular favour,
but some lights of the great love Almighty God showed
me in working miracles upon me to the end I might
attain health, and so become His spouse. Yet at the
end of this Exercise St. Xaverius appeared to me for
my comfort and the good of another whom I had
recommended to him. This was the Sub-Prioress who
taught me Latin. Though she would often be chiding
me, yet I loved her entirely. She was frequently
speaking to me of spiritual things, and used to importune me to pray to St. Xaverius to obtain health for
her to go through the duties of religion. She would

often be asking me what he said to me concerning her,
but he had given me no answer all this year till now at
the end of this Exercise.

As I was one day walking in the Chapter House after
dinner, the time appointed for saying Beads (but I was
too much recollected for vocal prayer), St. Xaverius
appeared to me on a sudden in the place where the
Prioress sits in Chapter, not standing on the ground
but as it were elevated, he bade me tell the party he
would obtain for her what was most for God's glory and
honour. This was all, as I remember, at that time, yet
I was transported with joy and devotion, this being the
first time I had seen him since I entered into religion,
excepting that dream which I have already mentioned.
He seemed to me as I believe he was whilst he was
conversant in the world. He remained not long with
me but soon disappeared, yet left me in great devotion
and with a light and contempt of all things of this world
which cannot be expressed, and I do not remember
that I have at any time passed through that chamber
since without particular reflection on this favour and
great reverence to the place. My great trouble now
was to think how I should be able to relate this to the
person concerned as the Saint had bade me, having never
as yet declared anything of this nature even to my
directors. I recommended it much to God in prayer,
and begged Him to give me light that I might know
what to do. I passed days and weeks before I could
resolve. One day after Communion, I found myself
so much moved to declare it to the afore-mentioned
person that I could no longer defer. After Matins at
night I knew she was kneeling in the dark before the
Blessed Sacrament. I placed myself near her, and she
bade me to commend her to St. Xaverius. Then I began
to relate with great difficulty what the Saint had ordered

me to tell her, namely, that he would obtain for her
that which was most for God's honour and glory and
the good of her soul.  At which she was transported
with joy and asked me many questions, how I knew
it was St. Xaverius, if I had seen him when he said this
to me, and the like.  I could tell her nothing but only
that I knew it was so.  She was much moved to devotion
and much consoled, as she told me afterwards, and slept
but little that night for thinking of it, and did always
her whole life after increase in devotion to St. Xaverius
to the admiration of all, for though she was a good
religious before, yet from this time she began to run the
way of perfection to the astonishment of all the Community.  Though they knew nothing of this, yet they
pointed out from this time the change which was in her.
Two years after this she was chosen Superior, and in
something more than a year after that died most happily,
particulars of which I shall hereafter relate, which I
think much to the glory of God, and will move others
to devotion to this great Saint who assisted her to the
last, and ten days after her death (as I have reason
to believe) procured the release of her soul out of
purgatory.  But I will now leave speaking of it till its
proper place that I may make an end of this first year.

A little before my profession I was much moved to
declare to my director some of the supernatural favours
God had done me, which I did.  As soon as I had
done speaking, he chid me grievously, and asked me
if I, who ought to do penance for my sins, pretended
such things.  Neither would he permit me to say any
more at that time.  I do not remember that I was
troubled in the least by what he said to me.  This being
the first time I had spoken of any such favours, I found
difficulty enough in declaring myself, but after this time
I spoke with less difficulty, for seeing he slighted them

and did not seem to believe them, I spoke more freely to him. I thought Almighty God required that I should relate them to him for the future, which from henceforth was my constant practice, having light now that it was more for God's honour and glory than to keep them to myself, and the proceedings of my director confirmed me in this, seeing he did not esteem me more on this account but rather slighted me more.

The morning I was to make my profession, after I had confessed, as I was going to make my vows, I told my director the great confidence I had that St. Xaverius would help me to perform what I was about. He reprimanded me and spoke as if my too great confidence were a great fault. At that I was troubled and I think moved to tears, but I hid this from him, neither did it last long nor in the least diminish my confidence in the Saint. I made my vows with great alacrity and devotion. When I had done and according to custom had prostrated myself on the ground, I found such a sense of devotion in considering that what I had so much desired was now accomplished, and that I was become spouse to the King of kings, and I think I fell into a rapt, when the Sub-Prioress came to raise me up as usual she found my hands stiff and cold and could not make me move at first. She told me afterwards she was so surprised that if this had happened to any other she would have cried out and supposed them dead, but she imagined this was some fit of devotion. I remember I was obliged to use force to myself before I could rise. I had that day a Mass of music in the church in honour of St. Xaverius, which I looked upon very providential. It was given by a lady who on this account made me promise to perform some devotion to St. Xaverius for her, which I did afterwards, and something happened very extraordinary upon it, but having forgotten the particulars I shall say no more of it.

I here end the first year of my noviceship.[1]

[1] 'I shall only add in this place that from the first moment that she entered this religious Community she drew upon her the eyes of everybody, and her exemplary life made her be looked upon as a perfect pattern of regularity and virtue. This is the character she gained in her noviceship, and which she continued to her dying day. Her mistress, who taught her, was so charmed with her virtue, that where she could speak in confidence, she could never sufficiently admire the treasure they possessed in this virtuous novice. She attributed great part of the graces, which she received abundantly afterwards from Almghty God, to this novice's prayers, and became herself in a manner her disciple or novice, choosing, as we may say, to die in her arms, being wonderfully helped by her in this last conflict of death, as shall be mentioned afterwards. Her director, though he did not fail to mortify her, had so great an opinion of her virtue, that from this time to his death, he kept a constant correspondence with her, thinking himself happy in the confidence and direction of a person who he thought highly grateful in the eyes of God. We may easily conceive the esteem which the Community had for her from her first entrance, seeing, that when, as we may say, scarce out of her noviceship, they cast their eyes upon her for Sub-prioress, and the next election chose her to be Superior of the monastery. She observes herself, which is very true, that people frequently begged her prayers; it was done usually, not only by those who were shut up with her and eye-witnesses of her virtues, but also by others from abroad who heard of her virtue. Thus whilst this humble soul proposes to herself to live unknown, and for these ends conceals, even from her directors, what God wrought in her, God is pleased to raise and exalt her in the esteem of others by a way which must give the reader, if he reflects on it, a strange notion of her exemplary virtue : for all this time of her noviceship when every one had conceived such an advantageous opinion of her, there was nothing known, not even to her confessarius or director, but was gathered from her exemplary life. Had it indeed been known that she had been favoured before by so many revelations and visions, I should not have wondered to see people flock after her, but to see this esteem raised universally in the minds of others, purely by the conduct of an irreproachable and exemplary life, argues more than a common virtue, which shone in her actions, by which she became so pleasing to God and man. *—Collector.*

# CHAPTER XVI.

*She advances in prayer. The effects of it. She is forbidden by her director to indulge the sweet caresses she finds in prayer. What happened whilst she strives to obey. The trials put upon her by her director, and her resignation to want their spiritual comfort is followed by greater favours. St. Xaverius promises to be to her a father, friend, physician, and director, and performs all these parts, foretelling her she shall be Superior. She not without difficulty acquaints her Superior with this. She finds frequent Communion her chief support in difficulties.*

As St. Xaverius had foretold me, I had this year more supernatural favours, and higher prayer than formerly. It is our custom to prostrate in the choir and renew our vows on Twelfth Day, at which time I begged of our Lord that I might ever keep them entirely, and after Communion I thought our Lord showed me them engraven on His own Sacred Heart, in some imaginary way which I know not well how to express. I found great joy and deep recollection in my soul. This often returns to my mind with singular comfort, and I confide in the goodness of God that I shall keep them faithfully, for I have often failed, yet so as not to commit any deliberate great sin, which God of His goodness preserved me ever from.

This year I advanced even much in prayer, without myself knowing how or by what means, but Almighty

God was pleased to do it, to show His power in so weak a creature. I often found myself elevated, and my body so light that I was not able to keep myself steadily upon the ground, though I would endeavour to prevent my rising by holding what was next me when I knelt, to the end others might not perceive it, for I had great difficulty and fear lest this should be observed by any. After this sort of prayer and these impetuosities, I found my mind and thoughts drawn so forcibly to Almighty God, that I was not able without great trouble to think of anything else. When I gave account of this to my director he chid me much, he bade me resist all these motions and feelings of devotion, to neglect and slight them, charging me to obey on this point. He added, though they should prove not to be from the devil, at least they were fancies and imaginations which might do me much harm. I was extremely troubled at this, and in great anguish of mind, and I could not forbear showing him my concern by weeping, for I was confident the prayer and favours I had were from God, by the effects I found in my soul of humility, mortification, and contempt of all things in the world. The only comfort and consolation I had was to converse with God and to consider the favours He had done me. So that now being ordered by obedience to resist these favours, and look upon them as temptations, was a torment beyond what I can express. This made me afraid to put myself on my knees, or recollect myself, for fear I should find my former devotion and favours. But the more I resisted them the more I felt them, and this created new anguish, making me apprehend I had not followed the orders of my director, and that I had therefore failed in obedience. My mistress perceived me one day to look more than usually pensive, and calling me to her to know what the matter was, I told her my director had mortified me and did not let her know in what.

Three or four days after my director sent for me, demanding if I had been obedient. I answered, the more I resisted this fervour of prayer the more it came upon me. This notwithstanding he bade me go on as he had ordered me eight days longer, till he came out of the Spiritual Exercise (he was then entering into it). At this my grief was renewed, and I wept bitterly to think I should remain in this conflict eight days longer. My mistress, seeing me so concerned when I left him, was desirous to know if he had offered me no comfort, supposing, as I believe, that I was under some great trouble, because she had not usually seen me weep. I told her I had received no comfort at all. I hope this resentment was not displeasing to Almighty God, for when I came to prayer our Lord appeared to me, and I complained to Him how hardly my director had dealt with me in bidding me resist these sweet feelings of devotion and caresses which His Divine Majesty was pleased to give me. At this I thought our Blessed Saviour had great compassion on me and caressed me the more. I had not enjoyed this consolation long when I began to have a scruple that I had not been obedient to my director in resisting these favours. I told our Lord so, but He sweetly replied that if He would caress me it was not in my power to hinder it. This I must confess was great comfort to me. Notwithstanding this, I entreated our Lord to retire, lest I should be the cause of His staying longer, that I might go on delighting and solacing myself with Him contrary to the orders I had received, and by this means should come to be disobedient. This was so great an affliction to me, I knew not how to express it. On the one side I knew not how to resist these sweet caresses of our Blessed Saviour, Who seemed now to be continually following me, comforting and compassionating my case, that I should be thus restrained and retarded from Him, neither could I forbear to make my moan to Him on the other side. Then I considered that my director had said he must try my obedience, and if these favours were from God I should obey. Seeing I could not resist them, but had them more frequently, I thought I had to fear they were illusions. I knew not what to do with myself in this perplexity and anguish, but thought it long till I could speak to my director, hoping he might be moved to set me at liberty, seeing me in this desolate condition, for I apprehended some great sin in not obeying him. But I had no hopes of seeing him yet, this being only the second or third day of his Exercise, as I remember, though I thought every day a week, and to continue thus till the Exercise was ended seemed insupportable.

In this perplexity I took my recourse to St. Xaverius, begging him by some means or other to obtain that my director might come to me. I knew all the means I could use would prevail nothing on account of the difficulty he had of interrupting his Exercise. The blessed Saint had compassion on me, for the next day an unexpected accident obliged him to come to the monastery. One of our ancient sisters, a jubilarian, at the end of our morning prayer coming hastily down stairs, chanced to fall. I heard her, and was the first who came to her assistance. I found her lying at the bottom of the stairs as if she had been dead, without any motion. The Superior and Community frightened at this sent in all haste for the Father. She continued in a strong agony after she began to stir, till he came, and then she revived and mended presently. The next day she was so perfectly well that she felt no more of it, which was surprising to all, considering her age, and that she was a very gross body.

I looked upon the Father as sent to me by the Saint,

and went to him and told him the trouble I was in,
fearing I had offended God in not obeying, for I found
the more I resisted these favours and caresses of our
Lord the more I had them, and withal I told him our
Saviour's answer, that if He would favour me, it was not
in my power to help it. He was moved to see me so
troubled, and said it was not in his power to limit
Almighty God's favours, that I need not be concerned,
that I had committed no sin of disobedience, and withal
gave me leave to go on the way God led me, at least till
this Exercise was ended, for I believe he thought, as well
as I, that this was the cause of his coming at that time.
I was overjoyed to see myself at liberty, and cared not
how long he stopped away, for fear he should restrain
me, which he did frequently the four years he stayed
after this.

Once he mortified me in a particular manner, and
would not speak to me for a long time, nor give me any
direction in a thing I much desired, but as soon as I
came to the grate, he used to leave it and go down stairs.
This I resented, and going down to prayer one night, in
this my second year, in great desolation, I complained to
St. Xaverius, thinking it hard to be left by him too. But
I was resolved to seek no other comforts, and to place
my confidence in him, being content to want all comfort
else, and even to that which I received from him, if it
were more pleasing to God. After this act of resignation,
I was rapt in spirit, and I saw as it were into heaven,
represented to me as a delightful garden in the spring
time, and there, as in a solitary place, beset on each side
with odoriferous flowers, I thought I beheld St. Xaverius
and St. Ignatius walking, as it were, absorbed in God,
and consulting about things which concerned His honour
and glory. But St. Xaverius seemed, as it were by
accident, to cast an eye on me, and perceiving the

desolation in which I was, he left St. Ignatius, and, as it
were, flew to me, saying: "Child, since you seek no
other comfort, I come myself to comfort you, I have
promised to be your father, physician, and friend, and
now I will be your director." He caressed me much
and seemed to have great compassion on me, and at his
departure, he gave me three blessings, one for myself
and two for two others, and bade me tell my director
that he would have him write down what I had told him
of the favours God had done me. I remained after this
in great consolation, and from that time took the Saint
for my director, and was in no haste to go to any other,
but in all occasions found a most sensible help from him,
and though he would advise me to go to others for my
humiliation, yet I never remember that they contradicted
any light I had concerning my acting in any difficulty,
even in this office of Superior in which I now am, either
in spiritual or temporal concerns, or that they gave me
any other counsel but what I had from him. Sometimes
they give me the same before I told them, and though I
now seem to myself in great darkness, yet I have a great
confidence in this blessed Saint.[1]

[1] 'This method of God's proceeding with the Saints by corporal
representations is not unusual (see Acts x. 11, seq.) We must always
observe here that what we read in these papers is of a very different
nature from those things which are commonly penned down in the
lives of the Saints. In those lives you find the hand of Almighty God
working wonderfully in them by producing exterior acts of heroical
virtues, or working by them prodigies in testimony of their sanctity.
Here you find those interior methods and ways by which God led her
step by step to that great sanctity to which she arrived by the help of
His grace. Not that other Saints were not led by those or the like
lights in an interior way to the height of perfection, or as if she was
to be noted for her singularity in this point. No doubt, they felt these
sweet motions of Divine grace, and their sanctity was perfected by their
attention to them, as we find them in the life of St. Teresa, who was
commanded to make known what God wrought in her soul, and in the
few notes of St. Ignatius, which casually escaped the fire when he consumed the rest of his writings. In a word, in the lives of the Saints we

When I found a convenient time, I told my director what St. Xaverius had told me to tell him, namely, that he would have him write down the things which had happened to me. I found a difficulty in doing this, thinking he would either be angry or else laugh at me, as he did, and when I told him the Saint had promised to be my director, he asked me if that was all, and whether I had any more to say, for he would seem to hearken to all with great attention, but then like one in a surprise when I had done speaking, he would treat them all as fancies, or the effects of a weak mind. I was not much concerned at this, but was satisfied I had complied with my orders in speaking. I found afterwards, my director was something uneasy that I had written nothing, and began to inquire further about it. Before he left this place he made me write down some things, but pretended it was only to see if I had a good pen. He knew I had a great difficulty in writing.

I constantly found the more he mortified me the more I was caressed by the Saint. About two months after this, being in prayer in the same place in the choir, and at the same hour ordained by our constitutions, in the evening from five to six, in the beginning of my prayer, I found great devotion and recollection, the Saint appearing to me with signs and demonstrations of most familiar, affectionate, and tender love. Here he performed at once all the offices he had taken upon him the last time he appeared, of which I never had a distinct light till now that I was going to write this down. When I lifted up my heart to the Saint, to beg him to teach me and

commonly read the exterior effects of Divine grace, either in their heroical acts or in the prodigies God wrought for them and by them. In these papers we find the interior motions of grace, sometimes, indeed, breaking out into exterior acts of virtue, but chiefly in an inward way, raising the devout soul from one degree of perfection to another, till she arrived at a high degree of sanctity.'—*Collector.*

direct me in explaining it so as to make it to be understood, I had a perfect knowledge given me of all the
particulars.   He appeared to me very beautiful, in his
habit, surrounded with a heavenly light and splendour,
not seeming to me to be much above the age of thirty,
yet with a great gravity and angelical modesty.   He gave
me his blessing like a tender father, making a cross upon
my forehead, and put his mantle over my head to show
he would protect me from all dangers.   He showed
himself a friend in foretelling me some crosses that I
might be prepared for them.   Standing after this, at a
little distance, he held in his hand a crucifix before me,
saying in a very solemn voice, but in an interior way, as
all favours happen to me : " Child, if you will imitate me,
you must embrace this and prepare yourself for crosses
and not expect me so frequently to visit and comfort
you."   I was a little afflicted at this, and I think the
Saint had a feeling of my grief, notwithstanding at the
same time he foretold me I should be Superior, by which
I understood that the chief of my crosses should proceed
from this employ.   Then, like an able physician, he
presented me the Heavenly Bread to strengthen my
frailty, and to enable me to go through all for God's
honour and glory.   For in that hand in which I had
seen just before a crucifix, I saw now a Host, and he
gave me to understand that when these crosses came
upon me, this Living Bread by frequent receiving should
give me strength.   After this, as a good director, he
advised me what to do on any sudden cross, bidding me
take my crucifix in my hand and embrace it, and give
thanks to God for the cross He sent, praying Him
to unite it to His Sacred Passion, that none of my
sufferings might be lost by my impatience, adding
sweetly he would help me to bear them.

The Saint stayed longer with me than he had ever

done before, appearing to me immediately after I had begun my hour of prayer at five o'clock, and remaining by me till the bell called us to the refection at six. Oh, how short did the hour appear! I cannot express the consolation I felt in my soul to see myself thus caressed by the blessed Saint. I found so tender an affection that my heart was even ready to melt; but I could do nothing but enjoy, not being able to make any distinct acts of thanksgiving or offering of myself. Yet I thought I was all his, and desired to remain by him; but he made it known to me that it was his will I should make a sacrifice of this satisfaction, leave him then, and accompany the Community to the refectory, which I did with much ado, not knowing without forcing myself how to stir, for in these transports my strength would be, as it were, quite gone, and my hands stiff and cold. When I came to the refectory I began to lament my solitude, and loss of the company of the Saint, and I think it was at this time he appeared to me there, as I was sitting at table, only to caress me and show me how pleasing my obedience was in quitting him to follow the Community.

My greatest grief was to think I should be Superior, and that the Saint would not so frequently visit and comfort me. I went to my director, and acquainted him with what the Saint had foretold me, but with much confusion and shame, for I thought he might with reason tax me with pride in believing I should come to be Superior, since I then was only a novice. Yet I resolved to acquaint him because I thought the Saint required this of me. I do not perfectly remember what he said to me on this occasion, being so full of confusion in discovering the thing that I scarce minded his answer. I only remember he gave me some check, and asked when that dignity would fall upon me. I told him I could not justly tell the time, but I was sure it would happen.   I had not then light as to the time, but since then it was revealed to me when I was in prayer, that the reason why the Saint appeared to me so young as thirty or a little more, was because about that age I should be put into that employ, as it happened after-, wards.   I was about twenty-seven when this was told me.

I caused a picture of the Saint to be drawn as he appeared then to me, expressing all the particulars as well as I could get them represented.   This picture for the most part I wear about me day and night; and when I am in great desolation, as it now happens, finding the great weight of my burthen, if I cast my eyes upon this picture it comforts me and gives me hopes that as the crosses he foretold me are fallen upon me, I shall not fail to find the help and assistance he promised me. The crosses indeed have been heavy since I have been Superior, and more sensible than I could have imagined. It is very surprising to see how they have happened and have gone on increasing ever since that time.   I am unwilling to mention them here, being only ordered to mention what happened in my noviceship.   If I outlive this employ (there is yet a year to the next election) and be then appointed to go on writing, I shall bring them in in their proper place.   But few who know my weak health since I have been Superior think I can outlive that time.

I must in this place add that the chief strength I find as to body and soul is from my frequent communions. I have had leave both from the confessor and director for almost a twelvemonth to communicate daily; I have also been advised to it by my Lord Bishop, who is our Superior, and to whom we make our vows, and I have the same advice from the present Provincial of the

Society, whom I consulted upon this point, thinking it would be better to abstain sometimes out of humility, it not being the common practise to communicate so frequently. Though I had a great desire of receiving daily, yet I was willing to consult so often about it lest I should give occasion of disquiet by my singularity. But when I was told I ought to look upon these thoughts as temptations, and not abstain one day upon this account, it was a singular comfort, and I thought what the Saint had told me was come to pass, namely, that by frequent receiving this Bread of Life I should be strengthened to go through.

After this digression, in which I have said more than I designed in this place, I return to my former discourse. I had not in my noviceship a light of all these things which I since find Almighty God designed to manifest to me by the particulars specified in this last apparition of the Saint, neither could I interpret anything aright myself till God gave me to understand it. I thought now I should not see the Saint of a great while, because he said I must not expect him so often ; but on the contrary he, like a tender father, seeing me not yet strong enough to go alone, heaped upon me for some time more favours than before, and as from this time my crosses increased, so did my consolation too till I came to be Superior.[2]

[2] ' Though she lived several years after the election of which she speaks here, yet by reason of her bad state of health and continual employments, she never had leisure to write down what happened to her after she was Superior, by which we are deprived of a distinct knowledge of those crosses she here mentions, as well as of those documents we might have received from her manner of bearing them. On the same account we have lost knowledge of those lights she received concerning prayer, of which she says she could have written whole volumes ; so that notwithstanding all we know of her, the account we can give is very imperfect, because God alone, Who wrought in her, is conscious of what passed in that virtuous soul during the last thirteen years—that is, during the most perfect part of her life.'—*Collector.*

J

# CHAPTER XVII.

*St. Xaverius appears to her and instructs her in imitation of him. She gets leave to suck a loathsome ulcer. Her sentiments, and the instructions she receives upon this. She willingly submits to the meanest employs. Our Saviour on this account raises her to a great familiarity with Himself. His documents on this occasion about perfect disengagement. She falls into a rapt before her mistress, but procures she should keep it secret.*

In this last year of my noviceship I had familiar visits from St. Xaverius. I was ordered to help one of the religious in the vestry. She was of a good temper, yet she often chid me when I got leave of my mistress to hear a Mass more than ordinary, or to perform some little devotions, thinking by this means I cast the work more upon her. What troubled me most was that she opposed my making so frequently the ten Fridays' devotion in honour of St. Xaverius, for she knew I could then get leave to spend the best part of the morning in prayer. I endeavoured to hear her with patience, and said but little, that I had leave of my mistress, promising I would work for her when I was at liberty to do what I would. Though I saw her a little mortified, I did not on this account desist from asking leave; yet when my mistress denied me I was content, and looked upon it as the will of God. As for the other, I thought it an imaginary difficulty in the service of God, and so offered it up to

Him. This Sister loved me much, yet, as she told me lately, she never was so hard to any one who was ordered to assist her as she was to me, and that she knew not the reason why she was so, or something to this effect, being out of countenance when she owned it.

When she left me alone in the vestry I used to work upon my knees, this place being just over the altar of the Church where the Blessed Sacrament was always kept. Sometimes I opened a door upon the leads over the altar, just by the cupola or lantern, where I could distinctly hear the Mass in the morning; yet I worked in the meantime, having a scruple to do otherwise without leave. While I was thus working upon my knees— I think it was not in the time of Mass—St. Xaverius appeared to me as he was conversant in the world, and reprehended me, saying I must not do these acts of mortification without leave of my Superior, and he gave me to understand that the humiliation of asking leave, and the act of obedience in doing or not doing the thing according to orders, was more pleasing in the sight of God. After this I did nothing in that kind of my own head. He soon disappeared, yet I was glad of his company, though he came to reprehend me.

Another time I was much moved to ask my Superior leave to do a mortification in imitation of St. Xaverius, sucking sores and ulcers. My greatest difficulty was in asking leave to do it, and I durst not do it without leave, particularly after the Saint had given me the aforesaid caution. Upon this I overcame myself and asked leave, which was granted me. In performing it the corruption seemed no more disgustful, after the first attempt, than if it had been so much milk; which gives me light to know that Almighty God sweetens the difficulties we undertake for His sake, and makes them easier than we can imagine.

Awhile after, this blessed Saint appeared to me again in the same place as I was sitting solitary at my work. Upon seeing him I found inward sentiments of respect and reverence, and as I remember fell down on my knees before him like one surprised. But the blessed Saint would have me rise again and go on with my work, and I signified to him that, having done what I had there, I feared that if I went into the next room to fetch some more, he would be gone before I returned. Yet the Saint would have me go and mortify myself in this. I had much ado to stir, being almost in a rapt. Before I had advanced many steps I perceived the Saint followed me, and, by the way, he gave me, as it were, a caution, that I should not think I had done such a great act in licking the corruption from the sore, though I had done it in imitation of him. At the same time he gave me to understand there were many interior mortifications more acceptable in the sight of God, as the bearing injuries patiently, the endeavouring to do a good turn to those that had done me an evil one or displeased me. This gave me some confusion, and I feared I had thought too much on what I had done, and taken some complacence in it. After this I thought I had a true light of it, and thought it a very small thing; yet I think the Saint was pleased that I overcame myself in asking leave. I thought he would not have me go on studying new mortifications in this kind, but practise what he had already taught me, which I did, endeavouring from this time to do it more perfectly than before. The Saint returned back with me to the place where I sat at work, and then disappeared, leaving me in great peace of mind and devotion.

I had been one morning in the noviceship with the rest of my companions, learning my Breviary. My mistress chid me very much for being so dull and reading my Latin so false. I went thence to the vestry to sort the foul linen, according to the orders of my companion. Being more than ordinarily concerned to think my noviceship was almost done, and that I was still so backward in reading my Breviary, I complained to the Saint sweetly, as if I took it unkind that he had not been so good as his word in helping me. Whilst I was in this desolation and anxiety the Saint appeared to me, saying in a sweet way, ' Child, you shall have your Latin as perfect as any of them,' meaning, as I understood, my fellow novices. The Saint having comforted and encouraged me, soon departed. In less than two years I was chosen Sub-Prioress, whose office it is to take care of the choir and correct those who read in it.

It is our custom to make once a year the Spiritual Exercise. This we make at two different times for the convenience of the Community. I was not permitted to make them in the spring, but was ordered at that time to help the cook in the kitchen. I was well pleased with this mean employ, telling our Lord I was content to be His scullion, and to be employed in these exterior things since it was His pleasure ; but otherwise I greatly desired Mary's part, and was overjoyed when it was my turn afterwards to make the Spiritual Exercise, that I might entertain myself in solitude with our Blessed Saviour. Being, as it were, transported with these thoughts, the first or second day of the Exercise our Blessed Lord appeared to me, as in His Humanity, whilst I was sitting in our cell, saying in an interior voice, ' Since you were content the last time to be My scullion, I will now take you into My chamber of presence to converse with you,' at which I was much moved to devotion and almost in a rapt. He gave me light that we must rise to prayer and contemplation by humility, obedience, and humble actions. I was also in admiration to see the goodness of Almighty God, Who regards the least thing done for His sake.

This Exercise passed, as it were, with my Divine Spouse, enjoying His presence in a particular manner. He appeared to me once more in His Sacred Humanity in a most intimate way, taking care of me and delighting Himself with me, which made me say, in a simple and familiar style, 'Lord, it seems to me as if You had nothing else to do but to keep in my cell and converse with me.' To which He answered interiorly, as these voices happen to me, speaking amorously, yet as it were afflicted that He had so few to delight Himself withal, saying, 'Child, I leave the rich places of the world and come to seek out some little cell where I can find a heart disengaged from all creatures, resigned to My will, and who has no other desire than to please Me; in this solitary soul I delight as in the highest heavens, and will manifest My secrets to her, to the confusion of the wise and foolish.' This raised up my heart to love and admire the goodness of Almighty God, and gave me a desire to make my heart such that He might delight Himself in it, and manifest His secrets to me. Yet I found myself wanting in these virtues He had proposed, but had at the same time a great desire of gaining them. I found in particular a great want of that perfect disengagement, my affections being still tied to my relations, and myself passionately fond of my mistress who taught me. She often chid me for speaking so affectionately of my father, and expressing so longing a desire to see him. He was daily expected to take the habit of the Society in their noviceship at Watten, having had a promise to be admitted for a Lay-brother before I came over, but he was stopped at this time on account of business. I used to argue with my mistress on this point, saying it was not against perfection to rejoice in seeing my father, especially since he was to come on such a design. But she told me there was too much of nature; that the time would come when I should be willing to refuse myself the satisfaction of seeing him. The first news I heard of him after this was that he was dead, and from this time our Lord began to send me some crosses to disengage me from all sensible things. I felt this very much, but will say no more of it in this place, because it takes me off from finishing what I was about.

I was very sorry to be taken out of my noviceship, fearing my best days were then past. In this time I had no charge upon me: my only care then was to do what I was ordered. My companions also, whom I left in the noviceship behind me, expressed a concern in leaving me. My Superior sometimes asked me what our Lord had said to me. I imagine she perceived upon occasions that I seemed to have more devotion than ordinary. I do not know that any others were in any sort conscious of the favours I received in my noviceship from Almighty God, excepting my mistress, who taught me to read my Breviary. The morning I took leave of her at the end of my noviceship, being then to be removed from under her care, she seemed a little concerned to part with me, and I was no less troubled to part with her. She was earnest with me to tell her something about St. Xaverius and of the dream I had of him the first year, asking how I thought the Saint looked, with other particulars. In endeavouring to satisfying her questions, I was so moved to devotion that I fell into a rapt before her, and was not able to go on. I was not a little confounded at this, and soon after parted and left her.

The same day she came to our cell, in time of spiritual reading, and asked how I did, and began to take some notice of what had happened. If I had committed a crime, I could not have been more out of countenance than I was upon this occasion, and I begged upon my knees she would never speak more of it. She was moved to tears, and promised never to mention it: but if she would have owned what passed in her own soul, I believe she was almost in the same condition, though I could not take notice of it.

I here end my noviceship, praise be to God and St. Xaverius, and hope I have satisfied the promise made in my last sickness. The Community at that time made the Devotion of the ten Fridays in honour of St. Xaverius for my recovery, and several offered up other private devotions for the same end. I apprehended that I should be long ill, and was willing to do anything which I thought pleasing to God to move Him to grant me health. In this disposition, I resolved if I recovered my health to go on writing. This made me put pen to paper at this time, and considering the little leisure I have had, I cannot but admire to see how much I have written.

If there be anything well said, the Saint has done it for me. It has never cost me any trouble to consider what I am to say, and has not cost me so much pains in writing as if I had transcribed a paper put before me, because there I must have lost time in looking on it.

## CHAPTER XVIII.

*She continues writing by new orders from her director. She is ordered by St. Xaverius to change her vote in the election of a Superior. St. Xaverius succours her against the enemy, who visibly molests her. She receives the news of her father's death, and practises what St. Xaverius taught her to do on the like occasions. The sentiments she had on this account. She importunes heaven for the good of his soul, and sees him after some time among the saints. Her devotion to St. Xaverius increased by this.*

JESUS, MARY, JOSEPH, TERESA, XAVERIUS.

THOUGH I spoke, in what I said the last year of my noviceship, as if I designed to write no more till I was out of this office of Superior, yet I being bid by my director to continue, I made no reply. My difficulty in this is much lessened, considering the supernatural help I have found, and the peace and repose of mind which I feel constantly whilst I am writing. Nay, my devotion is then even greater than in prayer, and for this reason I begin to-day, being in more anxiety than usual, tired out with a multiplicity of affairs relating to my office of Superior. I chose therefore this half-hour to write, by this to quiet my mind, thinking that St. Xaverius is then particularly near me, by the sensible help I find from him then more than at any other time. Yet I do not remember that I have ever neglected any of my other duties for what I have written, though I should be glad in these spare times when I have sometimes a half-hour, sometimes an hour, to myself, to be in some solitary place. This cannot be done while I am in this employ. Nay, commonly I sit where all the Community may have free access to me ; and whilst I have been writing these few lines I have been interrupted by eight or nine of the religious. Yet, though this happens frequently, I cannot say it puts me out in what I have to write. Nevertheless it mortifies me. I design here to relate what happened the first year after I came out of the noviceship, hoping still to have the same help I have had hitherto.

About a month after I ended my noviceship came on the election of our Superior. It is always our custom nine days before the election to recite in Community the Hymn *Veni Creator*, to implore the aid and assistance of the Divine Spirit, and to beg light to direct us in the choice. During this time my thoughts were to give my voice to the re-election of her who was already Superior (our Constitutions leaving us to our liberty in this point either to re-elect the same or choose another). With this design I went up to our cell on the day of election, not thinking to make any change, but as I took the paper into my hand to write the billet, designing to give my voice to the Bishop for her, St. Xaverius appeared to me, and seemed to look something angry at me for not giving my voice for her who was Sub-Prioress. She was the person I spoke of before, who taught me my Breviary in my noviceship. He gave me to understand it was for this reason he had appeared to me in the first year of my noviceship (as I have related), in the chapter-house, over the place in which the Prioress sits, there ordering me at the same time to tell this person he would obtain for her what was most for God's honour and glory and the good of her soul.

I presently changed my resolution and wrote down

her name in place of the other designed before. The reason I did not choose her before was not for want of respect or esteem, but I believe I thought my voice would be lost, she not being likely to be chosen by the Community by reason of her weak health. Before I gave my voice, I acquainted my director (as we were permitted to do) with my design. He seemed surprised to see me change my mind, and gave me no encouragement, asking me if I thought her fit to converse with seculars, not knowing the language of the country. In conclusion, she was chosen Superior, but to the surprise of many, and I believe if she had wanted my vote she would not have had a sufficient number. I believe it was much to God's honour and glory she was made Superior, though doubtless it shortened her life, because she was now so much restrained from following her fervour and zeal.

I was scarce able to contain the joy I felt at her election, and the day she was chosen she demanded of me a picture of St. Xaverius, to which she had great devotion. I gave it her the same time as I delivered my obedience to her. The reason why I valued this picture so much, was this : one morning as reciting the Canonical Hours in the choir with the rest of the religious, the enemy seemed to appear to me in a very ugly shape, tempting me with despairing thoughts, saying, for all my high prayer I should be his, and that he would deceive me at last by prayer. I found myself a little surprised and frightened at this, but, as I remember, I answered thus interiorly— However, I would endeavour to love and serve God as long as I was in this life. Though he continued to stand before me in an imaginary and frightful shape, yet I went on with the rest in the Divine Office, but I believe thought it long till it was done, that I might get out of the choir before him, but he was too

quick for me.   I found him in my cell when I got
upstairs, seated under the table.   I was truly frightened
and loath to enter, but at last I took so much courage
and confidence in God as to go in, resolving he should
not hinder me doing what obedience appointed, which
was, at that time, to put in order my cell.   I had much
ado to stay, and thought if I was once got out I should
never more care to enter it, for the imaginations and
temptations were so abominable and impure that I knew
not what to do to defend myself.   I remembered I had
a picture of St. Xaverius about me.   It was one of those
in which the Saint is represented kneeling at the foot of
a crucifix.   I held this up before him, with great confidence in the blessed Saint.   At the sight of it the
enemy went away, saying, as it were in a murmuring
voice to two or three of his companions, which I then
perceived with him, 'We shall never get anything of her
so long as she has such a confidence in that man.'   It
seemed to me that this was the most contemptuous word
God would permit them to say of the blessed Saint.
I put this picture in the place where the devil had sat,
to keep him from coming there any more.   I went from
hence to Mass, and after Communion, as I remember,
I saw in spirit an angel standing over the place where
the foul spirit had been, and a most resplendent light
overshadowing this picture, which makes me esteem it
so much, and the whole cell adorned with odoriferous
flowers.   I longed now more than ever to be in it, and
when I entered it was with great respect, reverence,
recollection, and prayer.   I thought this was the angel
that appeared to me in my sickness, with a crown in
his hand, being very like to him.   My Superior often
borrowed the picture of me, and perceiving the devotion
I had to it, suspected something extraordinary, though I
never told her of the favour I had received by it.

I think St. Xaverius would not have it taken from me, for one who had been our director, passing by, and thinking, as I suppose, I had too great a tie to it, took it from me and carried it away, saying I should see it no more; but soon after he sent it me back in a letter, telling me he had sent me my beloved picture, on condition I should pray to my Saint for him. I wore it constantly about me. God forgive me, I am so tepid now, I am very little moved to devotion by that or anything else.

A little after my noviceship, I dreamt I saw my father in his agony. I was much afflicted, and it was as sensible to me as if I had been present at his death. It wrought also very much upon my spirits, and I told my Superior and others what I had dreamt, and the first letters from England after this brought me news of his death.

I had heard nothing of his being sick, but was in daily expectation of his coming over to enter into the Society. He had got leave to be admitted for a Lay-brother. I was willing then to look upon it only as a dream; but when I considered the thing afterwards, and by comparing found it to have happened the very night, as I think, on which he died, I was apt to look upon it as more than a dream, and that God had pleased to give me some light of it.

My Superior kept the news private for some time. She had great compassion for me, and knowing how sensibly I should be troubled at it, she was willing to wait some favourable occasion of breaking it to me; but she began at last to have some scruple of depriving his soul so long of prayers. Hence one morning she called me to her cell before Mass. She began to speak about St. Xaverius, and desired me to show her the picture I esteemed so much. She knelt down and kissed it, asking me if St. Xaverius was not my physician and friend, and if he would not also be my father. At these words I was struck, and asked her if she had heard my father was dead. She did not presently answer me, and could not, I believe, for tears; but after a little she showed me my sister's letter, which gave me the news of it. I had not then the comfort to hear any particulars; but some months after I understood he died of a fever, and very happily, having a Father of the Society with him to the last. At the first news of his death I shed not a tear, but disguised the grief I felt for a time, and went on doing some little things I was accustomed to do in accommodating my Superior's cell, at which she was surprised, seeing me contain myself so much; but as soon as I had done there I retired into our own cell and shut the door; my heart was afflicted more than ever I remembered it to have been in my whole life. In this distress I immediately cast myself upon my knees and took my crucifix in my hand, remembering what St. Xaverius had ordered me to do upon any sudden cross, when he appeared to me, as I have already specified, in what I wrote concerning the time of my noviceship. I kissed the Five Wounds of our Saviour, and thanked Almighty God for the cross He had sent me, begging Him that none of my sufferings might be lost by my impatience in suffering them, beseeching Him to unite them all to His Sacred Passion. I cannot express the resentment I had, considering how tenderly I loved my father and the reasons I had for it, and the daily expectation I was in of seeing him. I sweetly complained to St. Xaverius, thinking it unkindly done in him not to obtain that he should die in the habit, seeing his business was almost completed I must confess I was extremely afflicted day and night, and could not forbear showing it, sometimes by tears, sometimes by sadness in my countenance, for which my Superior would often chide me. Yet the trouble was not such as to hinder me in the least in any of my spiritual duties; for though I had a lively sense of it, yet in the bottom I found an entire resignation to the will of God. I thought this was one of the crosses St. Xaverius had foretold me, and I perceived his particular assistance helping me to bear it, for in my greatest desolation I do not remember that it was ever a distraction to me in my prayer : I was still more united to God, and more disengaged from creatures. My prayer was chiefly an amorous complaint to our Lord and St. Xaverius for my father's unexpected death, before he could accomplish his good designs. I believe he had acted according to all the rules of justice. I had also made several devotions for him, and told the Saint he had often granted my request for strangers and now denied it to my friends; that I never begged anything of him but with a perfect resignation, as it might be most for God's honour and glory, of which nature I thought this petition was. I also resented that he should be dead so long before I heard of it, to procure prayers for his soul. All I could now do was to importune St. Xaverius for the good of his soul; for though he was very virtuous, yet I know a soul must be pure and without stain before it can enter heaven, which made me apprehend he might yet have something to suffer. Thus I continued praying some weeks before I had any light concerning his state or any answer to my prayers; only once, I remember, as I was complaining to our Lord that I was left an orphan, that He had not only taken away my father, but had withdrawn Himself likewise, or to this effect, I presently found great joy in my soul and saw our Blessed Saviour standing before me, speaking in a most sweet and amorous way, and saying, ‘You are My dear Xaveria and darling child ; come to Me as to

your Father for anything you want.' He gave me to
understand He did not take my father away till He had
given me another besides Himself, which was St. Xaverius.
This was of great comfort to me, considering that five or
six months before my father died St. Xaverius promised
to be my father.

Though I had great feeling of my father's death, yet
my sentiments were very much changed from what they
were when I first left the world.   My sister and I told
the person who brought us over that we had left our
friends and should not have the grief to see them die.
He answered, we should have as great grief to part with
those we were to live with in religion; but we did not
then conceive how far a spiritual love surpasses a natural
one, but now I know it by experience.   I should have
greater concern to lose my present Superior than I had
for the death of my father, and when I was at first
so much afflicted at his death I cast myself upon my
knees before her and told her I thanked God for giving
me so good a mother before He took my father from
me.   But now Almighty God began to disengage me
entirely from creatures, for it was not much above a year
after this before He was pleased to take her from me.
I shall give the particulars in their due place, for I am
much moved in writing to bring things in their due
order of time, though I did not design this in the
beginning.

This, my dear Mother, awhile after the news of my
father's death, used frequently to tell me with a great
deal of confidence, that she believed his soul was in
heaven.   I was pleased to hear her say so, but I had no
light of it till five months after.

In Whitsun holidays I was reciting Terce in the choir
with the rest of the religious.   I had been some time in
desolation, yet had begged the Divine Spirit the Comforter

might come upon me and replenish my soul with His gifts. I do not remember I found myself disposed in any particular manner to devotion, much less did I expect at that time any supernatural favour, till on a sudden I heard a voice, as it were a fluttering of doves, which transported me, and I thought I saw the heavens open and the Holy Ghost descend upon me with great speed in the form of a dove, saying, 'My spouse, for deferring so long I come now the stronger;' resting Himself upon my breast with a mighty force which surpassed my natural strength and forces and put me in a rapt. I was not able to speak nor go on with the Divine Office, though I forced myself, and I think I felt then some of that Divine fire, and as much as I could bear and live. I stood like one in a maze at what I saw and heard, and at the suddenness of it. Oh, what a light had I then of all things in this world! I cannot express the contempt I had of it, nor the joy I likewise felt in seeing part of heaven open to my sight, where I discovered my father standing in his rank among those of the Society of Jesus, clothed in their habit. St. Xaverius seemed to cast a kind eye upon him, by which I understood he had obtained him this favour, though my father could not accomplish his desire of living among them on earth : Almighty God, knowing his good designs, by the intercessions of the Saint had completed all in heaven.

I do not remember that after this I had any grief or concern for his death, and some days I was so transported with spiritual joy and devotion that I could not, if I would, have put this out of my mind. He did not seem to me like one dead, but living, where I might have free conversation with him, and oftener than if he had been in the world. After this some of the religious would press me to tell them if St. Xaverius had not revealed that my father was in heaven. I never owned

K

anything of it, not even to my Superior, though my countenance sometimes betrayed me by blushing when they spoke of it, at which I was mortified, but could not help it. I related something of it to my director, but not so distinctly as I have penned it here.

After this my prayer and devotion were increased to St. Xaverius for this great favour done to my father, and I found I had no reason to complain for his not having so much kindness to my friends as he did to others I prayed for. I see the blessed Saint never forsakes them that confide in him, and if he refuse to do it in this life he will do it plentifully in the next. I must confess my father had a strange confidence and devotion to him out of gratitude for what the blessed Saint had done for me, which often puts me to confusion when I think of it, and it made me love my father with a more spiritual love on this account, though the Saint seemed to forsake him at the last, for I believe he died in great desolation. Yet now I see all was for his greater good. Almighty God gave me this knowledge and consolation, which I fear He granted not to my other brothers and sisters, who were extremely afflicted at his death, and it was thought it would have cost one of them very dear. I had most reason to love my father because, being sick, I most experienced his affections, not that he was partial, nor did I desire it more than the rest, but he thought it charity to give me all the comfort he could because I suffered so much by sickness. I think it best to say no more on this subject, lest nature should have any hand in it; but in what I have said I think I have no other motive than the glory of God, and to raise in them that read it a perseverant devotion to St. Xaverius.

## CHAPTER XIX.

*Her disposition with regard to exterior employs.*
*Our Saviour rewards her charity in serving the*
*poor. Our Blessed Lady appears to her. The effect*
*of this vision. She makes use of the favours received*
*to promote regularity. Her Superior's death, with*
*several particulars relating both to her and her dying*
*Superior. Almighty God makes use of this cross to*
*disengage her entirely from creatures.*

In this year I was ordered to assist the porteress at the
grate. I had no inclinations to the employ, knowing the
many occasions of distractions I should necessarily meet
with, and that I should frequently be called out of the
choir to answer the bell at the grate. Yet I made no
reply, but resolved to content myself where obedience
placed me. I knew God was not tied up to time or
place, and that when He has a mind to favour us He
can do it as well in exterior employments as in solitude,
if our actions are performed with a pure intention to
please Him. Though I had left solitude, I met with
more occasions of mortification and contradiction, which
I endeavoured to put up with in silence.

I had a particular delight in serving the poor who
came sometimes to the turn to beg an alms, and I
remember once as I was hurried about in serving the
brewers who were then in the cloister, I carried them
meat to the garden door, whence they were to fetch it.
On a sudden I thought I saw our Blessed Saviour pass

by the door in mean apparel. He seemed, as it were by
chance, to cast His eyes upon me, at which He stopped
a little, and looking upon me with great compassion and
sweetness, spoke to me interiorly to this effect, 'Poor
Xaveria, who used to be conversing with Me and My
angels, is tired and wearied in serving those poor men.'
At which I found great reverence and devotion in my
soul, and I returned this answer, 'I rejoice, O Lord, to
serve You in the meanest of Your creatures.' I thought
our Blessed Saviour was highly pleased at this, and I
found myself almost in a rapt waiting for these poor men
to give them their meat at the door. I served them with
more respect ever after, and had a clear light of what
our Saviour had said, 'Whatever you do to one of these
little ones, you do to Me,' and it gave me great comfort
to see our Blessed Saviour take notice of so small a
thing, and reward so highly as He did me by this vision.

In the octave of Corpus Christi, being in the choir at
prayer, the Blessed Sacrament exposed, I found myself
in very great recollection, when on a sudden St. Xaverius
passed by me, saying : 'Child, prepare your heart, our
Blessed Lady will come to visit you !' This the Saint
seemed to say with great tenderness and respect, but
departed immediately. I was surprised and very much
stirred to devotion, but how to prepare myself I knew
not. Before these thoughts were passed, our Blessed
Lady appeared to me with our Saviour in her arms. She
did not seem so resplendent as a glorified body, but
rather as she was conversant in the world, in an unusual
dress, such as I suppose she wore. But there appeared
in her face a wonderful grace, modesty, and beauty,
beyond that of an angel, which struck a great reverence
into my soul far beyond the apparition of any other
saint. She said : 'It is I, child, who appeared to you
in your sickness with a crown upon my head and a

sceptre in my hand, and laid my hand upon your head,
and now I have brought you to my house, where you
must bear example to others.   In relating these favours
to your director you do well, for by hiding them you
hide the mercy of my Son.'   I remained this time in a
rapt and in great astonishment and admiration at this
favour.   As our Blessed Lady was turning away to
depart, little Jesus seemed to take His hand out of her
bosom, and looking sweetly upon me put out His hand
towards me.   This gives me an unspeakable comfort as
often as I think of it.

This favour alone would have been sufficient to inflame
with the love of God any reasonable creature except
myself, whose heart remained so hard and stony, and
often insensible, after so many blessings and ardent
flames of love from my Beloved, and though they are
such and so intense that I often thought they would
have taken my soul out of my body, yet through my
fault and want of correspondence, they have not
yet rooted out self-love and my unmortified passions,
which makes me even tremble to think of it whilst
I am writing this.   This favour remained a long time
as fresh in my memory as when it happened, and
moved me to great favour and devotion, but at present
it seems so distinct and clear as if it had happened
yesterday.   I related this to my director presently, after
it happened, being encouraged to do so by what our
Blessed Lady had said to me, and I had now some
scruple to conceal anything in this kind.   In giving him
this account I was almost in a rapt, which made me not
know well how to proceed.   He also seemed much
moved to devotion, and what moved him chiefly was
that our Blessed Lady bid me ask him if he had not
dreamt of her.   He owned that he had, but what it was
I know not. I found about five years after this happened

but about three weeks before I wrote this, some papers,
by which I understood that this house was built and
founded by several persons, moved thereunto by different
revelations or visions from our Blessed Lady, which was
as a comfort to me in agreeing so perfectly with what
she told me when she said she had brought me to her
house.

I saw St. Xaverius another time in this Octave of
Corpus Christi, between the Superior and myself, as we
were reciting the Divine Office. I do not remember he
said anything at that time, but it was a comfort to see
him so near me. Since I have been in this office of
Superior, she being chosen at the same time my Sub-
Prioress, I have a clear light that the Saint will stand
between us, helping us to advance regular observance,
which I could not well do without her assistance. I
sometimes relate to her this passage, to make her willingly
concur with me for the keeping up of discipline. She
has a great devotion to the Saint, and is ready, with
great humility, to submit to me on all occasions, though
I was her novice but the other day, and she Superior
several years. St. Xaverius made me tell her, even when
she was Superior, what it was which hindered most her
progress in perfection. I did it, though with much difficulty. She took kindly the admonition, and mended the
thing I mentioned.

The great cross Almighty God made use of to disengage me thoroughly from all things in this world, was
the death of the person who was my Superior the first
year after my noviceship, at that time of which I am now
speaking. I did not think anything in this world could
be so sensible to me, and yet she foretold it to me pretty
clear about fourteen days before it happened. I came
one morning to her cell, and she bid me pray to my
Saint to send us a novice, and that soon, otherwise she

would not live to see her. I was surprised, she not
being accustomed to speak in this manner, yet I would
not seem to take notice of it, asking her in a familiar
way if she had dreamt this. She would not satisfy me
as to the reason of her speaking so, but told me I might
believe it, for it would be so, and that she should drop
down on a sudden even when she went about the house;
moreover, that she should not lie long sick. She bid
me remain by her and assist her in her illness, and not
forsake her. She ordered me as soon as she was dead
to close her eyes with my hand which St. Xaverius had
cured. This was spoken so positively that I was much
amazed and troubled; but much more some days after,
when I heard her speak to the same purpose in Community, on the account of a novice who was to be received to her profession. She changed the day designed
for this, adding that life was uncertain, and therefore she
would not defer it so long. That very day the Community were assembled in the choir for the reception of
this novice. She having ended her speech to the religious, was reciting the usual prayers which are always
said before we give our votes, and having just finished
that of St. Xaverius, she was suddenly struck with palsy,
and all apprehended she would have died upon the spot.
The other religious ran out of their places to assist her.
Being near the Blessed Sacrament, I immediately prostrated myself upon the ground, begging St. Xaverius to
obtain her life, or if it pleased God to do otherwise, that
at least she might have all the rites of the Church. After
this I went to the other end of the choir where she was.
I found her a little revived, but one side quite dead.
She looked compassionately upon me, gave me a picture
of St. Xaverius with some papers she had about her, and
asked if not all had come to pass which she had foretold
me. The confessor and doctor were immediately sent

for. She made us a fervent discourse, exhorting us all to love and fear God, Who could strike down in a moment, and to be always prepared for death, &c. Most present, and particularly the doctor, were extremely moved with her words. After her confession the palsy seized her tongue. She was then removed out of the choir to a lower room. I helped to carry her; and though we did it as gently as possible, yet by moving she lost her senses. This augmented my grief. I took my recourse to St. Xaverius. She returned to herself after the first night and received all the Sacraments. The nine days she continued alive she was for the most part sensible, to the admiration of the doctors, having a violent fever, palsy, and lethargy. I stayed by her constantly these nine days, and was never absent an hour at a time by day or night. I never heard her all this time speak one impatient word; but whenever she was out of her lethargy she was constantly calling on Almighty God and talking with St. Xaverius as familiarly as if she had seen him. Two days before she died she told me that she had seen him, that he was taking care of her, and as busy about her as if he had been her nurse. She described him to me, and spoke as cheerfully of him as if she had ailed nothing; but as she approached nigher her end these sensible comforts were taken from her.

One night as I was watching alone by her, she declared the deep sadness of her soul, and told me none in this world could give her any comfort. This oppressed me extremely, and I was inspired to tell her that St. Xaverius had once given me a blessing for her. I have mentioned this before, at which she was much revived, and asked me when it was and in what manner. She made me also lift up my hand and give it her, which I did with great difficulty, she being my Superior. She was extremely

comforted, and asked me why I had not told her this
before. There was a long time passed since it happened.
I could give her no good reason, but I think it was
God's will I should reserve it till this time, in which she
seemed most to want it. She begged me when she died
to importune my Saint for her speedy release out of
purgatory, and I, on the other side, begged her when
she came to heaven to obtain for me that I might soon
follow her. As ill as she was, she failed not to chide
me for this, saying I must live to advance God's honour
and glory, and did as good as tell me I was to live and
suffer much, and that I should be Superior, which added
to my trouble. She gave me care of all her papers,
with orders to deliver them safe to our director, who
said of her after her death, that she had never lost her
baptismal innocence.

## CHAPTER XX.

*She continues writing after a long interruption. She is chosen Sub-Prioress, and soon after Mistress of Novices, though she had not been long out of her noviceship. St. Xaverius removes her fears on account of her insufficiency. Her deceased Superior appears to her. The documents she receives from her. The effects she finds in herself from this apparition. She sees her twice more. Her fears lest others should come to the knowledge of the favours she received.*

IT is now about a year and a half since I left off writing, and the troublesome charge of Superior having again fallen upon me for three years longer, I think I shall have little time to write, yet, in compliance to obedience, I begin again. I hope this may draw my Saint nearer to me, for if I go on writing, he must be by me and dictate to me as he has already done. As to myself, I remember little or nothing when I take my pen; but in short I recommend myself to St. Xaverius, begging I may write nothing but what may be to the honour of God, and that he would please to help me. It would be impossible for me to descend to all particulars which happened so many years ago unless he then brought them to my mind, and unless I found this supernatural help I should suppose it to be the will of God I should desist from writing. Relating to my office, I do not lose confidence, though I think what I have written was not so hard to be remembered as what I have to write.

I have none of my former papers by me, but, as I think, I had there finished my first year after the noviceship.

Some days after the death of my dear Superior, of which I have already spoken, I was chosen Sub-Prioress, to my great astonishment and affliction. I knew myself ignorant of many of the duties of a simple religious; I was backward in the Divine Office, and was often obliged to go to others to ask direction. I was now full of confusion to think that, by my post, I was made Mistress of the Choir, to direct others when they failed. I should have been glad to hide myself in any corner, that nobody might see me, for I thought I should never be able to perform the office without an extraordinary help from God, of which I knew myself unworthy. Hence I shed many tears, believing when I came to the choir I should only distract others and make them laugh at me. I had a singular mortification to see myself placed in the choir and refectory above the rest, in the place next to my Superior. This trouble was increased when she was absent, for then I was obliged to supply her place, which happened very often. I found that some of the religious were likewise concerned to see that one who had been so short a time in religion should be promoted before others, both elder and fitter for the employ than myself, whom they had reason to look on as a poor ignorant novice. Something of this kind was once told me by one who seemed a little angry at it, and who added that I might thank my Superior for this promotion. I do not remember I made her any return, nor could I be angry at anything of this kind, knowing how much reason they had. When she cried and showed herself troubled I embraced her tenderly and with true love, for I thought she pitied me.

After some small time my Superior gave me care of the novices, which increased my trouble and confusion.

One of them had been my fellow-novice, and was much
older than myself, but she was very humble and willing
I should be over her. This charge increased my desolation, but seeing myself thus loaded with obligations,
not knowing how to perform them, as I was one day in
the choir, full of these pensive thoughts—I think it was
in time of Mass—St. Xaverius appeared to me, and said
I had nothing to do but what he bade me. This gave
me great comfort and confidence, that he would teach
me all things belonging to my office. It seemed to me
from that time that I was only his deputy. After this
I presently knew all things concerning my office. I
was not only ready at the Breviary, but taught the
novices without difficulty, and corrected what was failing
in the choir. Some were surprised to see me go on so
well beyond expectation. I do not remember that I
had ever any thought of vainglory for anything of this
kind, for God gave me light to see from whence my
help came. I thought now St. Xaverius had fulfilled
the promise he made in my noviceship, that I should
know my Breviary or Latin as well as others, for though
I cannot say I am so quick at it, having been always
dull in this point, yet I think it was given me to understand that I have it as well, because I can acquit myself
of my obligations and perform my duties as well as they.
One of the religious, who owned she had not given me
her voice, told me that though she had been many years
in religion, she had never seen this employ performed
better. Praise be to God and St. Xaverius, for I see
my own disability. One thing which added to my
punctual observance was the perfect health which I
enjoyed these three years, which made me continually
the first and the last in the choir, which many before
me had not been able to do.

My first four months in this office were passed in great

desolation, particularly on account of the death of my
dear Superior. I saw myself placed in the same station
she was in the two years of my noviceship. I had her
cell, her place in the choir, refectory and the noviceship,
where she used so often to move me to the love of God.
I called to mind the consolation I had in talking to her
of St. Xaverius and spiritual things, and being now
separated from her was a grief which I thought I could
never outgrow. At the same time, I cannot but say, I
was in the bottom of my soul entirely resigned to the
will of God. Yet I thought as long as I lived I should
find a sensible resentment on this account, having
nobody in whom I found that spiritual comfort as in her.
But I see since it was a great goodness of God to take
her from me, thus to disengage me from all creatures, for
though my love to her seemed altogether spiritual, yet I
often found when I was deprived of her company, or
when she was sick, I was much troubled and disquieted.
But now having none of these ties, I found myself free
from these disquiets, and reposed much more in God,
and loved all in Him. I endeavoured to hide the
kindness I had for her, from others, and to carry it so
that the troubles I felt might not be perceived, and I
cannot say it was in any kind so much as to take my
mind off from Almighty God, or ever hinder me in my
spiritual duties, it rather drew me more to Him.

I found great oppressions and desolations this four
months till I went the Spiritual Exercise. My Superior
appointed me a gallery to walk in at those hours in
which, according to the distribution of time, we were
to say our beads. On the second or third day being
in this place, I saw on a sudden my deceased Superior,
as I have mentioned before, and as I shall now more
particularly set down. She appeared to me in no form,
but like a white cloud, yet I knew she was there. I was

no longer able to continue my vocal prayers, nor even
to walk, being, to my thinking, almost disjointed. I
fell down upon my knees before her, and asked her
interiorly if she were in heaven. She answered yes. I
asked her if she had not been in purgatory. She said,
in an interior way, she had been there for ten days,
and that St. Xaverius had then obtained her release;
that she went to heaven the same day I was put into
the office of Sub-Prioress, and she gave me to understand that she saw joy in heaven upon my being placed
in this station; saying that by this she saw the house
of God would go on increasing and rising, as I understand, in virtue and religious observance. I asked on
what account she lay in purgatory; she let me know
that one reason was the following her own will even in
things which seemed to tend to devotion, by which she
impaired her health, particularly towards the end of her
life. I believe this was manifested to me for my own
direction, for about this time I lay under the same
temptation, being carried to much penance, and though
I did nothing without leave, yet I endeavoured to bring
my Superiors to my own will in point of fasting and
other extraordinary penances, which our Rule did not
exact of me. She exhorted me not to be too much
troubled nor to disquiet myself when I heard others
speak of the imperfections of her former life. She had
been always very weak, and on this account unable to
live up to the strict observance of the Rule, hence-she
was led by the way of humiliations which she said had
advanced her much. She gave me to understand she
had a particular reward for having mortified me to
advance me in virtue. I had always a difficulty to tell
this to my director, lest they should follow the same
method of mortifying me. As these things were made
known to me, I perceived the shape of an arm lifted up

which gave me a benediction. This, she gave me to
understand, was sent me by St. Xaverius in recompense
for that I gave her from him when she was dying. She
added, though I had more of the Saint's favour when
we lived together, yet being now in heaven she had
more power with him. After this I arose and walked.
The spirit accompanied me like a cloud over my head.
When I came to the end of the gallery she seemed in
some form which I cannot express, but broke out into
great acts and impetuosities of the love of God. One
word I remember which she said to me in an interior
way, as all this happened: 'Oh, love then this great
God of Love,' which moved me much to the love of
God. In this apparition I seemed to have lost all my
natural force. She disappeared, and I strove to get
to my cell, which was not far off. This great favour
which God did me took away all the grief I had felt
so sensible at her death, and though I thought it was
such that it never could be removed, yet after this
I never felt more of it; though this apparition gave me
a singular comfort, yet at the same time it struck me
with fear beyond what I had ever felt before. I cannot
express the dread it gave me to see one I knew so
well come now to me as a spirit from the other world.
When I passed afterwards through this place in the dark
I found myself seized with great apprehension, but at
the same time with great respect, and when I came to
the place where she gave me the benediction, I seldom
passed by, if alone, without kneeling down and kissing
the ground, and I cannot but blame myself for being
so much afraid of a soul which I undoubtedly believe to
be in heaven. But God permitted this that I might see
the weakness of my own nature, that I might humble
myself, knowing how unfit I am to converse with the
least of those who are enjoying Him, and whereas on

the like occasions I have never found these apprehensions of fear, I understand now I am writing this,
it is a gift of God not any desert of mine. I am fully
satisfied this apparition was from God, neither would
it have encouraged me as it did, to advance the observance of regular discipline, nor have taken away that
trouble I had felt hitherto. From this time I thought
I enjoyed her company in Almighty God in a far more
perfect and delightful way than I did when she was in
the world.[1]

---

[1] 'There is something in this passage which will seem as strange and
extravagant to those who are imperfect, as it will appear edifying to
those who are acquainted with the ways of Almighty God. Persons
who are apt to carp at everything that seems miraculous or extraordinary
will easily persuade themselves that this apparition was nothing but a
fiction of her own fancy, heightened with an imaginary conceit of her
own worth, which made her think that heaven rejoiced at so small a
thing as her preferment to a private religious order. They will
wonder how this deceased Superior would merit a crown by mortifying
her novice in her life, and they will suppose this hint given, not to follow
her own will in extraordinary penances, is only calculated to give her
and others a pretence of indulging nature. These or the like reflections
may seem very natural to several who read this passage, but then they
must reflect that persons arrived to a great degree of perfection (in
which number I think we may place this virtuous woman), are as much
above pride as they are above their other passions, and as they suffer an
injury without bearing resentment, so they can bear their praise without
indulging vanity. I have often made her relate some of those extraordinary favours, being in circumstances in which I could oblige her to
it, and I always found they raised in her so deep a sense of the goodness of Almighty God Who is the sole author of them, Who bestows
them as He pleases without any desert of ours, that the knowledge of
the favours received grounded her in a most solid humility. She
owned, indeed, with the most Sacred Virgin, that God had done great
things for her, but then she saw it was a God Who had done them for
her, and by this Divine light, which was then so plentifully bestowed
upon her, she saw how little part she had in them, which made her
constantly break out into the praises of God without attributing anything to herself. She was at the same time sensible how much God
requires of those to whom He gives so much. Hence she lived in
continual apprehensions of not corresponding duly to these great blessings, neither was she ever observed to put the least value upon herself on
account of them. That heaven should take part in whatever regards

Whilst I was Sub-Prioress I saw twice more this, my deceased Superior.  As I was one day singing Mass in the choir with the rest of the religious, St. Xaverius appeared to me in his habit, and I saw, as it were, under his cloak this my former Superior in the same form and manner in which she had made my picture be drawn in the vision I had in my noviceship.  It was a great comfort to see my Saint, and that he should bring her along with him for my consolation.  I had not now the least fear of her, but I was very apprehensive of falling into an ecstasy in the sight of the Community, for I was so transported and absorbed in God that I could not sing with the rest, and being chantress in the middle of the choir I knew not how to return to my place when I had ended, which would have made them take notice of it.  I was in the like occasions very apprehensive of this, and often begged of Almighty God that nothing in this kind might appear in public, and I return Him humble thanks that He has hitherto granted my petition.  But I fear I did not ask this purely out of humility; perhaps I might be moved to it by thinking others would expect from me a more exemplary life, or that they would laugh at me, imagining they were only fancies.  And I am confounded when I reflect what our Blessed Saviour told

the spiritual advancement of a religious Community will not seem strange to those who know that the angels rejoice at the conversion of a sinner.  Her deceased Superior had acted the part of a true friend in endeavouring to correct whatever she found amiss in the comportment of this young religious, and this being done with a design of advancing this chosen soul in the way of perfection, no doubt it was grateful to Almighty God Who is so good that He lets nothing pass unregarded which is done for His sake, on the other side it is not unusual to see some, particularly in the beginning, carried on with an indiscreet zeal, and willing to undertake more than they are able to perform.  This being the case of this holy woman, God was pleased to let her understand that this submission to the will of another was to be her rule, and that the greatest austerities are not so acceptable to Him as the submission of our own will to the law of obedience.'—*Collector.*

L

our holy mother, St. Teresa, on the like occasions, to wit, that those who believed these favours would praise Him, and those who did not would condemn her, so that by both she would be a gainer. But I must confess I have not yet humility enough, nor can I resign myself that anything of this kind should appear in public, and I think I had rather a thousand times have all my sins exposed than what I have writ of the favours God has done me. At present I need not be in any apprehension about this, for my thoughts are so disposed with the concerns of my troublesome office that I rarely feel any of these favours.

## CHAPTER XXI.

*Her different employs carry her to Almighty God.*
*Her deceased Superior appears again. A remark*
*on these her visions. She sees her vows engraven*
*on the Heart of our Blessed Saviour. His strict*
*union with her. The effects of these visions. She*
*is transported with the love of God and zeal for*
*souls, and scarce able to contain these flames of*
*Divine Love. She is ordered by St. Xaverius to*
*write her life.*

IN these three years of which I am now speaking, I
had many supernatural favours from Almighty God, and
advanced much in the way of prayer. I enjoyed
frequently the prayer of quiet recollection and union.
Both my offices of Sub-Prioress and Mistress of Novices
contributed to my prayer. I seldom came out of our
cell or noviceship but to the Choir or acts of Community,
and so both these employs tending to the advancement
of spirit, were a help to my prayer. They imposed
upon me afterwards a third employ, which was very
troublesome, by this I was obliged to consult with the
Prioress and some others once a month about the
temporal concerns of the monastery. When at other
times my Superior spoke to me about these affairs, she
easily perceived how troublesome it was to me, and
she used to say I loved to hear of nothing but spiritual
things, yet I always answered as well as I could, and
strove to make show of as little difficulty as possible.

I had very little experience in temporal affairs, but since
I have been Superior I have been obliged to turn my
head to them.   It was not then so necessary, but yet
at the same time I did my best, for I always sought
to do the will of my Superior as near as I could, and
when I found any repugnance I confessed it, though
nothing appeared to the exterior.   In some cases I
believe I need not have been so scrupulous in confessing
it, but I always desired to be simply obedient and not
to be of a contrary opinion to my Superior.

To return to what I was saying in relation to my
deceased Superior.   She had often told me, particularly
in her last sickness, and, as I remember, two or three
days before she died, that when she came to heaven
this house should find her help and the effects of her
prayers.   I assuredly believed she was in heaven, and
I had found in my own particular help by her, yet I
was very much concerned to see several things pass in
the Community which I hoped she would have remedied
by the power of her intercession, and I was uneasy to
think she had not complied with her promises in this point.
Whilst I was in this trouble, I communicated one day
and found myself in more than ordinary devotion with
great recollection, and our Saviour placed, as it were,
in the centre of my soul attendèd on by serveral saints
and angels.   I thought my deceased Superior was one
that attended there, not that I saw her in any form, but
I knew it by an interior light which I cannot express,
and she answered me interiorly to the doubt I had
about her performing her promise made to the Community.   Her answer was made in these words, more
distinct than I can express, with a kind of a reprehension
for my dulness, but yet full of sweetness and comfort :
' Did not our Lord say to St. Peter, " Thou art a rock,
and upon this rock I will build My Church ?"'   These

words took from me all doubt and filled my soul with peace and light, and she questioned me if I had not found her help. I remained awhile astonished and confounded within myself and confessed I had in a most particular manner. Then she turned the sentence of St. Peter upon me, saying upon me the good of the house did depend, and that by helping me by her prayers she helped all the rest of the Community. I cannot express the confusion the thoughts of these words gave me, which came often into my mind, to think how ill I have put in practice the designs of Almighty God. For in place of being a pillar of this house of His, by giving good example and settling a firm foundation of virtue, I have hitherto been a weak reed, I am full of imperfection and sin, I have given ill-example for which I am full of confusion, and I must humbly ask pardon of Almighty God for my ingratitude after so many favours and supernatural graces bestowed on me, merely out of His own goodness, without any desert of mine. I am very sensible that if I do not comply with them, I shall suffer for these very favours in the next life. That they are favours from God seems to me clear beyond dispute, neither can I say I ever had the least doubt or utmost apprehension of illusions in any that I have written or in many others I am to write. Neither do I remember that I ever prayed or desired Almighty God to lead me this way, but I believe His goodness saw me very weak, and perhaps if I had not had these wonderful helps I should not have saved my soul. I pray God I may save it now. I am indeed full of confidence that I shall, by the mercies of Jesus Christ and the intercession of our Blessed Lady, St. Joseph, St. Xaverius, my holy Mother St. Teresa, and all the saints and angels.

Since I began to write what happened these three

last years, I have been obliged to break off several times
and lay my papers aside, being taken up in making
the Spiritual Exercise and complying with the other
duties of my charge. I should have a great scruple
to neglect anything on account of writing, and when
I get time to write what I do, I know not. This I
observe, when my mind is quite dissipated with the
many concerns of my troublesome employ, I have been
moved to write for to recollect myself, and though I
find repugnance at first, as I have often said, when I set
myself to it, after a small space of time I find myself
quieted, recollected, and comforted.

During these three years that I was Sub-Prioress God
gave me great consolation in prayer. I no sooner put
myself on my knees but I could say ' I have found Him
Whom my soul loved, I will hold Him, neither will I let
Him go.' Thus I seemed to be united to God by a
strait union. It is our custom to renew our vows and
to prostrate in the choir on the Twelfth Day in Christmas. The first year after I was in this employ I begged
earnestly of Almighty God at that time that I might
keep these vows perfectly, and after Communion our
Lord showed me in an interor and intellectual way that
He would keep them in His own Heart. I seemed
to see my vows engraven there, *obedience* and *chastity*, in
gold and silver letters, very bright, but I was something
troubled for a considerable time because I did not see
anything of my vow of *poverty*. I was afraid this was
a sign I should not be exact in this vow, till I had light in
prayer, that if I kept those two in perfection, the other
was included in them, and I should not break it, which
was a great comfort to me. I am in some doubt whether
I have not mentioned this before, and whether this
happened at the time I mentioned. It would be no
great wonder if I should mistake, having so bad a

memory and not having my former papers by me, yet I
hope St. Xaverius will not let me lose my time in writing
anything twice.

This Christmas I thought the little Infant Jesus gave
me a kiss of peace, or to speak more freely in the words
of the Canticles, 'a kiss of His mouth.' This happened
after Communion. This kiss was a strict union with
God, and, as I may say, not knowing how to express it
better, with a sweet breath He blotted out all sin and
imperfection and left me in a great purity of soul. It
was, I think, about this time that our Saviour spoke
these amorous words to my soul, in a most endearing
manner. 'I have manifested to the world, My spouse,
how much I have loved you, in working so many
miracles to bring you to be My spouse,' which was
giving me to understand how this, my dear Spouse (for
methinks He gave me leave to call Him so), had preserved my life in this world, many times by miracles,
had at last cured me by the same manner, and by no
less a miracle had brought me to this place to be His
spouse. And He added: 'Manifest to the world how
much you love Me,' which was exhorting me to be an
example to others, particularly in the Community where
I am, of the exact performance of all religious duties
and of patient suffering on all occasions. I cannot
positively say I have written all the words just as they
were spoken, yet I think I have said rather less than
more. When things which have happened long ago
seem a little dark, so that I cannot clearly remember
them, it is in vain for me to lose time in studying them,
being after all reflections as far off as before. When
God puts them into my mind they occur clearly, and
indeed I have seldom occasion to study what I am to
write, and God knows if I were to take that pains I
should neither have time nor I fear mortification enough

to undergo it. Hence St. Xaverius is forced to help me, knowing the weakness of my own abilities, and my want of virtue to undertake it. I have a great repugnance to writing, but God is pleased in this to give me so much supernatural help and has bestowed so many other favours upon me that I ought to submit cheerfully to everything He requires of me, and I wish I could bring all the world to love and serve Him. I have been moved to lament sometimes when I have felt these darts of Divine love, and considered the sin and misery there is in the world, and what may happen even to us religious. I have often repeated these words : ' Oh, my Love is not loved!' and with so great feeling and with such impetuosities that I thought I could neither think or speak of anything else, but desired all the world might love and know what then I felt, which cannot be expressed by vulgar tongue. These impetuosities would seize me on a sudden without knowing what moved me to them. I remember sometimes in the Spiritual Exercise, in the time allotted for walking and saying some vocal prayers, I used to be seized with such impulses of love and knowledge of God, that I thought it was as much as my natural force could bear. It was indeed a great pain but a delightful one, none can tell it, I believe, but those who have experienced it, though it be a pain so great that it is of force enough to deprive one of this mortal life, yet those that feel it desire not to be free from it, but that it might increase, and even that they may lose their lives with it.

I have often found in these three years those impetuosities with such heatings at my heart and such oppressions for want of breath, that it seemed as if my very breast would have opened, not being able to contain all I felt, but I was advised to do all I could to hinder these motions which I endeavoured to do to the

utmost of my power. Yet I was commmonly moved
to cry to our Lord, but in an interior way: 'O Lord,
let an act of Your pure love separate my soul from my
body and break this heart of mine; and, O my God,
let me be all Yours, live or not live.' I found myself so
moved when the Community met to recreate together,
and when they discoursed on this subject, as our holy
Mother St. Teresa advises us to do in the like
occasions, that sometimes I was ready to betray my
thoughts. My countenance would change, as I have
been told by my companion who sat by me. Once, in
particular, I was so transported in speaking to one of
the Sisters, that she was surprised, and, as I remember,
she told me she thought I would fall into a rapt, but
I put it off with a jest, for I did not know well what I
had said or how I had carried myself, but I knew I
was very much moved with the love and the desire that
others might love my Beloved. When anything of this
kind happened in time of recreation, I was glad to
hear the bell ring to call us to solitude or the choir,
that I might give more scope to my devotion without
being taken notice of, yet I was not without fear of this.
I was often raised from the ground in reciting the Divine
Office, but as the place of Sub-Prioress is somewhat
distant from the rest and at the end of the choir, it
could not easily be perceived. I did what I could to
hinder this elevation, but I had often much ado to keep
myself on the ground, and my body appeared so light
that it was ready to take its flight up to heaven.

The works of Almighty God are beyond all human
understanding, much more above my weak capacity.
Learned men know much of the power and the Perfection
of God and of His love to creatures, yet I do not think
they have such a knowledge as those souls have which
experience these favours and are taught immediately by

God Himself. I believe some of those, even simple
women, may be more learned in mystical divinity. In
saying this I do not mean myself, for God knows I
cannot tell what mystical divinity is, I only know what
Brother Giles said, that a simple woman might love God
as well as the greatest divines, which is as much as I
desire. Yet I rejoice much God is pleased to bestow
these favours on learned men, as He did on the great
St. Xaverius, because they bring many souls to the knowledge and love of this good God. Now I have written
this I have great confusion within myself, remembering
what our holy Mother, St. Teresa, says, to wit, that
some young beginners who have felt these consolations
were presently for perfecting others and think they would
do great things for God, when afterwards these fits of
devotion being passed, they are scarce able to kill a gnat.
By this comparison I believe the blessed Saint reflected
on herself, which was humility in her, but in me it is
a real truth, for in these fits of fervour I could wish
to go with my blessed Saint and patron into the Indies,
there to suffer as he did, to bring souls to God, but
in small occasions I find both the want of patience and
courage in advancing the Community and this little flock
committed to my charge. I find myself full of self-love
and very weak on several occasions since I have been in
this employ.

About this time St. Xaverius appeared to me as I was
sitting in our cell at work, and ordered me in gratitude
to Almighty God for the favours received to write down
my life; but I have already spoken of this, and of the
difficulties and repugnance I found in complying with
these orders. 'Lord, give me grace to do what You
command, and command what You please.'

## CHAPTER XXII.

*One of the religious is helped in an extraordinary
way by her prayers. Her practice in instructing her
novices. Her mortification on account of the illness
of one of them, and her behaviour in all this troublesome affair.*

ALMIGHTY GOD was pleased to help one of the religious
by my prayers, which I think fit to mention here. She
was a very virtuous soul, but troubled with scruples to
that degree that her confessor was afraid she would lose
her senses; he told me as much to move me to pray for
her. She had leave to have recourse to me whenever
she pleased, and I spent a great deal of time in comforting her and animating her to obey and follow the
advice of her confessor. I was afflicted to see this poor
innocent soul suffer so much. Her confessor being
obliged to absent himself for ten days to give the
Spiritual Exercise to another monastery, called for her
before he went, and, knowing the innocence of her life,
ordered her before me to communicate, in his absence,
with the rest of the religious on the days appointed, and
he bade me put her in mind of his orders; but she would
seldom obey him in this point. One day I met her
in the morning by chance, a little before Mass, and made
her a sign to come to me, which she seemed very loath to
do, fearing, as she said afterwards, that I should be persuading her to communicate, which she was resolved not
to do that day, and all I could say to her was then

to little purpose.  I told her if she would communicate
that day I would, and had offered myself to change
Communions with her.  When I came to the choir I
found myself moved, more than ordinarily, to pray to
Almighty God to take away these troubles, forasmuch as
they hindered her in the way of perfection, and I offered
myself to suffer some troubles, if it pleased God, in
exchange, to bestow on her some of those favours He
had designed for me in Holy Communion.  I used at
those times to enjoy most high and sublime in most
familiar and amorous communication with Almighty God.
She, on the contrary, was like a soul in purgatory, in
continual anguish and pain, as she told me afterwards,
and this continued till the Elevation at Mass ; then on a
sudden, like one awaking out of a slumber, she found an
unusual peace of mind, all her trouble being at once
removed.  Upon this she came to me, having leave to
do so, and asked me, ' Did the Father bid me communicate to-day ? '  I answered, ' Yes, he did.'  ' Then,' she
said, with a quiet and calm voice, ' I will.'  I was much
surprised at this sudden change, having often told her
the same thing before to little purpose.  When we went
to Communion I found in the beginning the same consolation I used commonly to feel these three years and
rather more.  I thought I saw our Blessed Saviour,
seated in the middle of my heart, speaking most
amorously to me, as if He designed me some great
favour ; but on a sudden He seemed to ask my consent
to go and caress this Sister instead of me.  I consented
to it, but presently wondered to see myself in anguish,
desolation, and dryness, thinking of the sins of my life
past, fearing I had not confessed them well, and several
of the same scruples she used to have ; but all this while
I did not reflect on the bargain I had made, and that
I had offered myself to change Communions with her,

till a little before dinner she came to me cheerfully, in an unusual way, and asked me how I did. She added, she feared I was in great desolation, but for her part she had got well by the change, that she had never felt such consolation in all her life as she had done that day after Communion. This peace, as she told me herself, con- tinued for ten days after, which time she desired to communicate oftener than we were generally allowed, and this most earnestly. I was amazed at the change, and thought it the work of God. As to myself, I was all this time in the greatest darkness, thinking how to pre- pare myself for a general confession against the return of my confessor.

He had given me a particular charge of this Sister, as I have said, and to satisfy her importunity, when she was in her trouble, I had promised her if she was obe- dient in his absence he would give her leave to make a general confession at his return, for nothing else would satisfy her. When the Father returned she told him what had passed between her and me, and how we had changed Communions, what peace she had enjoyed. I went to him soon after and told him some troubles of my life past, desiring him to give me leave to make a general confession. He let me go on awhile to hear what I would say, for he had never seen me disturbed in this kind before. He then asked me if I had made no agreement with anybody, or offered myself to suffer in place of them. I was then in such anguish that I had forgotten the change I had made with that Sister, or at least did not think that was the cause of my disquiet, but he saw it and would not give me leave to make a general confession. Soon after, this Sister fell into her former scruples and I enjoyed my wonted peace of mind, with the same fervour of devotion in prayer and after Communion. It often gave me a great deal of confusion to think of the good use she made of these favours God did her during these ten days, how exact she was in all spiritual duties, so true it is that he goes on easily whom the grace of God carries, and she continues so grateful to Almighty God that she keeps every year the anniversary, as I may call it, of this day on which we changed Communions with great devotion and thanks giving. She told me that though her troubles returned for a time, it was nothing to support when she remembered the kind expressions our Blessed Lord used to her at that time, and the assurances He gave her of eternal happiness. When she enjoyed this favour she had light that her troubles would return, but since that she seems entirely free from them and advances daily in the way of perfection, which I perceive by her often desiring me never to forbear mortifying her when I think it is for her good.

I have often been in admiration after I had felt some of this good Sister's troubles, to find myself so soon again enjoy as great peace of mind as ever I enjoyed since St. Xaverius cured me. I thought I should never have recovered it without a general confession ; but I believe, had my confessor consented to it, that would have engaged me further in trouble. I had heretofore consulted my former director, under whose care I had been five or six years, whether I should make a general confession to his successor. He bade me by no means do it, yet in these troubles I could not satisfy myself without proposing it, but I acquiesced when it was refused. That same director, whom I loved and esteemed very much for the care he took to advance me in the way of perfection, seemed commonly to slight what I told him of the favours I received from God, and used to mortify me very much, yet he said he would tell me before he went away what he thought of them. The last time I saw him I was coming away without laying claim to his promise (I had either forgot or else was so well satisfied in my own interior that I did not care to ask him). He called me back again, saying he would fulfil his promise, and assured me I needed not to fear but that the favours I received were from God, that it is true he had seemed to slight them, but that was only to try my spirit. He added several things by word of mouth to my commendation, and repeated them afterwards in his letters, which is not fitting for me to put down in paper. The assurance he gave me raised in me a new sense of gratitude and fervour in the service of God. When he treated them as women's fancies, though it was mortifying, yet it gave me comfort to think that nobody knew the favours which God did me. I took much to heart the care of the novices who were under my charge, and often begged light of Almighty God, through the intercession of St. Xaverius, to know how to advance and instruct them, and when to admonish them, that it might have effect. I never spoke to them by way of correction when I found myself moved to anger or impatience; and when I was to explain any point of the Constitutions, I used to kneel down before the altar in the noviceship, putting myself in the presence of God with an humble distrust of myself. I begged light of God through the intercession of our Blessed Lady, our holy Mother St. Teresa, St. Joseph, and St. Xaverius, and I used to tell my novices they must take these not only for their patrons, but for their masters and mistresses. I found great difficulty in admonishing them and in explicating the Constitutions; but when I had once begun all difficulty ceased. I never wanted words to instruct them, and often found myself moved to practise what I taught.

One of the novices under my care was very young. She seemed to be a soul in a particular manner prevented

by Almighty God, but I have found in her afflictions one
of those black crosses which heaven designed for the
sanctification of my soul. I loved her very much for
her pious inclinations, and observed in her (beyond what
could be expected from one of her age) a great humility,
contempt of the world, and confidence in Almighty God,
and a simplicity in treating with Him in prayer. I was
often moved to devotion in speaking to her of heavenly
things, and have sometimes been in a rapt before her;
but I charged her when I came to myself never to speak
of it, and I am confident she never did. She often put
me upon these discourses. I once found myself dry,
and was therefore unwilling to yield to her importunity;
but in speaking I was so moved that I would say no
more. She knelt before me, and, seeing what passed,
embraced me, and with a great deal of innocency said,
'Mother, I have made you love God, though I cannot
love Him myself.' This novice gave me great confusion
to see how she advanced in all virtues, and used often
to wonder what this child would come to; but the
designs of God are secret and always adorable. He
advanced her in a short time, for she seemed to begin
in the practice of perfection where others end. I wish
I may attain at last what this child aimed at in her
beginning; but I cannot say she begun only when she
came to religion, though she were then so very young.
Before she came out of England she used to withdraw
herself from company and play, and seek some solitary
place for her prayers, and she was moved, after hearing
a sermon about religious perfection, to make a vow of
chastity. In her noviceship she seemed inspired to beg
to be despised and accounted a fool for Christ. When
I chided her and bid her beg of God more wit, she
answered she could not make that prayer, that there was
enough of that in the world, and as for her, she only

desired that wisdom which might make her love and
serve God. About a year after her profession she fell
ill of a sore throat and fever, which kept her from sleeping
some nights; but she concealed it, for she never complained of any indisposition till it appeared. We consulted the doctor as soon as we perceived her indisposition, but he did not apprehend it till on a sudden
she fell out of herself. I first perceived a great change
in her, but it was not then so visible to the rest of the
Community. However, I acquainted my Superior and
Director. Within a day or two she fell raving mad.

This, I think, was the heaviest cross I had ever felt.
I endeavoured to offer it up to be united to the Passion
of our Blessed Saviour, and I kissed my crucifix as
St. Xaverius had formerly advised me to do on the like
occasions. This afforded many trials of patience both
to me and the rest of the religious. She was heard, not
only in our own house, but by the neighbours. At first
she spoke of nothing but spiritual things, but afterwards
the enemy seemed to make use of her tongue to distract
and vex the whole Community. I have several times
gone from her in the middle of the night to prostrate
myself before the Blessed Sacrament bathed in tears and
oppressed with grief, but our Lord was pleased in this
great affliction to leave me in desolation and darkness
without any answer to my prayers. Many difficulties
were raised from within and without, that is, from my
own thoughts and from other persons. I feared as to
my own particular that I had been wanting on my side,
and indiscreetly permitted her to apply too much to
prayer. Others spoke with some distrust of me, imagining I must have seen some tendency to this before
her profession, which they had reason to suspect I had
concealed from them, but, God knows, I never mis-
trusted any such thing, neither did the two Directors,

M

with whom she had dealt since she was here, suspect anything of it.   On the contrary, they both esteemed her for her virtue and simplicity, and often desired me to put her in mind to pray for them.   The ways of God, as I have said, are secret.   I do and always shall believe that this soul was and is highly pleasing in His sight, that He first adorned her in a short time, and then permitted her to fall into this condition to increase mine and other people's patience.   This I had some light of in a particular manner.   I had offered my devotions and penances for her, complaining to our Lord to see this poor child continue in this condition, and suffering a great deal by remedies, and this without merit, which was a great cross to me.   As I was in great desolation on this account, walking in a solitary place, our Saviour seemed very near to me, but like one in the dark,   He spoke interiorly to me, and gave me to understand that He was more glorified by my suffering those crosses which her infirmity gave me occasion of, than He should have been if she had been well and in a condition of meriting, and that it was also a more secure way for her, as now she was not capable of offending, and that He had advanced her in a short time.   I also understood she was a soul very dear to Him.   I had indeed no other reason to think otherwise.   She seemed to have had some lights of what was to happen, for about half a year before she told me with some concern that thoughts came into her mind that she should be like such a one, naming a person that was out of herself, but upon my advice she strove to divert these thoughts, yet I perceived she was troubled at this, as well as for her brother's concerns.   He was fallen into the hands of a Protestant.   She prayed much for him, and procured several prayers.   Once after Communion she told me she had great hopes of her brother's conversion, for

reflecting our Lord had been so good as to call her to
be His spouse, she told Him that certainly He would
never permit her own brother's soul to be lost. She
spoke it with such confidence and simplicity that it
did me good to hear her.

About six months after she first fell ill in time of a
devotion which was made to St. Xaverius for her, I promised if she came to herself so as to be capable of the
Sacraments that I would take upon me again the care
of the novices. I resolved otherwise to use all the means
I could in conscience to avoid it. After this she came
to herself and continued perfectly well for three months,
frequenting the Sacraments and complying with other
acts of Community. We took care she should not apply
herself too intensely to anything, yet after three months
more she relapsed again and continued still in the same
condition. We perceived nothing of it when she went to
bed. About midnight I heard somebody come into our
cell, and being awaked asked who it was ; she answered
in a trembling voice, which made me speak very kindly
to her. She told me she was loath to awake me, but that
her head was so troubled that she was sure she should
lose her senses again and never more return to herself.
This she said God had given her light of. I did all I
could to make her put off these thoughts, though I saw
she was far gone. She spoke very sensibly of her condition, even to move a heart of stone. I exhorted her
to resign herself into the hands of God, and to make an
act of contrition, which she did, but wept and said it was
a sad thing to be without sense all her life, and have no
merit at all. But when she perceived I was troubled,
she embraced me and begged me not to trouble myself
for her, but leave her in the hands of God. After this
she went quite out of herself. I was at this time in
the office of Prioress, being chosen a month after she

fell ill first.  I have had much to suffer on her account, particularly cne time when she broke out from us.  I was ready to sink down when I first heard it, fearing it might bring some scandal upon the house among those who did not know her condition, yet God gave me so much moderation as not to lose my interior peace of mind, and I was moved to mortify myself and say nothing at that time to those who should have taken more care of her, but I secretly admonished them of it afterwards to make them more careful for the future.

I called the Community to the choir where, after some short prayers, I went where she could see and hear me, and she immediately returned again of herself.  She was only seen by two or three honest neighbours who soon perceived her condition and pitied her and our misfortune.

## CHAPTER XXIII.

*Her different visions of Purgatory, Hell, and Heaven
and the many instructions she draws from them.
Of the Purgatory of many pious souls in this world.
Some troubles which happened in the election of a
Superior. How she behaves herself in them.*

WHILST I was in the office of Sub-Prioress, as I was
making the Meditation of Hell in the Spiritual Exercise,
I was deeply recollected and seemed to see myself
transported into that sad region and placed near some
of that horrid crew, where I was to be racked and
tormented by them. I seemed laid upon a huge plank
in the middle of a place of fire under ground. Above
me was all dark and black, below me fire, not like
what we see here, but violently intense and unquenchable. The devils came round me to torment me in all
parts with red-hot irons, giving me to understand at the
same time with a kind of envious spite and malice that
the faults which I had committed during the two months
I was absent from my father's house, as I have elsewhere mentioned, were those for which I had deserved
these torments. I hope God has pardoned them. The
very thought of them gives me no small confusion.
I remained about half an hour in this transport
into another world. What I saw in spirit made
great impression upon me. It remained a great while
fixed in my mind, and I have still new lights upon
it. It was given me to understand in prayer that this

place was purgatory, and that I was to have remained
there for many years if I had died of the smallpox,
which I had about two years before my great sickness.
But it was revealed to me that our Blessed Lady,
St. Xaverius, our holy Mother St. Teresa, begged
Almighty God earnestly for me with my holy angel that
He would be pleased to spare my life and give me grace
to satisfy for my sins in this world.   All thought I
should have died of the smallpox, but I recovered;
and sometime after I fell into my great sickness.
Almighty God made known to me that He was fully
satisfied, and that if I had died then I should have gone
straight to heaven.   Of all the supernatural favours I
have received from God, I think I never found greater
benefit from any than from this: first, by seeing what
I had deserved for my sins.   This makes me think all
I can suffer in this world is little if compared with what
I have merited.   It often occurs to me in my pains and
sufferings, and helps me to support them.   Secondly, by
seeing my obligations to these my blessed patrons, when
I had, as I may say, no knowledge of them, nor
devotion to them, neither had I done anything to move
them to be my friends.   I had indeed always some
kind of devotion to our Blessed Lady, as all Catholics
are taught to have.

    This place of purgatory seems not to differ from hell,
but only in this that these souls are sure they will one
day see God.   The punishments are greater or less
according to their faults, which I suppose happens
also in hell.   During these three years of which I
am speaking I had one day a vision of at least some
part of hell, being deeply recollected in prayer.
I was suddenly called to follow somebody, neither was
it in my power to resist; but I was, as I may say,
hurried through a long dark place without seeing the

person I followed, neither did I know who it was. I seemed surprised, not knowing what the event would be, till I saw myself placed in hell among the damned. I was not much frightened, neither did I lose the peace of mind I had in prayer. This I take to have been a supernatural help of the Person Who conducted me, which I then understood to have been our Blessed Saviour, though I did not know it at first. He permitted or ordered me to examine some of these souls that I might know for what vice they were condemned to those never-ending torments. All the time I examined them, our Saviour seemed close by my side, which gave me courage. Some answered, as I remember, for pride, for gluttony, for impurity, and the like sins which we commonly read of; but when I came to one particular soul, which appeared to me in form of body a woman, I asked her for what she was condemned, she answered (though all this passed interiorly), that she had been once highly favoured by Almighty God and a religious person, but she had fallen from her fervour by degrees, and for concealing things in confession was banished from the sight of God for ever: she looked like one whose heart was breaking with grief.

After I had a sight of this horrid place, which seemed to me like that of purgatory, my guide conducted me back to my cell, for it seems to me that I was in another world, though I believe I was only transported in spirit. I remained many days meditating on what I had seen. I seemed to pass through the fiery furnace without being touched. What chiefly affected me was the thought of this religious; as if God had carried me thither on purpose to give me a caution that though I was favoured by Almighty God, I might come to fall. It made me search more narrowly into my confessions, yet without disturbance or scrupulosity though I was deeply struck with a sensible fear.  I have also seen another place which I may call purgatory, though it be very different from the other two places I mentioned.  This seemed a little heaven in comparison of the other: it was represented to me as I was praying in the choir before the Blessed Sacrament, where as I seemed to be transported, in spirit and body too, afar off into another world, when I saw these other places.  This appeared as a little round space hanging in the air full of brightness: in it I discovered several crosses of different colours, red, white, black.  It was given me to understand that this signified persons who had their purgatory in this world, which I believe many good people have by making good use of all the crosses which befall them.  I looked very earnestly on this place and the crosses, but knew little what they meant till Almighty God was pleased to let me know that the red crosses signified the martyrs who by shedding their blood gained heaven without any other purgatory.  I thought this was one of the lightest crosses.  The white crosses signified confessors, who suffered much by imprisonment and other persecutions for their faith.  I understood also that they signified religious persons living in an exact performance of their vows and holy institute, in all purity of life, who though they failed sometimes took care to do penance, thus to satisfy the justice of God.  The black crosses seemed heavier than all the rest.  I understood them to be Superiors of Orders who discharge themselves well of the obligations towards their flock.  Though these crosses seemed heavy and black in this world, yet they will shine bright not only on themselves but also on those they have advanced in virtue.  This favour was done me, as I remember, a little before I was elected Superior.  These black crosses seemed allotted to me, and I have groaned under them these six years.

Whilst I am writing this, I have some new light, by which I understand that everything represented to me in that vision was mysterious. The light of which this place was full is a heavenly light, which God does not fail to shower down upon those who have their purgatory here to enlighten them in all things for His honour and glory, if they do not darken or put it out by their sins. I said these black crosses will shine : they shine very bright if the office of Superior be well performed, but I think this black cross is the most difficult and hardest to carry well. Nay, if those who carry it are not purely spiritual, and all their passions well mortified, in place of having their purgatory in this world, by this cross, they will increase it in the next. I say this, pretending to have some experience, for, as I have already said, had I died before I came to religion, after my first year's sickness, I am confident I should have gone straight to heaven without coming near purgatory ; but I did not think the same had I died in the office of Superior, when in the beginning of it I had the last Sacraments, for I apprehended then I should have gone to purgatory for faults committed in that office. Yet I believe I should have increased my crown in heaven, and have gone laden with more merits, than if I had died after my first year's sickness. I have been always moved from a child to pray that I might have my purgatory in this life, and since I have seen something of purgatory, I still desire it more ; nay, I hope our Blessed Saviour has showed me those pains in spirit, that I may escape them, and that I may still see my greater obligations to Him, if He be pleased to give my punishment in this world, for I am truly convinced all we can suffer here is little in comparison of what souls suffer in the next life, for what we are apt to think very small faults. To return to what I was saying. The third place I mentioned, and in which I saw the three sorts of crosses, which is the purgatory of those to whom God grants the favour of having their purgatory in this life, is a heaven in comparison of the other two. The place itself I can compare to nothing I have seen. It was represented to me in an imaginary way, like a place of small compass drawn up from the earth by a powerful hand, and there sustained between heaven and earth, full of light and comfort, yet remote and in some sense void of comfort, like a thing hanging in the air. I think myself often now in this state, finding no gust in my spiritual duties, nor interior consolation from God, neither do I care to think I have received any particular favours from Him, for that only serves to add me greater confusion as having more to answer for. Neither do I care for comfort or anything in this world. If I seek to solace myself by speaking or writing to a spiritual friend, I find no help nor assistance from this, it rather adds to my trouble. In this case I seem like a creature hanging in the air. This has often happened to me these six years I have been Superior; but I do not remember I ever omitted my prayer or any of my spiritual duties on that account, or anything concerning my office which I thought might make to the glory of God, or contribute to the observance of our holy rule and to the constitutions of our holy and glorious Mother St. Teresa. I said this place was full of comfort and light, and then I seemed to contradict myself. I must beg St. Xaverius to help me to know how to make myself to be understood.

I had a particular light how the Blessed Trinity remains there with His heavenly court, saying there is His delight, and, as it were, protesting that to those souls who are perfectly disengaged from creatures and have no other desire than to please Him, to those souls He will even in this life manifest the secrets of heaven

He seems thus to give them heaven in security even whilst they are here. These have their purgatory in this life, and are not unlike the place I saw void of all comfort, though they possess the only Comforter with His heavenly court. There are some souls, I believe, in this state, who never know what they enjoy. They are strong souls, and need not this help : their faith and love of God is sufficient to carry them through. By this way of suffering they increase their crown in heaven. This knowledge of their own happiness is, for such weak souls as mine, who, perhaps, without this support would have fainted in the way. Our Blessed Saviour one day, to manifest how pleasing in His sight these souls were who went this way of suffering, said to me, ' Did these souls know their merit and how pleasing they are in My sight ?' I understood by this they would have a heaven in this life, and so lessen their crown in the other. I had a particular light imparted to me to show how pleasing souls were to God in these times of desolation, how perfect their acts of self-denial. God give me grace to walk this way which I see so secure and full of merit.

Perhaps those who read these papers will say I may well ask to walk in this path after I have received so many supernatural favours, helps, and lights from Almighty God. It is true God has been good to me, yet I dare not pray to be led this way of desolation for fear of my own weakness after all favours received ; but I leave it to Almighty God to carry me that way He sees most for His glory and the good of my soul. I continue to pray for my purgatory in this life, hence I expect to suffer as long as I live in this exile, and I have found something of this kind of desolation and aridities in these six years I have been Superior : I find no comfort from God nor help from creatures.

This place of those who had their purgatory in this

life was represented to me in the choir near the repository where the Blessed Sacrament is kept; and here,
when I was first Superior, I placed an image of St.
Xaverius, made according to my own devotion, with a
surplice and a black cross in his hand. I ordered the
workman to get an image of our Saviour fastened to the
Cross, but could not prevail with him to do it, at which
I was displeased; but a little after I understood that I
was the person who was to be crucified upon it, and that
St. Xaverius would obtain for me that I should make
good use of this cross, being frequently strengthened by
receiving the Blessed Sacrament.

As I have been transported into purgatory and hell,
so I have also seemed to be in a place of paradise of
pleasures and delights. I know not how to express
what this place was like, but I think I may say with the
Spouse in the Canticles, 'I found Him Whom my soul
loveth, and I will hold Him.' Neither did I care to
possess anything else: I had such delight and contempt
of all things in this world, and such an interior, I may
even say such an exterior joy, peace, and content, and
delight in all my senses. This place seemed something
like a delightful spring as to the exterior composition of
it, a place of great solitude. All the harmony I heard,
and whatever else I saw, served to increase the deep
recollection so as, I may say, to make me go more out
of myself and enter more into Almighty God. It suited
perfectly well with that sentence, 'I will lead her into
solitude, and there speak to her heart.' In this place
there is no speaking for the soul, she hears and sees so
much from her great Master; she has not time to speak
one word, nor does she desire it; she sees her Spouse
knows all her wants, and what she wants without noise
of words. By this I do not mean only vocal prayers,
but even mental, for here the soul languishes with love;

she is, as it were, wholly overcome, and can do nothing but enjoy. As for those who cannot or will not understand this, I beg my glorious Saint, who was so well versed in this divine art, to obtain for them some experience of it, or else I think they will never comprehend all that is contained in this divine way, though they be otherwise men of great sanctity.

I hope St. Xaverius will obtain for some that will read these papers a sense and feeling of those impulses of Divine love which will make them understand how this heavenly Spouse treats with His beloved, who are frequently simple and unlearned. I hope, I say, the Saint will obtain this for some who shall read these papers, because he has moved me, whilst I was writing, to pray to him that they might have some experience in this, and I do not remember that I am ever moved in this manner to pray to him for anything but that he obtains my request, because he first moves me to ask and then I am confident what I ask he will obtain, yet I do not say it shall be granted to all who read these papers ; yet, I think, the Saint promises me that none shall read them without benefit to their souls. I have some mortification in writing this, because it seems as if I invited others to read what I have written ; yet I have had and have still some concern and trouble to think that any one should see what I am ordered to put down in paper, and I fancied I should never be able to look anybody in the face who has read it ; but God has taken that so entirely from me that when I see the persons I can scarce say I think of it. If they be persons who know me, and if they believe what I write to be true and from Almighty God, I am sure they will wonder that I am no better, and they will have just reason for this. I am even confounded myself at the sight of it.

The delightful place to which I seemed transported

was neither on the earth nor yet in the heavens above,
but, as it were, drawn on one side towards the right
hand.   I think I may compare this solitary place to
some delicious lane which leads directly to the Celestial
Jerusalem, that is, those who are on this sort of prayer
and union with God, and follow what they are taught,
are in the straight way to heaven.   Although I am
certain I have not followed all these lights, but have
fallen far short, yet since I have seen so much of the
mercies of God and of His goodness, I do not remember
that I ever had anything like a doubt or even almost a
flying thought as if I should not be saved, or as if I
should not enjoy God for all eternity.   I know that as
long as we live in this world we are never secure; I
know that we cannot tell whether we are worthy of love
or hatred; and I have already mentioned that I saw one
in hell who had been highly favoured by our Blessed
Saviour.   Have I not reason to fear when it is also said
we should work out our salvation with fear and trembling?
These thoughts, I confess, keep me, as I may say, in
awe, and seem terrible; but on the other side I reflect
that love and confidence expel all fear, and since I know
our Blessed Saviour loved me before I was capable of
loving Him, He made me of nothing, He redeemed me
with His precious Blood, He sanctified me in Baptism,
He has called me to His true Faith, and after all this to
be His spouse in this holy Order (even setting aside all
other supernatural and abundant favours), is not this
enough, my God, to make me confide in You, that You
made me for Yourself, and to reign with You in Your
heavenly kingdom, to sing forth Your praises to all
eternity?   Oh, that this time were come !   Oh, that this
pilgrimage were at an end !   When dark thoughts occur
I often think of the passage related by St. Francis of
Sales between the divine and the poor man.   The divine

asks him what he would do if after all God should damn
him. I answered to my own thoughts with this poor
man. I have two arms to embrace Him, the one of fear
the other of love, and I had rather be in hell with God
than in heaven without Him; for methinks I would hold
those Divine hands so fast that He would never let me
go nor leave me there behind Him, though I know I
have justly deserved it. Yet, my God, I know Your
mercies exceed Your justice, and that You are called
the God of Mercies. This confidence which You have
given me is one of Your mercies, and when I have been
in great affliction You gave me, I thought, this light,
that all I suffered was little, seeing I had this confidence
in the bottom of my soul; besides, my God, among other
favours You have in a particular manner given me an
assurance that I shall never be separated from You, as
I shall hereafter relate, and which I look upon as one
of the greatest favours You have ever done me. I must
own and acknowledge this gift of God obtained by
St. Xaverius. I hope those that read this will not take
confidence for a presumption. I confide in no good
works of my own. If ever I did anything, God has done
them by me, making use of so poor and insignificant
a creature the more to show His omnipotence and
power.[1]

---

[1] 'When the reader meets with these visions of purgatory, hell, and
the rest, he may perhaps be raised to an expectation of greater things
than he finds under these titles, and may hence conclude that the
notions she pretends to have had from God at those times are scarce
worth penning down as things very remarkable. If, on the one hand,
he seems less satisfied, he must on the other reflect that a soul must
not pretend to dive farther into the secrets of Almighty God than He
is pleased to lead her. Everything in this kind which comes from God
is truly valuable, and though the graces and lights imparted to some be
much inferior to those which are imparted to others, yet the very least
of these, being gifts of God, and bestowed upon a soul by the effect of
His pure mercy, ought to be received with a deep sense of acknow-

I have said more here than I designed, and must
therefore repeat what I have already mentioned in other
places, I am obliged to take spare moments to write,
and have interrupted my writing for sometimes months
and sometimes years, hence, not having my former
papers by me, when I take pen in hand I often know
not what is to come next, but I think the Saint dictates
to me and when I once begin I never lose time in
studying. I think the Saint is near me when I write.
When I have a spare moment and am so dull that

ledgment and gratitude. That these representations of purgatory,
hell, &c., were extraordinary favours imparted to this devout soul by
Almighty God, seems to be beyond all dispute, by the effects they
produced in her. She thinks herself that of all the supernatural favours
she had then received from God, this sight of purgatory encouraged
her most to a love of sufferings and a true sense of gratitude. The
vision of hell produced also admirable effects in putting her still more
upon her guard lest she should prove so unfortunate after all He had
done for her, and the sight she had of paradise encourages her to
solitude and prayer, and to go, as it were, more out of herself, that the
whole soul might enter more perfectly into the ways of God.

The reader ought further to reflect on the time Almighty God gave
her them. This happened when she was first Sub-Prioress, about six
years after she had entered her religious course, and about thirteen
years before her happy decease. She was also moved to declare things
as they were delivered to her, with the lights and sentiments imparted
at that time, when every particular happened. Had she lived to pen
down the last thirteen years of her life, perhaps we should there have
found much more sublime thoughts and ideas of these very things she
now treats of. We have reason to believe this, because we find from
the very beginning of her life till this time, she went on, as I may say,
daily increasing in virtue, and was raised by Almighty God from one
degree to another, as is obvious to any one who peruses her writings;
and besides, she tells us that God discovered to her His own perfections
by degrees, according as she saw her strength to bear these lights, and
it is probable He dealt with her in the same manner in the discovery
of other Divine truths. But since it has pleased Almighty God to take
her out of the world before she could write anything of these last
thirteen years, this must not deprive us of the advantage we may reap
from what is known of her, which is the reason why her writings are
exposed, though we want the chief part of her life.

For the rest, I must own as to myself I am so far from being arrived
at a state which may seem above instructions from these, which some

nothing occurs I tell my Saint in a familiar way that he does not help me, . . . neither can I say what I designed if I think the Saint is not pleased, and if I see it proceeds from human respect, as this great Saint sought nothing but the glory of God, neither regarded what people thought or said of him. So he would have me do, particularly in regard of what I have written. I have mentioned before the advice given to our holy Mother St. Teresa by our Saviour Himself, according to which, if it be equally pleasing to God and as much for His

may term imperfect visions of purgatory, hell, &c., that I cannot read what she says here without having lively sentiments of apprehensions and fear. The many years she was to be condemned to purgatory for the sins of her youth (and yet her youth seems virtuous and saintly compared with what daily happens), these many years of purgatory, this dismal sense of intense and unquenchable fire, the envious spite and malice of the devils, ready to torment her, are notions which struck this holy woman so much, at a time when she was pretty well secured she had escaped the danger, that she thought after this she was never to repine at anything she had to suffer in this world. And shall not this light, with a certain knowledge that I have deserved greater torments, and that I have done little or nothing to secure me from them, have no effect upon me when I read this and the like reflections, drawn from the vision of hell? And I believe there are few so advanced n prayer who may not find advantage from what she says, discoursing of the glimpse she had of paradise. What she adds there of the purgatory which souls find in this world, and of the black cross of Superiority, was shown her, as she observes, just before she was chosen Superior, and seemed represented as a preparation for what she was to undergo. The state she mentions of souls who possess God within themselves, and are chosen temples of the Blessed Trinity, whilst in their own eyes they seem abandoned by God and are left for their own greater merit to act by the light of faith, without the feeling of any supernatural comfort, seems to have been often her own case in the latter end of her life, and may, I believe, serve much to encourage others who may find themselves in the same circumstances. She, it seems, would have thought it a presumption, after all the favours received, to have trusted so much to her own strength as to beg to be led this way of suffering, which she acknowledges so perfect and meritorious, and therefore leaves herself in the hands of God to lead her which way He pleases. If here, on the one side, we have reason to be edified at her humility, we are taught on the other a practice of perfect conformity.'—*Collector.*

N

glory, for me to be contemned for my writing, as for Him
to be praised, it is equally pleasing, so far as I can see
to myself, and if be not so I am sure it ought to be so,
since I say so often, it is for obedience and the glory
of God that I write, and that it is to do His will, no
other motives. Let them who see these papers make
what use they please of them, so it turns to God's glory,
I am sure my pains will be well bestowed. If I were
commanded by obedience to burn this and all I have
written, I would do it this moment and should not
repent at what I have written, nor the time I had spent
in writing, because I hope to have some reward for the
acts of obedience I have employed in it. I think it has
also advanced me in the way of virtue by often raising
me to a fresh sense of gratitude to Almighty God for
all these favours.

I must now return to my meditations. In the meditation of the Two Standards, I was carried as it were
to a place afar off, where I had great lights of several
degrees of prayer. If I were to treat of this and write
all I know of this heavenly science (which none can
understand but those who are taught by Almighty God)
I should spend much time and many sheets of paper.
It seems needless now, at least according to the lights
I have at present. I wish every one made use of what
they know, or what they with moderate care might know,
it would be sufficient. As for high prayer, it cannot be
gained by reading, it is a gift of God, which none can
attain but those to whom He is pleased to impart it,
but there may be greater saints without these extraordinary favours, which are given sometimes as rewards
in this life and to strengthen those that have much to
suffer. In this meditation I had a heavenly joy, with
contempt of all things of this world. Something of the
nature of this prayer was made known to me by the

representation of a most pleasant garden in which there
are several sorts of flowers and fruits. Some grow on
the out ranks and are called wild ones, and do not much
delight the gardener, yet this shows the soil is not
barren; they mark those who out of custom say several
vocal prayers, frequent the sacraments, and just take
care to save their souls. There are other flowers, though
single and slight, yet yielding a sweet savour, and representing those who have attention to their vocal prayers
and desire and endeavour at perfection. Thirdly, the
gillyflower, the single, is very sweet and agreeable, and
these are they who begin to make mental prayer, meet
with many difficulties and aridities, yet go on striving
to overcome their passions. They are agreeable to
Almighty God as beginning to flourish in His garden,
though the weeds about them are not pulled up by the
roots. Fourthly, the double gillyflower, odoriferous in
smell and lasting, whether it be let stand in the garden
or transplanted in flower pots, represents strong souls,
who by the use of prayer root out all that hinders them
in the way of perfection. These souls are highly pleasing
in the sight of God. The pains and labours they undertake are more agreeable to our Blessed Saviour than
the most odoriferous flowers or the finest perfumes
can be to us. And these courageous souls who can go
on thus without finding any sweetness in prayer, nay,
without knowing whether they are acceptable to God
or no, and yet persevere in this rough way of mortification, and, if religious, are faithful in their rules and other
observances, these souls, I say, are a pleasing spectacle
to heaven, and it seemed to me as if our Blessed
Saviour stood constantly looking on and watching these
souls with pleasure yet far off from them, He in some
part of the lower heavens and they still upon earth.
But I believe few attain to this without first having some

contemplation of God, which makes them enamoured with Him, thence they resolve to give and do all they can to possess Him at last. I was carried this way myself, which makes me judge the same of others, yet I know those that are carried on by faith may be greater saints.

In repeating the meditation of the Incarnation after Matins, as soon as I had placed myself upon my knees I fell into high contemplation, had great lights of this mystery, and was astonished to see Almighty God make this great descent from heaven to earth, not only for His friends but for His enemies. I also saw that they need not doubt but that all the favours that I have received are truly from God. And our Blessed Saviour said interiorly to me: 'If I have done this for My enemies I will not fail to communicate Myself in less favours to My friends.' I had besides a particular light, how this favour of God becoming Man for me, and clothing Himself with our human nature, did abundantly surpass all the supernatural favours He has been pleased to bestow upon all the saints, much more those bestowed upon me the most unworthy of His servants. Though nothing is hard to God, yet it is represented to me as a much greater marvel and more surprisingly admirable for God to become Man than to make men become as gods. This He could have done without suffering any indignity in His own Person. I could have remained till morning in prayer with much more ease than I could force myself out of the posture I was kneeling in. I found my hands stiff and cold, and had almost lost my strength, yet with much ado I got to bed, because I was ordered not to exceed an hour in my prayer, and I heard the clocks and bells go twelve. I forced myself to leave God for God, but when I slept I dreamt I was in prayer and awaked myself with making aspirations.

For the meditation of the Nativity I was much recollected. This day I had great and languishing desires
for Communion, with great impetuosities of love to God.
After Communion I found myself plunged in Almighty
God, my littleness in His greatness; I begged light to
know what I should do to make some return of gratitude
for all these supernatural favours and graces He was
pleased to shower down so plentifully on me. It was
answered me in an interior voice: 'Return Me back
all that is Mine, that is, all you have done and suffered
in your whole life, and all the good you shall ever do,
acknowledging that it was My grace that moved you to
it and carried you on.' In this prayer I had also
instructions not to trouble myself nor be in anguish, as I
had been some time before, in what manner I should
chastise my body, by importuning my Superior for extraordinary penances, but that I should leave myself in His
hands as a child in those of his father, corresponding
sweetly to all the designs He had on my soul, to which
I offered myself.

On these lights I made my hour of prayer following,
not being able to fix on the meditation of the Hidden
Life of Christ, but from these instructions I had in the
former meditation I found great humility and a clear
light of myself, and how it did not always happen that
great penances and chastisements of the body were most
pleasing to God. What He chiefly required was the
taking all things from His Fatherly hand, resigning,
conforming, and yielding up ourselves entirely on all
occasions of sufferings or crosses, which He was pleased
to impose upon us or permit to befall us. I endeavoured
to conform myself and have since that time had some
occasions to exercise these virtues more than ever I
had in my life before, and in different kinds, which if
I live and have time I shall relate, if not, there are some

that have been witnesses and have seen that my dear
Spouse, after He had strengthened me by these favours,
thought me fit to suffer something for His sake, for
which I thank God, and acknowledge it the greatest
favour He has been pleased to do me, as making me
in suffering the more like Himself, Who was never free
from them when on earth, unless it were those three
hours on Mount Thabor.

In the last day of the Exercise I had as great a desire
to communicate as before, and I saw our Blessed Saviour
after Communion settled in a higher place in my soul. I
had, as it were, a garden of flowers on one side, of fruits
on the other, with a fountain between. I had notions and
lights concerning prayer drawn from each of them. Seeing
myself thus closely united with Almighty God, I desired
to die, fearing and knowing human frailty, and that
living longer this union might come to be dissolved,
and I become so ungrateful as to offend this great God,
Who I now in some sort comprehended by lively faith
and love, and I wished to be in full possession of the
Beatifical Vision, that I might yet do it more perfectly.
But it was made known to me that it was the Divine
decree that I should live for His honour and glory and
the good of others. Yet God gave me assurance He
would continue this union with my soul till He brought
it to possess the Beatifical Vision. However, as not
content with this, I answered with importunity, tears,
and tenderness of devotion : You grant me this request
that I never more offend Your Divine Majesty by one
deliberate sin or imperfection! For do You think, Lord,
I can bear this and see Your goodness to me? No, no,
Lord, this cannot be, either grant my request or have
patience to suffer my importunity : for I know Your
goodness is so great and so sweet that You cannot deny
Your Spouse a request so reasonable. To this contract

I call for witnesses our Blessed Lady, St. Xaverius, and the whole court of heaven.'

This Exercise was made the second year I was chosen Sub-Prioress, and the year following I was, for the most part, carried by high prayer and contemplation, receiving many favours from God and lights from heaven. At the end of these three I made another Spiritual Exercise, according to the method of St. Ignatius, as the rest of the Community did, according to our practice.

In this Exercise I seemed to enjoy higher favours than in the former, though some, I think, were of the same kind. One great difference was this, in the former Exercise I seemed to be closely united with Almighty God with a Divine union, but now in this I seemed to be admitted to the spiritual marriage with my heavenly Spouse, which He Himself did declare, when, in His Sacred Humanity, He came to make His abode and habitation with me, as in His own palace, giving me to understand by clear and distinct words, that now these spiritual nuptials were completed He would make me partaker of His heavenly treasures and riches, giving part of them, even now, in my own hands, to dispose of them to my relations and friends. And this comparison was made to me, that when an earthly prince espouses a mean person, by this marriage all her poor kindred and friends are raised to some high dignities. So it should happen in a spiritual way to my relations, and I have seen this, in some sort, effected in them.

I was often favoured in this Exercise in visions of His Sacred Humanity, like as He was conversant in this world. He spoke to me by an interior, but distinct, manner these words : ' Unto your care I recommend this My family and house.' By which I understood I should be chosen Superior, which happened in the following election about two months after, though my

director, whom I acquainted with this, could not tell
how to believe it, thinking me too young both in
religion and age.   My dear Spouse (for I presume to
call Him so, because He used to call me so) then
strengthened me for this great cross of Superiority, by
giving me to understand I must then look after His
household affairs and seek the advancement of others,
whom He should put under my care; that I must not
now expect to spend my time at His feet in contemplation, but that I must act for Him.

CHAPTER XXIV.

*Some few passages of her life after she was Superior.*

[WHAT she has written hitherto gives us only an
account of what happened to her in the world, before
she was religious, and what happened the first years of
her religious life, before she was chosen Superior.   It
pleased Almighty God that she should be so afflicted
by sickness, or otherwise taken up with business, as
never to finish the remaining part of her life, by which
we are deprived of those instructions we had reason to
expect from it.   I find among her papers some few
passages which happened about or after the time she
was Superior, which I shall give here, as they were
penned down by her, without much order of time.]—
*Collector.*

    In obedience to my director, with the help of my dear
Saint who seems near me, I will relate what happened
when I was first chosen Superior, almost ten years ago.
Though I have much business on my hands, yet seeing

my director will give me leave for no extraordinary
penance, I will impose this upon myself by way of
mortification to prepare myself for the ensuing feast of
my great patron, physician, and father, St. Xaverius,
and will, on this account, endeavour every day to write
something.

When I heard the Bishop name me for Prioress, at
the election,[1] my natural strength failed me, and I was
ready to sink down, had not the religious supported me.
This gave me no small confusion. It is impossible to
relate the crosses, contradictions, and, as it were, con-
fused number of afflicting thoughts, which were represented to me, when I heard myself named. I saw
what God required of me in this office, the reforma-
tions I was to make, the oppositions which would be
raised against me, and what most touched me, that I
was to forsake my beloved solitude, which was indeed
a great sacrifice, and went most near me. I had light
since, that this extraordinary tie to solitude was much
mixed with self-love and inclination. In effect the difficulties here represented did so work upon me that I
came to lose my health. I believe I never passed a day
without a fever, though I did what I could to conceal it,
and would admit of no dispensations. In conclusion, I
was in a short time confined to the infirmary, where the
doctor, finding me very weak, and in a continual fever,
ordered me the Last Sacraments. I was very willing to
die, but feared I should not. I was also in great desolation, thinking myself forsaken by St. Xaverius, and
sorry to see myself fallen again into the hands of the
physicians. Whilst I had these, or the like thoughts, my
blessed Saint appeared to me, as it were, elevated on
high. His sight, with the good news the doctors gave

---

[1] 'This happened about two months after the Exercise she spoke of.
—*Collector.*

me of my approaching death, gave me so great joy that
my natural forces could not support it.  One of the
doctors who sat by me, seeing a change, felt my pulse,
and being surprised at the alteration, pressed me to tell
him what was the matter, saying he was sure there was
something more than ordinary, but I would acknowledge
nothing.  The doctors immediately ordered my confessor
to be called for, fearing he would come too late to give
me the Holy Oils.

['She was somewhat recovered before her director
came, but she owned in private to him that the transport
of joy upon hearing from the doctor that there was no
hope of her life, had wrought this change, and had
almost taken her out of the world.  Though she had
resolved to continue writing, yet I find after having
written this short passage she was obliged to leave off
and write no more for three years.  What follows is a
short account of the state of her soul a few years before
her death.']—*Collector.*

I am now, for the most part, in desolation, expecting
the time of the Spiritual Exercise, for then Almighty
God is rather pleased to increase His favours to me,
though most unworthy, by new lights and passive union
with Himself.  I cannot say I ever received comfort
from creatures.  I have treated very little with any one
concerning these favours, they lie hid between God and
myself, till He be pleased I shall have time and His
Divine assistance to enable me to declare them, otherwise I think the best of pens and writers could never be
able to do it.  If I had not already experienced a supernatural help in writing, I should think it impossible,
though I know nothing is impossible to Almighty God,
and the weaker the instrument is the more His power is

manifested, so with confidence in this my dear Spouse,
our Blessed Lady, and St. Xaverius, I begin to write
what I could never otherwise relate.

In an Exercise some years ago I was very much drawn
to interior recollection with intellectual favours, particularly after Communion. I received one day new lights,
and what I had never before received, nor heard of, one
in particular. After these impetuosities and passive
unions were a little passed, I found in myself impatient
desires of solitude and to be freed from all exterior
employs, from this office of Superior, and of retiring to
my cell to live with God. After these thoughts and
desires, our Blessed Saviour discovered Himself to me
in the most innermost part of my soul, giving me, as
I may say, a gentle reprimand for being so solicitous
about this, bidding me make my cell in His Divine will,
teaching and instructing me never to go out of it, and
it seems to me as if He had brought down the chiefest
part of His Court for me to live, love, act, suffer, and
die in, so large and so well fortified, that it seemed to
me I could not get out of it, if I would. God grant,
by the intercession of all the saints, I never may, but
that I may always say as He has taught us, 'Thy will
be done on earth, as it is in heaven.'

It is about three years since I first received this favour
in the Spiritual Exercises of St. Ignatius, and ever since,
in all Spiritual Exercises, new and divine lights have
been communicated to me upon this subject, and in
such a manner that of all the supernatural favours I,
unworthy, have received from the hands of Almighty
God, I never found any advance me in so solid and
secure a way of perfection as this. From the time I
first received this light, when after the Exercise I was
obliged to converse with seculars, or be otherwise employed as my office required, notwithstanding in all

exterior dissipation, I always found peace of mind
when I reflected that this was the will of God; and
although I was called from prayer to the grate, I still
remained in prayer, though sometimes more sensibly than
others. Since that time many difficulties have happened,
both in regard of myself by sickness, and great torments
which have forced me to cry out loud in these words:
'Jesus, Your divinest will be done!' This often moved
those that heard me to tears of devotion. In one surprising extremity, which did not last long, but was so
violent for the time that I do not remember I ever felt
greater torment, and I think it was not inferior to some
tortures of the martyrs, I made this act of resignation so
heartily that the infirmarian has often told me since how
much she was edified at it.

I was in great desolation of mind in this sickness,
besides many other occasions of suffering; all I could do
was to endeavour to keep, and not to go out of, my cell
of the Divine will and pleasure of Almighty God, resigning myself to whatever He permitted to fall upon me, in
mind, body, or from creatures, but this with some repugnance, not with sensible gust as I have hitherto had; yet
this I had, I desired not to be freed from any of my
crosses, although it were in my power, till I knew it was
the good pleasure of Almighty God. So I hope I have
kept myself in this blessed cell, though sometimes it
seemed to me I advanced a step or two to go out of this
heavenly palace—I thought to have said cell, but I
think the other word much more proper, for a cell sig-
nifies a little place, and this Divine will of God is of vast
extent, and I have no comparison whereby to make it
sensible, there being nothing corporeal by which I can
frame an idea of it. For all these delightful objects and
sights which are found in the noblest palaces, are base
and gross; nay, what is said in the Apocalypse of heaven,

falls much short of it. When my Divine Spouse is pleased to solace me with Himself, by a most high and sublime favour of His Divine will He brings me into this heaven, or rather, I find myself there on a sudden, I know not how. But this favour is, for the most part, done me after receiving the Holy Communion, or in the Spiritual Exercise, when I can attend wholly to Almighty God and prayer. In this divine union the soul sees herself one with her Creator, as a drop of water falling into a vast ocean, which can never more be divided. Here my soul finds herself, in some manner, as secure of her eternal happiness as the blessed in heaven, and this through the goodness, mercy, and merit of its Saviour, Who discovers to her new lights of His admirable per-fections, and of the gifts and fruits of the Holy Ghost. She sees each apart in Almighty God,· since His Divine wisdom, knowledge, and understanding infused into the Apostles in small parcels, as I may say, like rivulets springing from the vast ocean, appear in them so admir-able, what must the source of them be altogether in Almighty God? Certainly the most perfect and con-templative may be drowned and lost in one of them, though I am apt to think (submitting myself in this and all other things to the Holy Church) that Almighty God does not discover any of His admirable perfections, as they are in Himself, to any in this life. As for myself, when He is pleased to discover Himself to me in these favours, it is by little and little, according as He sees my strength to bear it, seeming to hide part of them from me, either till I come to possess and see them in heaven, or else till I am stronger in virtue. Sometimes this seems to give me a supernatural strength of body to support life, but particularly of late, these intellectual favours seem to cherish and strengthen me both soul and body

[What follows is a short account of some lights she had in the Spiritual Exercises. The year is not marked down, neither was it her turn to make the Exercise, but she conformed herself as much as she could to the hours of prayer with the other half of the Community who made the Exercise.]—*Collector.*

In the first hour of prayer at night I found great recollection. I sat down the last quarter, being ordered not to kneel so much. As soon as I sat down, I thought I saw St. Xaverius very near me, on my right side, which increased my devotion. I would willingly have risen and knelt before him, out of respect, yet I could not. The Blessed Saint seemed to show me, under a black cloak, a very rich garment, by which he gave me to understand, that my soul should be left in great desolation, and be overcast with dark clouds, but yet it should remain rich and adorned with virtues, though it should not seem so to me.

The first day after Communion, I found great devotion, and I thought I saw our Saviour working as an overflowing fountain in my soul, washing and purifying it from all its sins and imperfections. Only one stain remained, which disfigured it; this troubled me much, fearing it was some hidden sin. Hence the next day before going to Communion I examined myself, and confessed, though I had no light to see what this stain was; yet it seemed so deeply engraved that I could not conceive how it could be taken out without great blemish, till the next day after Communion our Blessed Saviour, in a moment, seemed, as I may say, with one spark of His love, to meet my soul and purify it from all spots, as gold is purified from the dross. The fourth day after Communion I found great recollection, and I thought our Blessed Saviour applied one drop of His Precious Blood in a particular manner to my soul, which loaded it with much more merit than I had demerited by the dross which was to be taken away before. The fifth day our Blessed Saviour appeared in my soul after Communion as a bright sun, sending forth His resplendent rays on all sides. In this favour I found extraordinary devotion, tenderness, familiarity, and kind caresses, both interiorly and exteriorly from God, giving me to understand that He had permitted all that happened these nine months, and the enemy to work out his fury against me, to bring me the more near to Himself and His saints, and I understood that this appearance of a sun, was to show me how much my soul was advanced.

I think it was in the last Exercise that I thought I saw myself engulfed in Almighty God as a bright star shining forth in Him. But this was represented in an imaginary way as our Blessed Lord stood by me, but here I saw myself engulfed in God, and Him in me. I had wonderful lights, which is too long to express. I found a great tenderness towards all, but particularly those who might have given me any occasions of sufferings.

All glory be to God, from Whom all good does come, and to Whom it is to be returned.

[Here ends all that Mother Mary Xaveria has written of herself. The chapters which follow are the work of the Collector, Father Hunter. In the manuscript they follow immediately on the two chapters which are placed first in this volume.]—ED.

# CHAPTER XXV.

*A summary and short account of her state of soul drawn out of her own writings, with a particular regard to her prayer. The means and manner by which Almighty God advanced her in prayer. Her fidelity to God in the use of the means He afforded her, and the perfect union to which He was pleased to raise her.*

FROM her infancy she found sweet attractions to prayer, and was encouraged by a sensible devotion she then found in it. And her fidelity in these years to God, thus moving and encouraging her, was a means to draw down new blessings. At the age of seven years she began early to gain little victories over herself, and had the resolution and courage to quit her play that she might find time for her usual devotions. From this time she was carried on with great tenderness towards our Blessed Saviour's Passion, and not content to honour it alone, she strove to inspire these pious sentiments into others. But such is the weakness of man, after this she began to relent and lost in part that tenderness of devotion which she then felt, till Almighty God by a sudden glimpse of Divine light made her sensible of her failings. She was then about sixteen years of age. We may date from this moment the beginning of her sanctity. She cast herself upon her knees, begged with tears pardon of her past neglects, and began with inviolable fidelity from this moment to cultivate those seeds of devotion which God had so early cast into her soul.

By what I can gather from her own writings, from the
testimony of those who were most intimate with her, and
the knowledge I had myself of her, I have reason to
believe she was never known after this to be guilty of
any wilful fault, and was never wilfully negligent in
corresponding with any light which she thought was
imparted to her by Almighty God. She was carried on
from this time with a strong impulse from Almighty God
(as she expresses it in her own writings) with a desire
of pleasing God. Mortification and prayer were the
means by which she endeavoured to comply with this
desire. She was then young, inexperienced, had little
help from any books, and lay under this mistake, that
it was better even to conceal from a confessor what
pious sentiments she found in her soul, which deprived
her of the advantages she might have reaped from the
direction of others. At the same time she felt little or
no sensible devotion from her practices of piety, and
yet she passes days and nights in prayer, rises often at
midnight, steals into corners and private places to spend
her time in devotions, performs several stations in honour
of the Passion of our Saviour, and took care from this
time never to let herself be carried to anything which
she thought less perfect. Her prayer was mostly vocal,
though mixed, as she observes, with something of
meditation, though then she did not so much as know
the name of meditation.

Almighty God, Who was her sole director, was pleased
soon after to raise her to a much higher degree of
prayer. Her patience and resignation to the will of
Almighty God in her first year's most grievous sickness,
when she was at the age of nineteen, which we may
justly deem the fruit of her prayer and piety, drew down
more signal blessings. Upon the first attack of her illness
she offered herself, out of a motive of the love of God,

o

to suffer whatever He should please to send, with a determinate resolution of obeying for God's sake all that were to attend her; and she was so faithful in complying with this resolution, that she was never known to show the least sign of impatience in word or action. God on His side, to reward her fidelity and enable her to suffer, was pleased to pour down His heavenly lights in greater abundance.

She passed this year in a continual exercise of mental prayer, chiefly in consideration of our Saviour's Passion, in uniting her sufferings with His, with an ardent desire of suffering more, wishing she could have eased His pain in the violent extremities of hunger and thirst which He suffered to an excess. She was so moved with the Divine examples of His hunger in the desert and thirst upon the Cross, that she declared to Him if it were in her power she would not admit of any mitigation of her pain, if it was made known to her that it was His will she should continue to suffer. She lay for hours and days, nay once for a month together, speechless, and in appearance senseless, so that those about her thought her often to be dead. This was the state of her body while her soul was all this time taken up in high contemplation and prayer. For, as she acknowledges in the manifestation of her conscience, she endeavoured to use mental prayer before her sickness but found no gust in it, now God gave her the gift of contemplation, and her thoughts, particularly at those times when she appeared in these great extremities of suffering, were for the most part in heaven, with a strange light of the other world, and as great a contempt of all things in this. When in these extremities she lay deprived of all human comfort, then it was she found the sweet caresses of Almighty God, to a degree that she declares she never before felt such a joy in her whole life, nor so much comfort. She learnt here by experience that the less we have of human comfort the more we receive from Almighty God.

The solid fruit of her prayer during this first year's sickness was an entire resignation to the will of God and a wonderful patience under the sharpest trials, by which she prepared her soul for the further operation of the Holy Ghost, and satisfied so far the justice of God, that it was afterwards declared to her that she would have gone straight to heaven had she died at the end of this year. God was pleased during this time to favour her with several visions and apparitions, both of Himself and His angels, to strengthen her in her sufferings. It is true that these extraordinary favours are neither to be sought for, nor to be entirely relied on, as certain signs of sanctity of the person on whom they are conferred, yet when by their admirable effects, as it happened in her case, we have reason to believe they proceed from Almighty God, they furnish a continual subject of admiration and praise, and serve not a little to raise a soul above herself. And this she experienced, being so far weaned from the world, and so sensible of the goodness and beauty of Almighty God, that she could never more set her heart upon any created good. Yet she had a great deal to pass through before she was raised to a perfect union with Almighty God.

She passed the four following years in a languishing condition as to her health. The state of her soul was yet in appearance less comfortable. Almighty God had now withdrawn His hand, all sensible comfort was subtracted from her, she was oppressed with anxiety, troubles, darkness of faith, without almost any sense of Almighty God. She was fallen into that obscure night and passive purgation through which God leads His chosen souls. Her prayer was then without much consolation, yet accompanied with a perfect resignation to the will of God, and

a great contempt of all things below. This state of desolation continued by fits most part also of her last year's
sickness. She was violently attacked with thoughts of
diffidence and despair, with frequent temptations of
quitting entirely the devotions she had begun for her cure.
She was beset on every side with that darkness; she lost
almost all sense of God. She partly lost the knowledge
of those supernatural favours and caresses she had
received, partly endeavoured to banish them from her
thoughts as fearing they had been illusions of the
enemy. She was still in this false persuasion, that it
was an imperfection to seek any ease by disclosing her
mind even to her confessarius, unless just in things
where she apprehended any fault or sin. Thus she
lay, desolate of all human help, but still supported by
Divine grace, so as never to yield to any of these
temptations, nor even to let herself be overcome by an
act of impatience.

God was pleased sometimes, particularly during her
last year's sickness, not only to support her by His grace,
but also to make the effects of His Divine Presence most
sensible in sending her angels, in coming Himself to
comfort her, in inspiring a child of six years old to play
the part of a director. Whosoever reads this part of her
life, of which I am now treating, will learn to admire the
wonderful proceedings of Providence. He will find her
sometimes rapt, as we may say with St. Paul, into the
third heaven, caressed by the saints and angels, nay, by
our Blessed Saviour Himself, in frequent apparitions and
visions (we seem secure of the truth of them by their
effects, namely, an invincible patience in a complication
of violent distempers which kept her for years together on
her back). At other times he will find her abandoned to
herself, supporting the whole weight of her afflictions,
interior and exterior, by acts of resignation, and an

unwearied patience following the dim lights of faith, forcing herself by the assistance of Divine grace (which is never wanting, though its effects are not then so sensible) to a faithful compliance with the will of God, and thus languishing after her Beloved, though He seems to fly from her. 'O my all-powerful Father,' says she, 'if I must needs drink of this bitter chalice, endure this long and tedious sickness, suffer these sharp torments, Your holy will be done. Lord, what will You have me to do? what is Your pleasure? Behold Your servant ready to accomplish it. What dreadest thou, my fearful and faithless heart? Behold Christ thy Captain is gone before thee, take up thy cross and follow Him, He leads to a kingdom. Heaven is worth thy pains.' 'Lord,' says she again, in this anguish of mind, 'Your will be done. Grant me patience and unite these pains to Your Passion.' Yet she confesses at the same time that her anxiety and pains were so great, that she had scarce sense of what she said, and the very knowledge of so many favours received was then so entirely taken from her, that she could find no satisfaction in refreshing the memory of them. Thus did God proceed with strange vicissitude to humble and exalt, to depress and to raise her, 'to bring her soul to the gates of hell and to reduce it back again.' Good God! how wonderful are You in Your Saints, and in the ways You take to purify their souls! 'I will boil out all thy dross till it be pure, and take away all thy tin,' says He by Isaias.[1]

The reader must not imagine that I treat here of a person trained up in a religious community encouraged, by the example of others who make it their study to aim at the height of Christian perfection, assisted by the lecture of books proper to instruct the understanding and discover the many deceits of the enemy, guided by the

[1] Isaias i. 25.

direction of the ablest men to secure her conduct. The person I speak of is a young, unexperienced woman, living in an heretic country, destituted of all instruction and example of virtue, excepting what she saw in her father, brothers, and sisters, in a private gentleman's family, assisted now and then by a missioner whilst in his circuit he comes to the house to administer the Sacraments. When we consider a person in these circumstances, and reflect on what she suffered during her seven years' sickness, and in what manner she passed through this fiery furnace of tribulation, directed by no other lights than those she received immediately from God and by her prayer, we shall conclude with the royal Prophet that God was her illumination or light, and that her conduct speaks an immediate direction of the Holy Ghost. But these were only preludes to what God designed to work in her.

Upon the eve of the last Friday (when she was making the ten Fridays' devotion in honour of St. Xaverius to obtain her health), and the day before her miraculous cure, whilst she was employing herself in making acts of entire resignation to the will of God, submitting to sickness or health, to life or death, she found on a sudden a wonderful peace of mind infused into her soul, it descended, as she expresses it, like a sweet dew from heaven. It so calmed her in God, that she says that she wants words to express it, and it was something above what she had ever felt in her life. At the same time, though she had neither rapt nor vision, she found her patron, St. Francis Xaverius (to whom she had now a tender devotion), very near her, making an intimate union with her soul. This great favour, which we may justly look upon as the crown and reward of her seven years' painful suffering, proved an inexhaustible source of benedictions for the time to come. It was a permanent blessing bestowed on her by Almighty God, for she declares, seven years after, when she penned down this part of her life, that this settled peace continued in her soul, and I have reason to believe it accompanied her till death.

She soon found the effects of this settled peace, for in this wonderful calm, the whole soul being intent upon God, when she found next day the admirable effects of His goodness and power, in the cure of her body,[2] she never stopped or had a thought of solacing herself in the new benefit of health, or the advantages of it, but passing further to the Author of the gift, she was totally taken up in admiring and praising Almighty God, Who was pleased in so wonderful a manner to exert His power in her behalf. It was for her a continual subject of prayer, admiration of God, and gratitude. She continued for several days almost constantly in prayer, whether alone or in company, but her desire was to be alone, pouring forth her heart before Almighty God. ‘I was willing,’ says she, ‘to be retired from company. I knew how to spend my time.’ When, some months after, by a wonderful effect of the power of God, by the intercession of St. Xaverius, she was cured a second time, her disjointed hip being immediately after Communion restored to its place, she not only found an increase of the former pious sentiments of devotion, love, and admiration of the beauty and goodness of God, but moreover being carried on with a sincere sense of gratitude she could never rest till she had consecrated herself entirely to the service of God in a religious course. She thought she could never do enough for God Who had done so much for her. She had a perfect contempt of everything below. She found herself very much disengaged from all affections to her kindred and parents, for whom she had a strange tender-

---

[2] See page 80.

ness all her life. She was now glad she had an occasion
of making this little sacrifice to Almighty God. She
was animated with so lively a desire of following the
Divine inspirations, and such a confidence in the protection of Almighty God, and her great patron, St. Xaverius,
that she not only broke through all difficulties, but, as
she expresses it, could have ventured to pass the seas
upon the water, if she had missed of a ship. Full of
these pious sentiments, she consecrates herself to God
in the holy Order of St. Teresa.

'My joy,' says she, 'was so great to see myself in
a religious habit, inclosed in a monastery, that I soon
forgot all other things.' She was totally taken up the
first year with the joyful thoughts of her future happiness,
in becoming the spouse of Jesus Christ by her vows
of Baptism. She began from her first entrance to count
the months and weeks, aspiring to this spiritual preferment. In the settled calm of her own breast she found
God continually and was, as it were, taken up with Him.
She had no difficulty in any rigour of their religious
observance. She was studying, indeed, to break herself
wherever she found any difficulty, but she had been
accustomed before to break her own will and practise
interior mortification, so that everything seemed rather
too easy. She was moved to a tender confidence in
Almighty God and her great patron, St. Xaverius. She
ran to him as a child to the best of parents, in all
her wants, both spiritual and temporal. Almighty God
at the same time gave her visible marks of His care,
in granting sensibly whatever she demanded of Him.
She was very easy in the subtraction of supernatural
favours, which were not now so frequent as in her
sickness. 'I thought Almighty God,' says she, 'sent
me these favours and apparitions at that time to enable
me to support my sufferings with patience, but now

He had brought me to religion to be a spouse of His. This was happiness enough, neither did I expect any more of Him.' In place of these she received new lights from heaven, manifesting still more clearly the great love God had showed in what He had done for her, and animating her to a still more lively sense of gratitude. She was so transported upon making her vows to see herself consecrated to Almighty God, that whilst, according to custom, she lay prostrate upon the ground, she fell into a kind of rapt, and could not be moved out of the place without difficulty.

From this time Almighty God began to advance her in prayer. Her heart in time of it was so inflamed with the love of God, that it broke out into violent impetuosities of love, as she terms them, which so much affected her body that she was frequently lifted up from the ground, and her mind so absorbed in God that she could scarce bend herself to apply to anything else. Her director, to whom she had now begun to manifest her interior, ordered her to resist these vehement impulses as prejudicial and dangerous, and she strove to obey; but the more she was restrained the more God seemed to caress her, till her director, at last satisfied, thought he might securely permit her to follow the sweet attractions of love, which he had reason to believe proceeded from Almighty God. She now thought herself at liberty, and giving herself over to the conduct of the Holy Ghost received several instructions, sometimes from our Blessed Saviour Himself, sometimes from St. Xaverius, who promised her to be her director. Her heart was so overpowered by the bounteous liberality of God, pouring down His favours upon her by the hands of St. Xaverius, that, as she confesses, she cannot express what at these times she felt in her soul. 'I found,' says she, 'so tender an affection that my heart was ready to melt, but I could

do nothing but enjoy, not being able to make any distinct acts of thanksgiving or offering of myself, but yet
I thought I was all His.' Being surprised at the wonderful familiarity with which our dear Lord was pleased to
bear with her, manifesting Himself to her in His Sacred
Humanity, and conversing with her, she told Him, as
she expresses it in a simple and familiar way, 'Lord,
it seems to me as if You had nothing else to do but
to keep in my cell and converse with me;' to which
He answered sweetly, but withal expressing a concern
that He found very few to delight Himself with. 'Child,'
says He, 'I leave the rich palaces of the world and come
to seek some little cell where I can find a heart disengaged from all creatures, resigned to My will, and
who has no other desire than to please Me. In this
simple solitary soul I delight as in the highest treasures,
and will manifest my secrets to her, to the confusion
of the wise and learned.'

The effects of these favours were an increase of humility
by a clearer knowledge of herself. She saw how little
part she had in them, the infinite goodness of Almighty
God in her regard, and this was a continual subject of
thanksgiving and praise. 'I do not remember,' says she,
'that any of these supernatural favours was ever an
occasion of pride or vanity to me, though some feared
they would.' Though she was already favoured so much
and raised to so high a degree of familiarity with Almighty
God, yet it seems His all purity, which can suffer no
blemish in His favourite souls, found still something in
her which interposed itself and hindered that Divine
union He was to make with her. She found herself
much disengaged from that too tender affection she had
heretofore for her relations and friends, yet it seems
she had some ties to creatures which she was less cautious
to avoid, thinking they had nothing in them earthly or

imperfect. She had a longing desire to see her father, who was upon the point of making himself a religious, and designed to pass through Antwerp in his journey. He had been the best of fathers to her. She was willing to see him, and thought she might please herself with the thought of this, particularly since he was coming on so good a design, but she saw clearly afterwards that she should have had too much natural satisfaction in his company.

She had also too great a tie towards a person who had advanced her much in the way of perfection, her Mistress of Novices. For though her love to her seemed spiritual, yet as she reflected afterwards, she was something disquieted when deprived of her company, but it pleased Almighty God by the death of these two persons to break these ties, and at the same time to give her a clear light to discover how prejudicial the smallest failings are to a person tending to perfection. Hence upon the death of the latter of these, she cast herself upon her knees before the Blessed Sacrament, begging of our Lord most earnestly that He would so possess her heart that she might never more be tied to any creature, and she found from this time that she reposed more in God, and loved all in Him. By this we see on one side the great purity of her soul, and on the other that entire disengagement which God requires in a person aspiring to the height of perfection. The enemy was some few times permitted to attack her visibly, both in point of purity and with temptations of despair; but her soul, which was now settled in a lasting peace with God, appeared like an invincible fortress, and these seemed only light attacks on the out-walls, without so much as touching the body of the place; in effect, he was soon put to flight, and her victories were generally crowned with new favours from Almighty God.

Her heart, now thoroughly disengaged from everything that was not God, became fit for the Holy Ghost.
She began to enjoy frequently the prayer of quiet, recollection, and union. 'I no sooner,' says she, 'put myself
upon my knees, but I could say I found Him Whom my
soul loves : I will hold Him, neither will I let Him go.'
This happy state seemed to be farther perfected when
the Infant Jesus, appearing to her, gave her a kiss of
peace, blotting out, as she expresses it, all sin and imperfections, leaving her in great purity of soul and perfecting
in her a strict union with God. The love of the Divine
Infant was not idle: He encourages her in a most
endearing way to act. I have manifested,' says He, 'to
the world how much I have loved you, My spouse, in
working so many miracles to bring you to be My spouse;
manifest you to the world how much you love Me.'
Those darts of love pierced her very heart. 'I have
been often moved to lament,' says she, 'when I felt these
darts of love, and used to repeat these words—" Oh, my
Love is not loved ;" but this with so great a feeling that
I thought I could not think of anything else, but desired
all the world might love, and know what I then felt. I
was seized with such impulses of the love and knowledge
of God, that I thought it was as much as my natural
force would bear. It was indeed a great pain, but a
delightful one ; none can tell it, I believe, but those who
have experienced it. Though the pain be so great that
it is of force enough to deprive one of this mortal life,
yet those that feel it desire not to be freed from it, but
that it may increase—nay, even that they may lose their
lives with it. I have often found these impetuosities
with such beatings at the heart, and such oppressions
for want of breath, that it seemed as if my very breast
would have opened, not being able to contain what I
felt, and I was often moved to cry out, "O Lord, let an

act of Your love separate my soul from my body, and
break that heart of mine. O my God, let me be all
Yours, love or not live !"'

As in her first beginnings her soul was prepared by
sufferings in her seven years' sickness for the favours of
Almighty God, by which in time she was all set on fire,
and now almost consumed with the flames of Divine
love, so Providence in her present state prepares the
same fuel to nourish, conserve, and augment these flames.
Her sufferings were now of a different sort. There was
in the bottom of her soul a serenity and calm which
nothing could reach, yet she was sometimes reduced to
a state by exterior crosses and a subtraction of all comfort from heaven and earth, that she was not sensible of
the treasure she possessed ! Clouds, says she, over-
shade the sun, all brightness disappears ; notwithstanding
there remains a sun, though hidden under a cloud. In
this state she remained, acting perseverantly by the light
of faith, like one of those strong souls actuated by the
love of God, which is sufficient to carry them through all
difficulties without any exterior sensible help ; for even
in those cases she felt no comfort nor assistance from
any creature, and was left to herself without feeling any
sensible favours from Almighty God ; yet, says she, I had
a peace of mind which nothing disturbed, and oftentimes
an inward joy when I was reviled and contemned. Our
Saviour, to encourage her, imparted to her a particular
light, to show how pleasing such souls were to Him in
these times of desolation, and how perfect these acts of
self-denial and resignation were in His sight, as if He
should mean they would have a heaven even in this life.
This made her put a high value on this state of desolation and darkness, yet such was her humility, 'I dare
not,' says she, 'pray to be led this way, for fear of my
own weakness after all the favours received, but leave it

to God to carry me which way He sees most for His glory and the good of my own soul; but I continue to pray for my purgatory in this life: hence I expect to suffer as long as I live in this exile.' These sufferings in the happy state she is in, serve only to increase her love. 'I found now,' says she, 'Whom my heart loves, neither do I care to possess anything else.' Everything helps to make her go more out of herself to enter more into Almighty God. 'Here,' says she again, 'there is no speaking for a soul; she sees and hears so much from her great Master, she has no time to speak one word, nor does she desire it. She sees her Spouse knows all her wants and what she desires without noise of words; but I do not mean vocal prayer, but even mental, for here the soul languishes with love; she is, as it were, wholly overcome, and can do nothing but enjoy.'

This high prayer was accompanied with a wonderful confidence in Almighty God. 'Since,' says she, 'I have received these supernatural favours, since I have seen so much of the mercies of God and of His goodness, I do not remember that I have had anything like a doubt, or even almost a flying thought, as if I should not be saved, or as if I should not enjoy God for all eternity. I know as long as we live in this world we are never secure. I know we must work out our salvation with fear and trembling. These thoughts, I must confess, keep me in awe; but on the other side I reflect that love and confidence expel all fear, and since I know our Blessed Saviour loved me before I was capable of loving Him, He made me of nothing, He redeemed me with His precious Blood, He has sanctified me, He has called me to be His spouse; is not this enough, my God, to make me to confide in You, that You made me for Yourself, to reign with You in Your heavenly kingdom, to sing forth Your praise for all eternity? Oh, that this time were come ! oh, that this pilgrimage were at an end ! Besides, my God, among other favours You have in a particular manner given me an assurance that I shall never be separated from You.' She looked upon this confidence as one of the greatest favours God had ever bestowed upon her, and she acknowledges it, as granted by the merits and intercession of St. Xaverius. 'I answered,' says she, 'the flying thoughts of despair suggested by the enemy with the poor man in St. Francis of Sales' works. I have two arms to embrace God, the one of fear, the other of love, and I had rather be in hell with God than in heaven without Him ; for methinks I would hold those Divine Hands so fast that He should never let me go or leave me behind Him. Though I know I have justly deserved to suffer, yet, my God, I know that Your mercies exceed Your justice, and You are called the God of mercies.'

Our Blessed Saviour, raising this happy soul still higher from light to light, seemed now resolved to take a full possession of her heart. One day at the Elevation at Mass He manifested Himself to her, as attended by the saints and angels, and as removing His court from heaven, to keep it in the most innermost part of her soul. 'The door of my heart being wide open,' says she, 'my King and Lord entered in, accompanied with our Blessed Lady, attended by other saints. Thus He entered the first and second room, being very large, I must say so, not knowing how to express it better.' After the heavenly court had taken possession of her soul, she seemed to be turned out of doors, as not being able nor worthy to stay in such company, but like one standing by seeing what passed, astonished, amazed, not knowing what to say or do. 'At last,' says she, 'I broke out with holy Simeon, "Lord, dismiss Thy servant," and, soon after, taking courage, I cried out with St. Paul, " I

live now, not I, Christ lives in me."' She received at the
same time, a lively impression from a great light, discovering her own littleness, and the greatness of God,
which made her cry out in an interior way, 'Lord, will
You come from the highest heaven to keep Your court in
this little worm?' She seemed to herself still most vile,
and she received for answer from her dear Lord : 'Yes,
where I can find a soul disengaged from all creatures, in
this soul I will manifest my secrets.' 'This,' says she,
'was one of the greatest intellectual favours God had
then done me.'

Though she found all her life languishing desires of communicating, yet now after this favour they were redoubled
with great impetuosities of the love of God, and one day
after Communion she found herself plunged in God, her
littleness in His greatness, with great desires of knowing
what she could return to Him in gratitude for all His
favours, and she received for answer : 'Return Me back
all that is Mine,' that is, as she understood it, all she ever
had done, or could do, acknowledging all as an effect of
the pure grace of God, moving her, and carrying her on.
Some days after this, she found our Blessed Saviour after
Communion, settled in a higher place in her soul, and
finding herself thus closely united to Him she desired to
die, that by enjoying the beatifical vision she might
complete this union; 'fearing,' says she, such is the frailty
of human weakness, 'lest by living longer, this union
should come to be dissolved, and I become so ungrateful
as to offend this great God, Whom I now in some sort
comprehend by a lively faith and love.' It was made
known to her she was yet to live for the greater glory of
God and the good of others, but at the same time she
received an assurance from our Blessed Lord that He
would continue this union in her soul till she came
to possess Him in glory. 'However,' says she, 'as not

content with this, I answered with importunity, tears, and tenderness of devotion, then grant this request, that I never more offend your Divine Majesty by any deliberate sin or imperfection; for do You think, Lord, I can bear this and see Your goodness to me? No, no, Lord, this cannot be, either grant me my request, or have patience to bear my importunity, for I know Your goodness is so great and so sweet, that You cannot deny Your spouse a request so reasonable.' To this contract I called for witnesses, our Blessed Lady, St. Xaverius, and the whole court of heaven.

This was the state of her soul when I had the happiness to be acquainted with her, thirteen years before her death, when she was first chosen Sub-Prioress, and we have no reason to doubt but that she was daily advanced to higher favours of prayer. Her director, whom she chiefly treated with during this time, being dead, and she being prevented by death from continuing the history of her life (she has only brought it till she was first chosen Superior), we shall remain in great part ignorant of those great wonders God wrought in her during the last thirteen years, that is, during the most perfect time of her life. All I can find of it is that she says in general, that God so increased His favour to her by new lights and passive union with Himself, that she believes the best of pens and writers would never be able to explain what had passed in her, without a particular grace and light from God. Among her writings I find besides the following short account by which we may in some sort be able to guess to what perfection she was then raised in prayer. This happened several years before her death.

She tells us she was much drawn to interior recollection, with intellectual favours, particularly after Communion; that one day she received new lights above

P

whatever she had received or heard of, and that after these impetuosities and passive unions she found impatient desires of solitude. Upon this our Blessed Saviour discovered Himself to her in the innermost part of her soul, and after a gentle reprehension for being so solicitously bent on solitude, bidding her never to go out of it, 'It seems to me,' says she, 'as if He had brought down the chiefest part of His heavenly court for me to live, love, act, suffer, and die, in so large and so well fortified a place, that I cannot in some sort get out of it if I would. Ever since this I have had new lights communicated on this subject, and in such a manner that, of all the supernatural favours I unworthy have received from the hands of God, I never found any advance me in so solid and secure a way of perfection as this.' After this, notwithstanding any exterior dissipation, she was almost constantly in prayer. 'Jesus, Your divinest will be ever done,' was frequently in her mouth. In her most violent fits of sickness, in crosses, exterior and interior, this was her comfort, here she reposed. 'When my Divine Spouse,' says she, 'is pleased to solace me with Himself, by this most high and sublime favour, He brings me into this cell, this palace, this heaven of His Divine will, rather, I find myself there on a sudden, I know not how. In this Divine union the soul finds herself one with her Creator, as a drop of water fallen into the vast ocean which can never more be divided. Here my soul finds herself in some manner as secure of eternal happiness as the blessed in heaven, and this through the goodness, mercies, and merits of her Saviour, Who discovers to her new lights of His admirable perfections, and of the gifts and fruits of the Holy Ghost. She sees each apart in Almighty God, and since His Divine wisdom, knowledge, and understanding, infused into the Apostles in small parcels, like rivulets, as I may say, springing from the vast ocean, appear in them so admirable, what must the source of them be altogether in Almighty God? Certainly the most perfect contemplative may be drowned in any of them : as to myself, when He is pleased to discover Himself to me in these it is by little and little, according as He sees my strength to bear it, seeming to hide part of them from me, either till I come to possess them in heaven, or else till I am stronger in virtue.'

It seems this virtuous soul did not rest here. She found herself indeed by this strict union drowned, lost, absorbed, and, as we may say, made one with God, in a state of conformity, as the divines express it. But about a year after this, by a more powerful operation of the Holy Ghost, she seems raised to a higher state, even of Deiformity, as we may gather from what she says, speaking of these former favours : ' I saw myself,' says she, ' in those favours engulfed in God, as a bright star shining forth in Him, but now, by the power of God, transformed into a more perfect resemblance of the Divine perfections, I saw myself engulfed in God and Him in me.' She mentioned at the same time wonderful lights received from God ; but, as I said before, it pleased His Providence to take her out of the world before she had time to pen down in particular what happened to her the last thirteen years, by which we are deprived of the knowledge of them.

I thought fit to give this short view of the state of her soul, rather to point out the means God made use of to raise her to perfection, than to give a full account of her interior. The many sheets she has left written are nothing else but a manifestation of what God wrought in her and for her, and if we can trust the truth of what she says, we must conclude she was a soul highly favoured by Almighty God and closely united to Him.

For the better knowledge of this, I must refer the reader to the first part of this book. I shall only observe that what God seemed chiefly to regard in her, and what was the immediate means towards her advancement in perfection, was first, constant fidelity to every motion of Divine grace, from the age of sixteen, when she found that first glimpse of light which made her enter into herself and turn herself entirely to God; and secondly, unwearied patience under her great and long sufferings. These were the means she pursued to draw down the blessings of Almighty God, and the whole tenour of her life corresponded so perfectly with the state of a soul enlightened and directed by the Holy Ghost, that it was the most satisfactory and most authentic testimony that could be required for a proof of all these wonders, which she says God wrought for her.

Her life was so regular, that for the twenty years she was religious I could never hear that she was wilfully guilty of the breach of any one rule. She was so perfectly mistress of her own passions, that even in the most unforeseen accidents she always acted with that presence of mind, with that sedate calmness of temper, as if she had been for some time deliberately preparing herself to act in this encounter. She was so inflamed with the love of God, that she never lost the sight of her Divine Spouse, even when obedience called her to exterior duty. Hence upon any occasion her love was ready to break into a flame. I have often observed, when she gave an account of herself, she was not able to contain this fire, which burned in her breast, though she endeavoured to hide it. It broke out in her very countenance. Nor was she able to continue speaking, but was often forced to interrupt her discourse, and I easily perceived her heart was more where it loved than where it lived. Her words at those times were sufficient to inflame a frozen heart, and nothing but my great infidelity to Almighty God could have made me neglect this favourable occasion of advancing myself by my conversing with her upon this Divine subject.

To frame a most just idea of the state of her soul with regard to Almighty God, we must have an eye on those endearing tokens of Divine love which she received so frequently from Him. The sweet title of the *beloved* Disciple of Jesus Christ given to St. John the Evangelist in the Holy Gospel has been looked upon in all ages as a sufficient panegyric to commend the high merits of this great Apostle, for, in reality, the extraordinary marks of God's love to a soul find or make her an object worthy of His love. Perhaps among all the servants of God whose lives and memorable actions have been transmitted to posterity for our instruction, we shall find few who have been favoured by Almighty God in this extraordinary way of visions or revelations, more than the person whose life is here written, and indeed those wonderful tokens of God's love, that perpetual, as I may say, familiar intercourse between her and St. Xaverius, by whose intercession she was twice so visibly cured, those endearing expressions from the mouth of St. Xaverius, our Blessed Lady, of our Saviour Himself, would with reason startle us, unless we knew on the one side the infinite goodness, bounty, and mercy of Almighty God, His more than maternal bowels of tender love and affection towards mankind in general, and particularly towards those who, by a faithful correspondence, quit all affections to creatures to give themselves entirely to His conduct, so far that He declares His delight is to converse with the sons of men ; and unless, on the other hand, we had some security from her virtuous, religious, and exemplary life, that they were the operations of the Holy Ghost. The fruits

prove the goodness of the tree, and the effects manifest
the cause from whence they proceed.

The solid virtue which appeared in the whole course
of her life made her directors easy, and gave them
security that there was nothing of illusion in her conduct,
as did the happy death which crowned her virtuous life,
together with some extraordinary things which happened
after it, and which shall be mentioned afterwards.    I
give to the public these papers, that God may be glorified
in His works, and that those who read these sheets may
find for their own edification and instruction the rules
and precepts suggested to her by Almighty God in the
whole conduct of her life.    I wish the reader also
would reflect on some lights imparted to her in prayer.
I had,' says she, 'a particular light, how this favour of
God's becoming man for me and clothing Himself with
our human nature, did abundantly surpass all the supernatural favours He has been pleased to bestow upon
all the saints, much more those bestowed upon me, the
most unworthy of His servants.    Though nothing is hard
to God, yet it is represented to me as a much greater
marvel and more surprisingly admirable for God to
become man than to make men become as gods.'    If
the reader reflects on this, he will wonder more that
there are so few that strive or dispose their souls for
these operations of the Holy Ghost than to see this
virtuous woman thus favoured, who, by an inviolable
fidelity, endeavoured in all things to follow His call.
St. Xaverius performed, as he had promised her, in her
regard, the part of a *friend*, a *physician*, a *director*, a *father*.
No wonder this should inspire her with the greatest
sense of love and gratitude and the tenderest affection
of a dutiful child towards the best of parents.    Hence,
seeing these heavenly favours were so frequent and
that her whole study was to make a suitable return to

Almighty God, we may say in some sort that her whole
life was a state of prayer. I must refer the reader to the
first and second parts of this book, written by herself,
and I wish he may come, by an imitation of her fidelity
and patience, to reap that fruit which St. Xaverius promised to those who should peruse what she has written.

### CHAPTER XXVI.

*What others observed in her of her affections towards
Almighty God. She inflames others with the love of
God. Her exactness in complying with all the duties
of the Church. Her devotion towards the Blessed
Sacrament, our Blessed Lady, and St. Xaverius.*

I MUST refer the reader to what is written in her own
life, as I have already hinted in several places, for a
just idea of her virtue in these points here mentioned,
and in others which I shall have occasion to mention
afterwards. What I design in these following sheets is
to put down what her religious observed in her exterior
carriage, by which her hidden virtue, which she always
industriously strove to conceal, broke out and discovered
itself. The account may serve to convince us that her
life was, as I may say, all of apiece, squared most perfectly in all points according to the rules of Christian perfection, and her practical examples of virtue in the daily
occurrences of life may help to engage us in an imitation
of her virtues.

'I perceived in our dear Mother Mary Xaveria,' says
one of her religious, 'during the ten years I had the
happiness to live with her, a most constant practice of
all sorts of virtues, and in all occasions, in particular an

ardent love to Almighty God, and a great zeal for His honour and glory, which she endeavoured to inspire into others. Meeting me sometimes she would say, "Love God, love God, child!" At other times, "Oh, when shall we be so happy as to do nothing else but to love and praise that great God!" At which words, though never so tepid and dry before, I found a great sweetness in my soul with tender inflamed affections towards Almighty God, and indeed to be nigh her only, though she did not speak (as being taken up in writing, reading, or some other business), was sufficient to wake in me a tenderness and feeling of God's Divine presence, which thing seldom or never happened to me when I was not nigh her. I understood at the same time that this was the effect of God's Divine presence in her soul.'

This was not the only person who found these effects. 'She had,' says another of her children, 'a very religious comportment in all her actions, and in her behaviour, which showed her continual presence of God. Her countenance was oftentimes more than ordinary sweet and angelical, particularly when she spoke of Almighty God, and upon great feasts, so that one might easily perceive an unusual joy, zeal, and devotion. I could never look upon her but I was struck with a great love and reverence, and I have heard several persons say that there was something in her countenance which moved them to respect and devotion.'

Her tenderness of affection to Almighty God carried her on to a perfect zeal for everything which regarded His honour, or that of His saints, as will further appear by the following extract of a letter from the present Superior of the English monastery at Antwerp, who lived several years under her: 'We saw evidently how much she was animated by the spirit of the Holy Church by the preparation she made for all the prin-

cipal feasts of the year, speaking in the chapter-house
of every particular mystery with such zeal and fervour
that it drew tears of devotion frequently from the eyes
of those that were present. She celebrated herself each
of these feasts with unspeakable piety.

'She had a most tender devotion to the Blessed Sacrament of the altar. When she was sometimes very weak
and quite sunk by the violence of her sickness, the
religious, out of their concern for her, would beg her
to be absent from the choir. Her answer was, "When
I am tired with sickness or labour, I go to the choir
there to rest and solace myself in presence of the
Blessed Sacrament." And indeed all her delight was
to be in the choir with our Blessed Saviour. Her
devotion was so great that she communicated every
day, yet she did not do this but by the order and
advice of my Lord Bishop her Superior, of her confessor, her director, and other learned men who approved
this her practice. All spare time she had was spent
before the Blessed Sacrament, and when we wanted her
we were sure to find her there in prayer and deep
recollection. I have heard her say, "If I have any
good in me it comes from frequenting the Blessed
Sacrament. I was cured a second time when I had
disjointed my hip, on the tenth day of the devotion
I made in honour of St. Xaverius, the very moment
that I had received the Blessed Sacrament."'

She told one of the religious not to be scandalized
at her frequent communicating, that she did not think
herself fit or worthy, but finding herself very weak in
virtue, she went to obtain courage and strength, since
God could do all things. 'And her example,' says the
same person, 'did very much augment our devotion to the
Blessed Sacrament, and our desire of more frequent communicating.' She acknowledges that she used to wake in

the night with joy that she was next day to communicate.
The same person adds, 'That she showed great concern
when any of the religious lost Communion, and when
Superior, she endeavoured all she could to prevent this.'
Others observed that, 'She never seemed to be in any
proper sphere but when she was treating and speaking of
Almighty God, for which she never wanted words, or a
subject, because she found matter from everything that
occurred: that she had a perfect longing after the Blessed
Sacrament, and before she had leave to communicate
daily she used, as she termed it, to steal our Lord, by
finding several pious pretexts on account of which she
got permission to communicate upon extraordinary days.'

The reader will find in her own writings how Almighty
God all along nourished and strengthened her soul by
this Divine Food.   When in her first year's sickness she
lay for a month speechless, and in appearance almost
senseless, without being able to swallow down any nourishment, yet whenever she gave a sign to her confessarius
at the times when he thought fit to bring her the Blessed
Sacrament, she would always take this Bread of Life,
though she could neither before or after swallow down
any corporal nourishment.  Her great physician, St. Francis
Xaverius, prescribed to her in her noviceship this
Heavenly Bread to strengthen and enable her to go
through all she had to suffer for God's honour and glory,
and the wonderful caresses she received from our Blessed
Saviour at these happy moments in which she enjoyed
His corporal presence, shows how much she was advanced
by this Divine means prescribed to her by the Saint.
Then it was He secretly took possession of her soul,
imparting to her a kiss of peace, distinguishing her by
the endearing title of His spouse, removing His heavenly
court, as it was represented to her, to make His abode
in her, inflaming her with His Divine love to that degree

that she had scarce power left her to act, but was totally
taken up in enjoying the Divine presence of God-Man,
Who acted so sensibly in her happy Communions, where
a soul feels these lively effects of the presence of her
Beloved, and where she is so sensibly taught to under-
value all that is not God, thus to prepare herself for
those great blessings He is ready then to pour down
upon her. (See the many passages of her written life.)

I cannot omit here two or three expressions of hers,
from which I think we may gather both the liveliness
of her faith and the tenderness of her affection to Almighty
God. When she was first Sub-Prioress, five or six years
after her entrance into religion, writing down what had
happened in her sickness, she gives an account of that
favour in which, when she was deprived of the happiness
of hearing Mass, which they were obliged to say in
another room of the house, and not in her chamber
by reason of the extremity of her pain, our Blessed
Saviour about the time of the Elevation appeared to
her, telling her sweetly, 'Child, I am come Myself to
comfort you.' No doubt her faith then was very great,
for she owns that she bore a great deal and was willing
to submit to a great many inconveniences that she might
at those times have the happiness of hearing Mass; and
besides, this great favour done her by our Blessed Saviour,
with this sweet expression, shows how lively and acceptable her acts of virtue were, which deserved to be recom-
pensed in so singular a manner; but what I observe is
her candour and sincerity in expressing herself on this
occasion, and which shows to what perfection this gift of
faith must have been raised when she penned down this
favour some years after it happened. 'I always loved,'
says she, 'to see the Sacred Host elevated, and had
a lively faith, though not as I have now.' In the like
manner, speaking about the time she allowed for prayer

in her infancy, she gives an account that she was very
punctual and constant in allotting the full time for her
prayers, though, says she, it was more difficult to continue
one hour upon my knees than it was afterwards to continue so four or five.   From such expressions we have a
great light both of the disposition of her soul and of her
practice.   When she wrote this revelation towards the
end of her life, complaining to her religious upon the
distractions she found sometimes in exterior employs,
'Lord,' says she, 'how dissipated are my thoughts now,
whereas I used to be always in prayer!'   I must add that
the time she was obliged to allow to her natural rest
seemed not to interrupt the continual intercourse she
had with God in prayer.   She was overheard frequently
by those who on account of her illness were ordered
to lie in the same room with her, in her sleep to break
out into fervorous aspirations and pious affections towards
Almighty God.

'She had a tender devotion to our Blessed Lady, the
ever Immaculate Mother of God' says the present
Superior, 'and showed upon all her feasts a particular
joy.   Once in the Exercise I had occasion of going to
her, after she had made the Meditation of the Annun-
ciation of our Blessed Lady, I found her all inflamed
with the love of God, and in such a transport of joy and
admiration of the greatness of God's love towards man
in His Incarnation, that all the time I was with her (I
think it was above an hour) she could speak of nothing
else but the high lights God had given her concerning
this mystery; but at the same time her discourse was so
sublime, and of such a nature, that I had never read or
heard the like.   I was amazed at it, particularly because
she was never accustomed to speak of her prayers or the
favours she had received from Almighty God.   Presently
after she took occasion to make an excuse for what she

had said, being in pain lest I should esteem her more
for it, 'I know not,' said she, 'what made me run on or
speak in such a manner.'

'Several of the religious remarked her tenderness of
devotion to our Blessed Lady, which she seemed to have
sucked with her mother's milk, having been committed
in a particular manner to the care of our Blessed Lady
by her mother, who apprehended her in great danger
soon after her birth. She often called upon her in her
sharp sickness, and found her once sensibly performing
towards her the office not only of a mother but of a
nurse, laying her sacred hands upon her head to assuage
her pains; at other times she appeared to her with that
wonderful grace, modest beauty, and majesty which
becomes the Mother of God, and which struck her with
reverence and respect, admonishing her, in acknowledg-
ment of the many favours received from God through her
hands, to make herself an example of virtue to others
that God might be glorified. What is remarkable in the
many visions and revelations of which mention is made,
the favour was not done her, as we may say, for the
favour itself, but was commonly accompanied either with
some instructions adapted to the present state of her
mind, or with some admonition and encouragement to
some point of higher perfection, from which the reader
with due reflection and application to himself may draw
great help for his own advancement in virtue and perfection. She was much devoted to our seraphical mother
St. Teresa, to our glorious Father, St. Joseph, to her good
angel, to St. Mary Magdalene, and I have heard her often
speak (says another of the religious) of this blessed Saint
going to the Sepulchre with that ardency of love and
inflamed affection towards our Blessed Lord that her
very countenance was changed, and her eyes sparkled
in an extraordinary manner. When she came to speak

of our Lord appearing in the likeness of a gardener, her joy and transport was more than I can explain. She used then all the expressions of a soul which could be· satisfied with nothing else than Almighty God ; her words were so inflamed and penetrating that they could not but make impression even on the hardest hearts.

'Whoever reads her cures by the great Apostle of the Indies, St. Francis Xaverius, and of the other favours she received from him, will not wonder to hear of the great devotion she bore to this Saint, whom she called her father. She was in a perfect transport of joy even to hear him named. She celebrated his feast with extraordinary devotion, and many years before her death she procured of some friends money to have his feast celebrated with music. Three or four years before she died, one who entered among us was inspired to found a perpetual Mass in music in honour of that Saint, to be performed every year, either on the day of his feast or on the day that Reverend Mother Xaveria was cured by the Saint. Our Mother chose the latter, viz., the 12th of May, old style, our 23rd, and it was to be offered to God in thanksgiving for the favours received by his intercession. This solemnity is still and will be always kept on the day aforesaid, and I doubt not but this was obtained by prayer.'

It is needless to add anything in particular. Her whole life was a series of repeated favours heaped upon her by St. Xaverius, who by an effect of that ardent love with which his heart was inflamed on earth, and which is now perfected in glory, seemed wholly taken up in promoting this chosen soul, and advancing her in the way of perfection. On her side, when she saw this Saint had begged her life, even before she had any particular devotion towards him, that by a wonderful effect of the Divine power she had been

twice so miraculously cured at his intercession, that
he himself had so often visibly played the part of a
director, teaching and instructing her by his own mouth,
that he had proved himself a father in sensibly protecting and defending her, that on all occasions he
prevented her wants in a way so familiar as if he had
nothing to do but to attend to her advancement—her
heart was so moved with so tender a sense of devotion,
that no child was ever so tenderly affected to a parent.
Her love was not idle, it did not content itself with
an indolent enjoyment of favours, but her whole life
was a continual study how she should make some
suitable return, and how she should transcribe into the
copy of her own actions this perfect original of his
great virtues, which she had always before her eyes
for her imitation. His inflamed love of Almighty God,
his zeal for souls, his ardent charity was that which
animated her in all she undertook for the love of God,
and in all her crosses she represented St. Xaverius as
he once appeared to her, presenting her with a Crucifix,
with this sweet admonition: 'My child, if you will
imitate me, you must embrace this.' There needed no
more to make her break through the greatest difficulties.

## CHAPTER XXVII.

*Of her confidence in God. The monastery is several times supplied in their wants by her prayers and confidence. Several particular persons find the effect of her prayers.*

HER tenderness of affection to Almighty God, and her inviolable fidelity in pursuing whatever tended to His glory, were followed with a filial confidence in His Providence. She was so far advanced in this virtue before she left England, and thought herself so secure in the hands of God, under the protection of her patron St. Xaverius, that she would have made no difficulty in passing the seas alone, though she knew nothing of the language where she was going. Her director observed afterwards that she never missed of obtaining what she asked of Almighty God. Her father at her departure from England, upon her prayers, found himself wonderfully supplied with money to facilitate her designs of going over seas. In all her wants, both spiritual and temporal, she took her recourse to St. Xaverius without further concern on her side. She found others ready to prevent her in supplying of their own accord all that was necessary, and she particularly observes herself that whenever she was moved by God to ask anything she never failed obtaining what she thus asked. As to what regarded herself, she reposed so securely in the arms of Providence, that she knew not what it was to admit any diffidence or uneasy doubt of her salvation, yet, as she observes very well in the place in which she mentions this, her confidence, grounded on the known goodness of God, and the infinite merits of Christ, was very different from that vain presumption with which the proud soul sometimes deludes herself. The present Superior of the Community at Antwerp, who was not only an eye-witness, but had also some part in the following passages, assures me, that in Mother Xaveria's lifetime the Community was sensible of many favours God did them for her sake, both in spirituals and temporals. ' Her first care was to advance them in spirituals, and as to temporals, her confidence,' says she, ' and faith in Almighty God were so great that whenever we wanted anything, if Mother Xaveria recommended our necessity to God, and her great patron Xaverius, we were always assured that God would inspire somebody to send us a supply of alms, as we have seen so many wonderful effects of her prayers in this kind, that it would be needless to mention them all.' She adds these following :

' In the year 1709, when all things were so excessively dear by reason of the hard frost, that a quarter of wheat, sold at other times for seven or eight shillings, was then sold for above thirty shillings, and so proportionately of other things, I had care of buying in provisions, and told my Superior, our Reverend Mother Xaveria, that we were almost out of beer, and wanted money to buy malt. She bade me, nevertheless, bespeak it, not doubting but God would provide money before the malt was delivered. I did so. The day it came in, as I was seeing it weighed, a gentleman came to the gate desiring to speak to the Superior, and told her he had brought her an alms. He gave her about ten pounds, which was about a shilling or two more or less than the sum we wanted to pay for the malt. She immediately gave it

Q

me, and bade me pay one of the men who stayed for
their money.  We who knew this passage gave thanks
to God, and admired His Providence, Who had thus
assisted us by the prayers of His servant.

'Another time she was obliged on a fixed day to
pay a sum of money, which she endeavoured, but in
vain, to borrow against that time.  The day came, she
waited for the person who was to call for it.  She told
me she was to have it in about two hours' time ; and
that, though then she had not one farthing, she confided
still that God would find some means to help her.  Our
bell rang for Mass, she went to the choir to recommend
this affair to God and her Saint.  Mass, I think, was
scarce ended when a gentleman, a stranger, and one
from another town, called for her.  He told her he was
travelling farther, and found he had more money than he
wanted for his journey, and therefore desired she would
take it, thirty pounds sterling, and give him a note for
it payable upon demand : this was exactly the sum she
was to pay that morning.  She had time enough to
procure the money again : it was not called for till some
months after.

'In the dear year above mentioned, we had great
losses and everything was at excessive rates, hence we
were in continual want of supplies.  Our Reverend
Mother Xaveria recommended continually the necessities of the Community to her great patron, who moved
a devout gentleman to bring us constantly money to
supply our wants.  The gentleman confessed he found
himself so strangely moved, and as it were forced to
do this, at that time, that he could but wonder at himself.
This lasted above a year and a half or two years ; after
this, he seldom came to the house, and when he did,
he gave nothing.  One of the religious took notice of
this to our Reverend Mother Xaveria : " Dear Mother,'

said she, " this gentleman comes not with alms as usual," to which she answered smiling : " Dear Sister, this gentleman will never more be a benefactor ; what he has done, he could not but do," at that time intimating that St. Xaverius moved him to it, and as she foretold it happened. It is now more than eleven years since, he never comes, nor takes more notice of our house than if he were a perfect stranger to it. She frequently said it was a great joy to her to be sometimes reduced to necessity, because it raised her confidence in Almighty God, Whose Providence never failed to inspire somebody to assist her. This is, says she, a joy which they who are rich cannot experience.'

As the Community in general, in the aforementioned instances, and several others which would be too long to put down, found the wonderful effects of her prayers, the same happened to several other particular persons. ' I have often seen,' says she, ' and felt the efficacy of her prayers, the same happened to several other particular persons.' ' I have often seen (says one of her religious) and felt the efficacy of her prayers, not only in clearing my doubts and removing my difficulties even to a miracle, but also in several exterior accidents. I had a mortification in my jaw, which the surgeon judged incurable. He proposed, indeed, the raising of the flesh and applying fire to the bone, as the only remedy, but doubted much of the success. The excess of pain was followed by a violent fever, in which it was judged proper to give me the Viaticum. I procured our Reverend Mother Mary Xaveria to stroke my face with her hand, in which St. Xaverius had left the mark of his cure, and presently it grew better, my fever left me, the wound soon healed up without leaving any scar, and in three or four days I went to the choir. Another time, being dangerously ill of the small-pox (she was then advanced in years) and ordered to receive the Viaticum, our Reverend Mother Xaveria told me she had obtained my life by promising a certain number of Communions for that end.'

'I have,' says another, 'in many difficulties and troubles, found great help and relief by her prayers, and once in a particular manner, going to her after a Spiritual Exercise with anxiety, I told her I had spent entirely the eight days in endeavouring to make one particular resolution, naming what it was, but had not yet the courage to do it, and that hence I was come out of the Exercise in the same disposition I found myself in when I began it. She told me, as she had done many times before, that God required it, but yet I must not be uneasy, for He would do it when I least expected it. I then earnestly begged for prayers for that end, which she promised me, and some time after, to my great admiration, I found myself entirely changed in that particular, and never since have had the least uneasiness concerning it, though I might reasonably have expected, if I had used my best endeavours, that it would have been the combat of many years.'

Another of the religious being obliged to go to her several times, both in time of Mass and at the hours of prayer, 'found her often so absorbed in God that she scarce seemed sensible of what was said or done, and yet at the same time, was always fully satisfied in what she demanded of her. She often gave me signs,' says she, 'when she seemed to me not able to speak, being totally taken up with Almighty God, and though what I had to say required several answers, yet I understood how she would have me act by the least sign; nay, in some fears and trouble of mind in which I had a desire to speak to her, I found myself perfectly satisfied, with some little inclination of her head, or the like, for I did not perceive that she saw me, she understood I was there, and knew what I would say before I could or did speak, which was plain by her preventing me with a sign, even before I would speak, and at those times I always received as much comfort and satisfaction to act as if she had spoken to me. Afterwards when I mentioned to her what I would have said, she told me she designed I should act just as I had done, and that I had understood her right. She had a great gift in comforting and helping those who had interior troubles, with few words, which were so clear and expressive that nothing could be more satisfactory, removing whatever doubt, and never raising new ones, and she left the person she treated with in peace and tranquillity of mind, as I myself have often experienced.'

One who thinks herself very happy in the possession of a religious life at Antwerp, attributes her happiness to the prayer of Mother Xaveria, of which she gave me the following account. Before she discovered her design of being religious, as she was one day praying in the English nuns' church at Antwerp, she begged of Almighty God to inspire Reverend Mother Xaveria, then Superior of the house, to speak to her mother, if it were God's will she should be religious in that place. Her mother, who lived at Antwerp, came some days after to visit Mother Xaveria, who presently, without having been spoken to, told the gentlewoman that her daughter had a vocation to be religious, and asked her consent. The mother, who was a widow, and had only this one daughter, was very unwilling to part with her, but the Reverend Mother replied that when God calls children, parents should be resigned to give them to Him. About a year after she gave her consent, but even then with difficulty, though she was much pleased to have her daughter under the conduct of Mother Xaveria, for whom she had a great veneration and esteem. She used to say afterwards that God gave her great comfort to see her child so happily settled, and that she would always persuade parents to resign their children cheerfully to the service of God in a religious state. 'Blessed be God,' adds this religious woman, 'Who has made me partaker of that happiness.'

## CHAPTER XXVIII.

*Of her religious comportment. Her mortifications and penances. The instructions she receives relating to these virtues.*

I ALWAYS observed and admired in the Reverend Mother Mary Xaveria an unalterable, quiet, sedate temper, which could not be said to proceed from stupidity or insensibility : she was rather, from an infant, of a high spirit, a good wit, and solid judgment. By an admirable effect of Divine grace she was so perfectly mistress of her own passions, that you could never observe the least sign of any irregular motion. I have reason to believe, both by what I know of her and by what may be gathered out of her writings, that she passed at least the twenty years she was in religion in almost a continual practice of the presence of God, in a continual conformity with the will of God, with as deep recollection even in exterior employs as most people arrive at in meditation or prayer. This Divine peace of God was fixed and settled in her soul, the night before her first miraculous cure, as has been observed elsewhere, and we may reasonably look upon it as the fruits of her long and painful sufferings, and as the crown of her heroical courage and unwearied patience. As she was born to a spiritual life by sufferings and crosses, she maintained herself in it by the same nourishment. When she lay under the grievous fits of sickness in England, that the use of her whole body was almost totally taken from her, 'I thought then,' says she, 'that I had nothing else to do but to suffer what God sent me.' But when by her wonderful cure she was restored, as I may say, to herself, she thought she was to make up by voluntary penances and mortifications what was wanting to her sufferings. Her confessor, before she left England, finding how much she was bent on mortification and penances, gave her a strict charge to do nothing without leave, and her great director, St. Xaverius, in her noviceship gave her the same caution, but withal let her know that the act of humiliation in asking leave, and the act of obedience in doing or omitting what was proposed, would be accepted by Almighty God in place of these penances which were not omitted out of a principle of self-love. The Saint reprehended her then for performing her work upon her knees, though she did it out of a spirit of penance ; and soon after, when she had performed an heroical act of mortification with leave, in imitation of him, he instructed her what mortifications were most acceptable to Almighty God, namely, the bearing of injuries patiently, endeavouring to do a good turn to those who had been less kind to us, and the like, and he showed himself more pleased at her submission in asking leave to perform that act of mortification than he was at the act itself, though it was a thing very repugnant to sense.

However, she was not wanting on her side in the exterior practice of mortification, as to the acts of penance which were performed in public. She always asked leave for those to which she found the greatest repugnance, and, as I am informed by those who lived with her, and observed her by her, penances and mortifications she had brought herself to a state in which she seemed quite dead to sense and all sentiments of flesh and blood. She was observed several times not to warm herself even in the coldest weather, never to show any difficulty even in the hardest matters, to bear with silence and cheerfulness many mortifying things said to her and of her, on account of some failings in the pronunciation of Latin when she learnt her Breviary. Nothing but obedience could have moderated her fasts, disciplines, and other practices of mortifications. She appeared dead to sense by the generous victory she gained over herself in sucking a loathsome ulcer in imitation of her patron; and the noble sentiments with which God inspired her on this occasion are sufficient proof of the Divine disposition of her soul with which she accompanied and animated these exterior acts of virtue.

I am informed by another, who observed nicely all she did, that she discovered several secret and rigorous penances, sufficient, says she, to have ruined her health, had not God in a special manner preserved her. 'She enjoyed perfect health till she was chosen Superior, but from that time was subject to great and almost continual infirmities; among the rest, her stomach was so disordered that she would seldom retain anything, but was perpetually subject to vomiting, all which she concealed as much as possible, lest she should on this account be obliged by those over her to absent herself from some acts of Community. I observed her on these occasions retire to the remotest places of the house, and yet, as soon as the bell called to the choir, or to some act of religious discipline, she came with that cheerfulness and charity as if she had been in perfect health, though at the same time, by watching of her, I found her totally exhausted and often ready to faint, notwithstanding all these infirmities, which, as another tells me, would have justly confined any one of less courage and virtue to her room. She constantly (excepting some fits of sickness which tied her to her bed) led the Community through all religious observances with an unwearied patience, peace, and tranquillity of mind till her last sickness.'

Whereas a great part of her life was a state of rigorous penance, in which she had nothing to do but to suffer, I must refer the reader to the first part of her life and to what is said afterwards of her last sickness, where, we are told, 'she particularly and pressingly recommended a pure intention, especially that of fulfilling the will of God in all my duties and ordinary actions, and, for correcting my immortification in the manner of performing them, she insisted upon the presence of God as a certain and necessary means to effect it. To encourage me to the practice of mortification, she would sometimes perform together with me some exterior acts of penance; but after she had thus taught me to overcome the reluctance of my own will in that particular, she then required interior acts of penance, being very cautious in permitting anything which appeared singular in that kind, but, in place of it, recommended a greater care in the performance of my spiritual duties, exactness, silence, recollection, and the like.'

This was the milk with which she nourished those under her care in their first entrance upon a religious course, often inculcating to them, as another observes, the happiness of a religious state, 'first to raise in us a sense of gratitude to Almighty God for so singular a favour; secondly, to move us to pray for those who live in the world; of whom she spoke so feelingly and with so lively a sense of the dangers to which they are exposed, especially missioners, that I believe she often beheld the particulars of the circumstances those were in of whom she spoke to us.'

# CHAPTER XXIX.

## *Of her last sickness and happy death.*

'SHE gave us a perfect example,' says the present
Superior, 'in all her great fits of sickness, of the greatest
mortification, patience, and obedience to her infirmarians
and those who attended her; but in her last most painful
and violent illness she carried these virtues to their
highest perfection. She seemed to have a certain foresight of her death in the year 1713, when the triennial
election was near at hand. She told her director that
either she should not be re-elected (she had been
Superior the six preceding years), or else that she should
die soon after. She spoke this to him with great assurance, but so as if she knew not which of the two would
happen. In that election she had all the votes but her
own, and was consequently to be declared Prioress. She
desired all the religious to retire, and then, on her knees
before the Bishop, begged her director (she could not
speak herself for want of language) to declare to him the
difficulties she found in Superiority, on account of bad
health, &c., to which the Bishop replied, "What can I
do? they will have her." Whereupon, at her request
(she could not bring herself to be satisfied with the
acceptance of the charge without this), he laid a precept
of obedience on her to submit to it. After this she said,
very positively, she was to die soon, and signified about
what time she should die. Before this election she was
heard to say that, if the Community would not free her

from the charge, she should soon be taken from them;
to which the person she spoke to replied, "I hope, my
dear Mother, I shall not live to see it;" but she was
answered by the Mother that she should, and that she
had very good assurance of what she said.'

She seemed prepared for her last sickness by what she
had undergone some months before, as I have it from
the pen of her who attended the sick at that time. 'I
had,' says she, 'in this office particular occasions to be
an eye-witness of her heroical courage and patience in
a painful and tedious sickness, for though I never knew
her enjoy any tolerable health (this religious had not
been many years in the house), yet she forced herself
to be constant in all acts of Community, and was not for
any considerable time confined to the infirmary till the
year before her happy death, in which she was obliged
to remain there near six months, by reason of an inter-
mitting fever, which reduced her to a great weakness, at
the same time she had a great disgust to all nourishment,
together with a painful hunger and faintness for want of
meat. She could seldom retain what she took, and had
been subject to vomiting for many years. At this time
it was increased, and attended with greater pain and
sickness of stomach. On those days she had suffered
thus in the greatest extremity, I observed that, notwithstanding the care which was taken to provide such diet
as was thought proper for her, and to her liking, yet it
always happened that by some accident or other it
proved to be what she could not take, or if she did,
it increased her disgust and sickness of stomach, insomuch that I have often stood by, with tears in my eyes,
to see the increase of sufferings, yet could not but look
upon it as an effect of Providence for her greater merit,
knowing there was nothing wanting in the goodwill of
those who had prepared it. When she perceived me

troubled on that account, she would smile, and bid me
not be concerned, saying withal, "Our Lord knows how
much I neglect to mortify myself, and He is pleased to
supply it in this way, which I look upon as a particular
favour." And indeed she always appeared more pleased
and cheerful when that mortification happened, than with
any relief and refreshment she received at other times.

'I also often perceived her great but secret manner of
mortification, in not asking or refusing according to what
might seem necessary to her, or to her inclination, but
wanting or taking according to the will of others. Once
I remember to have given her some physic which was
very nauseous, and I perceived the mortification she had
to take it, nor was she able to retain it, yet she expressed
no uneasiness in that suffering; at which being surprised,
I begged to know how she was able to suffer it without
complaint, to which she answered, "I think it was the
most disagreeable thing I ever took; but our Lord
brought into my thoughts the gall He had taken for us,
and by this reflection I had no regard to the great
bitterness."

'She suffered very much in this sickness, and with
great equality of mind and alacrity expressed often her
desire of suffering as long and as much as was pleasing
to Almighty God. Once upon the application of some
remedies, she suffered a most intolerable torment, insomuch that it obliged her to call out aloud (this I believe
is the time mentioned in her own writings in which she
seemed to suffer no less than the pains of death). I
remember I was much moved with the sight of her
suffering, and as much edified to hear her often repeat,
"Jesus, my Jesus, Your Divine Will be ever done in me."
Notwithstanding her great weakness, she daily heard
Mass, unless forbid by those to whom she was to submit.
Her ardent desire of Communion made her suffer much

by abstaining to refresh herself when most faint and thirsty, because she would not lose Communion, which she never omitted when she was able or permitted by the doctor to rise. When it rung to the choir, she would always bid me go to praise God, and offer up her tepid heart, as she was pleased to call her fervent one, to our Lord, and beg Him to make it according to His own. She said many things to me in this sickness, by which I plainly perceived she had a certainty of being freed from her office of Superior, as she earnestly desired; and when she heard me tell her that since it was the will of God, her submission in this point was to be preferred to all things else, she always answered, " Doubt not but I shall be freed the next election ; but if I am mistaken in this, at least death will release me." Upon the feast of the Purification, the year before she died, as I was assisting her in going to bed, she being then sick, she asked me where I thought she would be that day twelve-months ? "Where you are now, dear Mother," answered I, intending by this she would be in her office. To which she replied, " Say nothing of it, but only remember to remind me this day twelvemonths of my having asked you this question." Which proved but too remarkable, for upon that day twelvemonths she lay upon her death-bed, in the same place, and died upon the octave of that feast.

'A short time before she fell into her last sickness, discoursing one day very cheerfully with her religious, she told them that in her dream there was represented to her a martyrdom she was to suffer, but so grievous that it was impossible for her to express it. Another time she told them she had seen in the same manner a chalice, extremely bitter, which she was to drink to the bottom. Whether her humility made her conceal the knowledge she had of her future torments under this notion of a dream, cannot be determined, but by the event she seems to have had a more certain knowledge of them. Hence in her greatest pains she would say sometimes that this was the chalice she was to drink.'

On the 17th of January, 1714, she fell ill of a violent fever, and was confined to the infirmary, and though the doctor at first apprehended no great danger, yet the symptoms were so very different from what she used to find in her former illness, that her religious were not without great apprehension for her. Within a few days the doctor pressed her to tell where she felt her greatest pain. She answered, in her back. He ordered it should be rubbed with an oil he prescribed. This she submitted to, but not without difficulty. 'By this,' says the religious person who was employed in it, 'I came to discover a wound grievously inflamed, even already mortified, and the inflammation was spread over a great part of that side. She perceiving I had discovered it, earnestly begged—nay, commanded—me to keep it secret, and said she hoped I loved her too much to occasion its being exposed to a surgeon, a mortification a thousand times greater than death to her; but my zeal for the good of the Community and the knowledge I had that her command could not oblige in this case, made me presently acquaint Mother Sub-Prioress with it. She told the director, upon which she was immediately ordered to discover her wound to the surgeon, to which she acquiesced. I desired her,' continues the same religious, 'to tell me what she had suffered before this was discovered. She said, "Tongue cannot express it." I begged further,' says the same person, 'to know if she had not offered herself to suffer for the salvation of some particular soul. And she owned she had; but when I questioned her further, she was silent.'

It is inexpressible, according to all the accounts I have, what she suffered during these eighteen days. New incisions were made for the most part twice a day, and not one day passed in which they did not cut out large pieces of the flesh. She lay all this time without the least complaint, and as those who constantly attended her assure me, without the least motion or sign, nay, as if she had been insensible, or as if they had been cutting a dead body, to the amazement of the doctor, surgeon, and all that saw or heard of it. When I had received from eye-witnesses this account of her wonderful patience under the incision knife, I was apt to believe the surgeon had never touched the quick flesh. I thought it was above what could be expected from flesh and blood, to bear such incisions without the least motion, groan, or sigh, unless we suppose the part to be entirely mortified. This made me write to the monastery in the year 1722, to be fully informed of the matter of fact, and to my great surprise I find it to be all literally true, and this apparent insensibility to be the effect of an heroical courage and a determinate resolution of suffering for Almighty God.

'I was once present,' says one of the religious to me in a letter dated November 7th, 1722, 'when the surgeon was dressing her wound in presence of the doctor. Having made a deep incision with his lancet, she did not make the least sign, or show that she had any feeling of it, so that the doctor, supposing the flesh so mortified that she had not felt it, ordered the surgeon to cut in deeper, till she came to have some feeling. She, hearing this, replied calmly he need not do so, for that she had felt it very sensibly.'

For greater certainty, the surgeon himself who dressed her wounds was consulted upon the same subject, and he has given to the monastery an authentic attestation of

what happened, which I shall put down here for the
edification of the reader.

'I, the undersigned, surgeon in the city of Antwerp,
was called to the Rev. Mother Mary Xaveria of the
Angels, Prioress of the English Teresians at Antwerp,
upon the 22nd of January, in the year 1714. A religious
having discovered a mortification upon her side, near her
hip, I came twice a day to dress it, till her death, which
happened on the 9th of February. To prolong her
life, I found it necesary to make daily deep scarifications
in the live flesh, whence issued great quantities of blood
with great pain to the patient. Notwithstanding, I never
heard her complain of her pain, or show the least impatience, which struck both the doctor and myself with
great admiration. I often thought and said we should
afterward hear strange things of this Reverend Mother,
and I wished that I might live to see her grave opened.
The veneration I had for this Reverend Mother made
me procure a medal, which after her death I applied to
her body, which I still keep with great respect and
esteem in my house. In testimony of the truth of this,
I sign my name, at Antwerp, August 1st, 1722.

'JOHN GOBEL.'

But the greatest sacrifice she seemed to make all
this time was in submitting to let the doctor and
surgeon dress her wounds, though she even condescended to this with great peace and tranquillity, and
without expressing her difficulty to anybody after she
was once ordered to submit to it; yet it was easy to
perceive how sensible a mortification this was, for upon
a sign given by the bell (which is usual when doctors or
surgeons come into the monastery), she would strike out
into a great sweat and pull her veil over her eyes. When

the wounds were dressed she did all they ordered her,
often with the greatest pains and torment. Thè Providence of God is truly to be admired. Before she was
religious He cured her by a miracle, importuned by
her prayers, lest her modesty should suffer by exposing
her disjointed hip to the surgeon's care. Now she is
arrived to the height of perfection, and certainly her
prayers were not wanting, though with due resignation
and submission, and yet God will have her drink this
chalice to the very dregs. My God, the ways you
take to sanctify your saints are truly secret but always
adorable !

The same pestilential humour which caused a gangrene
in her back spread itself, as the surgeon said, all over
her body, even to her hands and feet, with intolerable
torment, but she never made the least show of suffering
anything, though for the most part confined to the
same posture; and what seems the most surprising, she
continued these eighteen days always on her back, but
still much with her usual unaltered evenness of temper,
as if she had not been the person who suffered, as will
appear by the following account of her behaviour all
that time, taken from the person who constantly attended
her.

'Her distemper increased, with great oppression and
shortness of breath, caused by an inflammation of her
lungs. She frequently during this time received the
Blessed Sacrament in the night after twelve o'clock,
which was her only comfort. She was perfectly sensible
all the time of her sickness, offering up and uniting her
sufferings with those of her crucified Spouse, and said
her pains were her delights. When some of the religious
desired she would beg God to prolong her life, and told
her they would offer up their prayers to this end, she
answered that she offered herself as an entire sacrifice,

R

and neither desired life nor death, but that God's best
pleasure might be done in her, which she often repeated
during her sickness.    When I did anything about her
I was often struck with admiration to see her unwearied
patience in suffering so many torments, and things so
contrary to her inclination, with so much courage and
peace of mind.    I was often concerned, fearing I gave
her many mortifications and occasions of suffering by not
knowing her inclinations, for she left herself entirely to
those that were to take care of her, and never showed
the least difficulty in taking whatever was ordered,
though never so disagreeable.    When she found anything refreshing she used to say it was too good, and
that she must mortify herself in it.    She would sometimes
cry out with great ardour—"My God, my Lord, my
Jesus, my Spouse, I am wholly Yours, and," with our
holy Mother, "suffer or die!"    Sometimes, with her dear
patron, St. Xaverius, when in the greatest extremity—
"More, O my Lord, more!"    In time of her sickness
she reminded every one of her duties, speaking to them
with great tenderness and sweetness, though speaking
was very troublesome to her.    She sometimes lay very
quiet, so that I hoped she had been asleep, but going
softly to the bedside I still perceived she was awake, but
in great recollection and prayer.    Three or four days
before she died, the hand which St. Xaverius had cured
contracted again, after which I despaired of her life.    She
would often look upon it with great pleasure, and as if
she had taken it for a sign of her death, saying frequently
that it put her in mind of her former sickness.

'Since I wrote this I understand from the present
Superior that, in her illness, she hinted at a promise
made her by her Saint that she should never fall into
her former distemper, convulsions, &c., of which she had
been cured in England, but yet her hand, which she

called St. Xaverius' hand, should be again contracted, as a sign of her approaching death. "Three or four days before she died we perceived," said the present Superior, "that she could not open it, but used to look on it with pleasure, and when we took notice of it to her she smiled and said—'This is the sign the Saint has given me.'"

'She was perfectly sensible and present to herself on all occasions, and put us in mind what was to be done at and after her death, and when any spoke to her of suffering she said—"Something must be suffered for heaven. I hope it will satisfy for some part of my purgatory." She said once to me—" What a Mother you have! beginning to corrupt before I die!" and to another of the Sisters—"The poor nuns will be forced to bury me the same day I die." She expressed often great concern for the religious, fearing they would be fatigued with watching and attending her. She truly resembled her Spouse upon the Cross, having no part free from pain and torment, but it was particularly violent in her hands, feet, and sides. Her strength daily decreased, and we saw with sad hearts that we could not enjoy her long in this life. When I once begged her to pray for me she answered—"When I am so happy to enjoy Almighty God I will not forget you, for charity is augmented in heaven." As to her interior, there is all reason to believe, from what is known happened to her in her sickness before her cure, and from the disposition, she was in the latter part of her life united with Almighty God and absorbed in Him. All we know in particular is this—she continued making acts of love and showing the desire she had to be dissolved and to be with her Divine Spouse. She said to her director in her last sickness, not long before she died—" I thought my blessed Saint had left me, but I have found him again."

"And I have reason to believe," adds her same director,
"that he was with her at the hour of her death."'

Some days before she died she earnestly requested to
have the Holy Oils, which she received with a perfect
presence of mind, and great devotion, saying that to see
the pious ceremonies used at that time was to be half in
heaven.  Before she received them, she begged pardon
of all the Community for the scandal and disedification
which her humility made her believe she had given,
upon which all her children who were in tears about her,
begged pardon of her.  She made them a short exhorta-
tion, but sweet and instructive, encouraging them to a
perfect disengagement from all creatures, to a love of the
Cross, admonishing them that they were come to religion
for no other end than to live and die upon the Cross,
that all their content must be placed in Christ crucified, &c.

On Thursday the 8th of February, she was permitted
to communicate by way of Viaticum, which she did with
singular joy and comfort.  That night the religious
coming to her before Matins, she gave them again some
pious instructions, then, lifting up her hand with great
difficulty, she gave them her benediction, and added,
'God make you all great saints: pray for my eternal
repose.'  She suffered much that night, with great
oppressions upon her breath.  One of those who had
care of her said to her in the morning, 'Dear Mother,
what intolerable torments you have suffered this night!'
She answered: 'I assure you this has been a night to
me of joy and pleasure.'  But when she farther asked,
'in what manner?' she was silent.

Most of the religious watched by her all night, as did
also her director, Father Woods,[1] of the Society of Jesus,

---

[1] [Father Edward Woods, who entered the Society of Jesus in the
year 1683, æt 20, was raised to the degree of a professed Father on
the 13th February, 1701, and for many years served the English
mission.]—ED.

and she with a great presence of mind continued answer-
ing to the litanies and prayers that were said by him.
Towards morning, after some uneasy slumbers, she
desired with some eagerness to know whether she might
not receive again the Blessed Sacrament, but when her
director let her know she had the night before, and that
it could not be permitted, she answered : 'If I may not
have that happiness, I resign.' Some of the religious
told her she would end her ten Fridays in heaven (she,
with the religious, was then performing the devotion of
the ten Fridays, and this was the last Friday). She
sweetly smiled and said : ' Oh, shall I be so happy ! '

Between seven and eight she fell into her agony, which,
though strong, was sweet and comfortable in this, that
she was sensible of all that was said and done about her.
We easily perceived she was constantly offering up all
her torments and sufferings with great courage and
fervour. As long as she could speak she desired
absolution, and when she could not she made signs.
She often lifted up her head and hand in time of her
agony, to kiss the crucifix and blessed candle. Some
little time before she died she cast a most compassionate
eye upon the Community, who were in deep affliction
about her bed, and then fixed them upon the father in a
moving manner. He was very careful in watching the
last moment to give her absolution, which she received
with a great presence of mind, and at the quarter after
ten in the morning, with a sweet violence, she breathed
out her happy soul, upon a Friday, the 9th of February,
the octave day of the Purification, the last day of the ten
Fridays' devotion, in the great novena of St. Xaverius,
and at his age, that is, at the age of forty-six, in the year
1714.

As soon as she was departed, her director, who was
conscious of her great virtue, and witness of that happy

disposition of mind in which she left this world, in place
of the usual Psalm *De Profundis*, desired the religious
there present to join with him in saying the *Te Deum* in
thanksgiving for the many favours she had received from
Almighty God.    She left all her children in great affliction for the loss of such a mother, and though they were
not wanting in their obligation of praying for her, yet
they all confessed that this was accompanied with an
unusual joy in their souls, and a certain assurance that
she was already enjoying the beatifical vision.    When
they came to lay out her body, they were then more
sensible of the unspeakable pain she must have undergone.    Her body seemed all corrupted, and she was
extremely wore away considering the shortness of her
distemper.    Several found themselves moved with great
devotion towards her, and came to beg pieces of her
habit, or of anything else she had used, and in private
took their recourse to her, both in sickness and other
necessities, and, as they said, not without success.

Whilst she lay exposed in the choir, dressed up in her
habit (according to their custom), one of the religious,
putting her hand to her side, thought she perceived a
perceptible warmth.    This was spoken of before the vault
was shut up ; after her interment on Saturday, late at
night, and though nobody could reasonably doubt but
that she was certainly dead, yet to satisfy the desire of
the religious, the surgeon who had attended her, was sent
for to view the body.    He was glad of the occasion of
seeing her once more, having a great opinion of her
sanctity.    She was found certainly dead, but her countenance, which was much altered in her sickness, was now
become so sweet, and breathed such an air of sanctity,
that one present cried out, it was a pity they had not
taken her picture.    Upon this, a painter was sent for,
who took her features in crayon, and afterwards drew

her picture. Notwithstanding she had been so often moved, and as she had said herself, began to corrupt before she was dead, yet there was not the least offensive smell when the coffin was thus opened. Her features being taken, and the religious having satisfied their devotion in kissing her feet, and touching her body with their beads, pictures, &c., the coffin was nailed up, and deposited again in the vault.

## CHAPTER XXX.

*Of what happened after her death, and of the foresight she had in her lifetime of things to come.*

ON the same day Mother Mary Xaveria died, a lady of Antwerp, who always had a particular respect for her, being alone in her oratory at her prayers recommending her soul to Almighty God, she found herself in an unusual peace and calm, whereas in the like occasions, when any of her acquaintance or friends died, she used to be seized with strange apprehensions and fears. The night following, being in bed, she saw suddenly the venerable Mother Mary Xaveria standing before her at the bed feet, in her habit, but with her face partly shaded. She saw on one side a resplendent star, which dazzled her eyes, though she could not discover whether the light came from the star or her body, the greatness of the glory took up her whole attention. The lady with great devotion cried out—' Dear Mother, pray for me, pray for me!' after which she disappeared. The lady has ever since had a great deal of confidence in her intercession, and has recourse to her by several private devotions in her own necessities, and in the concerns of her family, and she is persuaded they have received many favours by this means. She was moved, about six months after this happened, to discover it to the Superior of the monastery for the comfort of the religious. She gave also a marble stone to be fixed where her body is buried, with this inscription—

'Hic jacet Sepulta Venerabilis Mater Maria Xaveria ab Angelis, quæ cum opinione Sanctitatis obiit 9 Februarii, Anno Domini 1714, Ætatis 46, Professionis 20, Regiminis 13. Cujus memoria in benedictione est, in pace requies.'

Some few days after Mother Xaveria died, Mrs. Barnwall went to the Jesuits' church to pray for her brother, who was dangerously ill, and despaired of the doctors. She found at the entrance a dead billet, by which Mother Xaveria was recommended to the prayers of the faithful (as is usually done in Catholic countries). Mrs. Barnwall was surprised at this, not having heard before of her death, but as she had always a great veneration for her, on account of her singular virtue, she was moved to have recourse to her dear Mother. Says she with a great confidence—'Your power was great with St. Xaverius while living; obtain now the recovery of my brother, for the good of his afflicted family and poor children.' At her return home she found him so much better, that when the doctor came to visit him he was amazed, and cried out, 'A miracle, a miracle!' In a few days he was perfectly well. Alms were afterwards sent to the monastery in gratitude for the favours received.

A priest of virtuous life, whilst he was in the church with others, singing for the repose of her soul, saw her body environed with glory, which was most resplendent about her head. He told it to a creditable virtuous person, who acquainted the religious with it, and at the same time assured them she herself had often seen her in glory.

Several in private had recourse to her, and the religious, partly at the request of others, who desired to be recommended to her, and partly to satisfy their own devotion, made several visits to her sepulchre, and were persuaded by the effects that these their private devotions were acceptable to Almighty God.

' How far I have experienced the power of our venerable Mother Mary Xaveria since her happy death,' says one of the religious, ' I refer to the judgment of those who shall read this following account. Some little time before · she died I was indisposed with rheumatic pains, with swelling in my feet and legs, which afterwards spread over my whole body, and remained particularly fixed in my stomach, which was extremely hard. I lost all appetite, slept very little, fell away in my flesh, and was reduced to an extremity of weakness. From February to the end of July I was in a continual course of remedies, but without effect. This made the doctors conclude my case was desperate, for, seeing the medicines did not remove the cause, which they said proceeded from a disorder in my blood, they judged my distemper too great to leave any hope of a cure. To ease the pains in my limbs they prescribed violent sweats, but my weakness increased to that degree that I could not go through with the course prescribed. Being then confined to the infirmary upon the 18th or 19th of August, I found myself much tempted with thoughts of diffidence concerning the sanctity of vene-rable Mother Mary Xaveria, with a kind of displeasure at the private devotions and frequent visits to her grave

which I knew some of the religious made; but after a
little reflecting as it were on these thoughts, I remained
with some scruple and anxiety, as believing in reason
they must needs be very displeasing to Almighty God,
and therefore, to overcome this temptation, which I was
subject to, I found myself moved to make a promise
that, if obedience and my health would permit, I would
daily visit her grave for a whole year, and say there the
*Te Deum*, in thanksgiving for all the great favours and
graces Almighty God had bestowed upon her. Having
acquainted my Superior with this, she answered that if
our Lord would give me leave in regard of my health,
she was most willing I should perform my promise. The
next day I was able to hear Mass, and went from thence
to her grave to begin my devotion, and from that time
my health continually improved without any other
remedy from the doctors; my swelling daily decreased,
and in a short time I was restored to my perfect health
and strength, which has continued about five years
without interruption.'

Sometime before she died, upon a Friday in Lent, she
advised some of the religious, who were to communicate
that morning, to chose for them some one of our Saviour's
Wounds according to their devotion, there to make their
abode. She chose it seems for herself, as appeared afterwards, though without telling them of it before, that of
His Sacred Side. Some time after, in discoursing with
Mother Delphina of St. Joseph, *alias* Catharine Smythe,
she asked her which of the Sacred Wounds she had
chosen. She answered, 'I desired to enter into our
Lord's Side.' 'I believe so,' replied Mother Xaveria,
'for having done the same myself, I thought my Blessed
Saviour gave me entrance, I seemed to find myself there
as in a most delightful garden, and on a sudden enter-
taining myself there I met you, and another of the

religious (she it seems had made the same choice in Communion that day), just, says she, as if walking in a garden one should unexpectedly meet two friends.' She acquainted Mother Delphina and the other person with this, for their comfort, but forbade them to speak of it to anybody, neither did they speak of it till after her death. Whilst Mother Delphina was praying by her corpse the night after she died, she found herself suddenly recollected, and in great peace of mind, and at the same time she seemed to find herself in the Sacred Wound of our Blessed Saviour's Side, where she met her dear friend Mother Mary Xaveria, who assured her she would always find her there in her necessities, and from this time she often in her private devotions had recourse to her. This passage will appear more credible to those who were acquainted with the merit of the person here mentioned.

The Reverend Mother Delphina, of St. Joseph, *alias* Mrs. Catharine Smythe, was contemporary to Mother Xaveria, and had always a great love and veneration for her, grounded on those eminent virtues she observed in this dear friend, and what is most to be regarded, she made it her business to copy out in her own actions this great pattern of virtue, which she had always before her eyes. She was of a most innocent life, of a tender conscience, of very good natural parts, much addicted to prayer, punctual, exact in all religious observances, and deserved for her virtue to be chosen Superior or Prioress of this religious Community, in which employment she died most piously, February 9th, 1721. She engaged me, some time before her death, to make a collection of those memories relating to Mother Xaveria, but before she received my letter, by which I desired her to transmit to me what she could inform me of, by her own knowledge, it pleased God to take her out of the world, by which we are deprived of many particulars relating to her friend.

Her brothers and several others assure me that she discovered to them many things relating to their own interior, only known to God and themselves. A young gentlewoman, a relation of Mother Xaveria, was recommended to her care, but her carriage was so unaccountable in regard to the lady under whose care she was, that it was judged necessary to send her back to England. Mother Xaveria saw that her return, on which she was violently bent, would prove infinitely prejudicial both to her body and soul. She had recourse, as usual, to her dear Saint, as she called St. Xaverius, and told one of the religious who was conscious of the whole thing that she was strongly inspired to beg a happy death for that poor creature. She was now at the water-side, if not already embarked. She fell there dangerously ill, confessed with abundance of tears, was perfectly resigned to die, and in three or four days departed this life. There are so many instances in the first and second parts of this book of the foresight she had of things to come, that I need add little in this place upon that subject, yet I cannot omit one remarkable passage. A young lady went to Antwerp to visit her brother, who lay sick in that city. Upon this occasion she paid a visit to the English monastery, and spoke to Mother Xaveria, who was the Superior of the house. Upon her departure, Mother Xaveria told some of the Community that young lady would one day be religious in that place. She neither spoke of this to the young lady, or had she any hopes of being religious, her father being then so averse to it, as not to bear the hearing it named. Mother Xaveria gave her a book of the ten Fridays' devotion to St. Xaverius, which devotion she afterwards performed, and at the end thereof he unexpectedly gave

his consent, saying it was not any longer in his power to
resist God, but could never bring himself to entertain
a thought of letting her embrace an Order so hard as
to the exterior. She, rather than to be entirely deprived
of the happiness she proposed to herself in a religious
state, chose another house; and though, as it appeared
afterwards, she was always uneasy and desirous to follow
her first vocation, yet submitting herself to the judgment
of those she consulted and relied on, she endeavoured
to banish those uneasy thoughts as temptations. She
took the first and second habit as they term it, and began
her noviceship in order to her profession. She never
kept any correspondence with the religious at Antwerp,
neither did any consult with them. It had, as it appears,
been said abroad that Mother Xaveria had foretold her
settling in the convent at Antwerp; upon which a letter
was written to some religious of another house, which
made a jest of her prophecy, and among other slight
expressions it was said they would now see whether
Mother Xaveria was led by a white or black spirit.
This very letter came accidentally into Mother Xaveria's
hands, who showed it to some in whom she could have
confidence; but concealed the names both of the person
who wrote and of her who received the letter. 'She
expressed even a satisfaction in seeing herself thus
undervalued and reviled, without showing the least
disgust to the persons concerned.

In the meanwhile, the time of the young lady's profession drew near; and some of the religious of Antwerp,
discoursing of her one day with Mother Xaveria, told
her: 'Mother, we hear that lady has taken the habit.'
She smiled and answered: 'She is not yet professed.'
In conclusion, the young lady we speak of called for
her Director. She let him know that the thoughts of her
first vocation to be a Teresian at Antwerp were still fresh

in her mind, that she had endeavoured to stifle them so long, in compliance to those she had consulted, and who told her that they were temptations and would cease in time. That she begged he would sincerely tell her his sentiments, she being then in a resolution of making this sacrifice of herself by professing in the house she was, if he would assure her it was the will of God. Though he had hitherto always appeared of a different mind, she found him immediately changed. He told her she might follow her first vocation, that it was always his opinion that God called her to be a religious at Antwerp, though nothing had been omitted to try her vocation. She was in a transport of joy, consulted her father without delay, and contrary to all expectation found him disposed to grant her request. Upon which she went immediately to Antwerp, begged the habit of Mother Xaveria, and after the usual trials was professed in that house. As Mother Xaveria was one day locking up the repository of the Blessed Sacrament (the Superior has leave to open a small grate in the choir, by which the Blessed Sacrament is exposed to the view of the religious) this young gentlewoman was kneeling by her, to whom she turned and said : ' Dear child, I never locked this door since I first saw you, without locking up your heart here with our Blessed Saviour.' And the gentlewoman says she believes it was so ; for though she was so far distant in body, she was always here in desire and affection.

This worthy Community, of which she was so long Superior, have found to their satisfaction and comfort that Almighty God gave her a wonderful foresight of things which were to happen to them, both in her lifetime and after her death, and they found what she told verified in so wonderful a manner that they cannot doubt of the singular protection of Almighty God, Whose watchful Providence has manifested His care over them by means of this His faithful servant.

I shall conclude this short account with a prediction of hers, which we have seen since her death verified in a most remarkable and miraculous manner in the face of the world. God gave her to understand that there was in the vault where the dead bodies of the religious were deposited an incorrupt body. She spoke of this to her director, Rev. Father Woods, of the Society of Jesus, with a certain assurance that what she told him would be found true. And several years before she had told the same to Rev. Father Matthew Wright.[1] It did not please God to discover to her in particular whose body it was, yet she opened several of the ovens (as they call them) or vaults in the dead cellar, and calling to her one of the religious who had about forty years ago been novice under the Reverend Mother Mary Margaret of the Angels, who died in repute of sanctity, she asked her several things concerning this her Mistress of Novices. The person, who is yet living, answered that this virtuous woman was always looked upon as a saint, but that she remembered that blood flowed out of her vault after she had been buried, which it is supposed made her believe that this was not the incorrupt body ; and upon which she desisted from opening the grave, yet this was the very person in whom the prophecy of Mother Xaveria was verified, as will more appear in the following appendix.

[1] [He was, we believe, a son of Mr. Wright, of Kelvedon Hall, Ongar, Essex, of which ancient Catholic family several members entered the Society of Jesus. Father Matthew was born in 1647, entered the Society in 1668, was solemnly professed of the four vows of religion while serving the mission of Kelvedon, 1684—5. He was subsequently Master of Novices at the Novitiate of the English Province at Watten. For the four last years of his life he was Rector of the House of Tertians at Ghent, and died at Dunkirk, August 22, 1711.]—ED.

## AN APPENDIX TO THE LIFE OF MOTHER MARY XAVERIA OF THE ANGELS.

*An incorrupt body is found in the dead vault of the Monastery of Antwerp, as she had foretold.*

ABOUT two years after the death of Mother Mary Xaveria, the religious found it necessary to enlarge their burying-place, and being for this end supplied with money by Mr. Bond, a worthy gentleman, who has a daughter, religious in that monastery, with leave of my Lord Bishop they set men to work and took down an entire side of the vault, in which eleven or twelve religious had been buried; some had been buried five, six, ten, and twenty years ago, and one only ten weeks. Some were found entirely consumed, the last entirely corrupted. As they had a great veneration for Mother Mary Margaret of the Angels, who had been buried thirty-eight years and two months, they ordered the workmen not to dis-order the bones, when they came to that grave, till some of the religious had viewed them, and accordingly that coffin was opened in the presence of three or four of the religious. They perceived when the top of the coffin was removed, something spread and drawn over the coffin and fastened to the edge, through which they discovered perfectly the body from head to foot. What covered it was like a thin tiffany, or gauze. They immediately gave notice of this to the rest of the religious. In the interim one of those present, being too eager to touch the body, broke through that which covered it. The Community was much surprised to find the body perfectly entire, fleshy, and formed. Thus they perceived it most distinctly when they had brushed off the habit in which she had been buried, which was all rotten, consumed, and moist. By pulling off the head-dress with too much eagerness, one of the Sisters plucked out one of the eyes.

The religious, not knowing how far this incorruption of her body might be attributed to natural causes, thought best to consult Mr. Troky, an experienced doctor, who served the convent, and for that end sent to him ; but he being informed of the reason for which he was called, brought with him Mynheer Vrylins, one of the best doctors of the town. They both examined the body, and were strangely surprised to find it so sound, flexible, &c., and being asked what they thought of it, they refused to give their opinion. But the religious could not hinder them publishing what they had seen. Another doctor, Mynheer Van Dycke, was called in afterwards, who had seen in his travels the body of St. Catharine of Bologna, and when he had viewed and examined the body he congratulated with the religious for the treasure they possessed. He declared his opinion that it was the body of a saint. He warned them to keep carefully the dust about it, and whatever belonged to it, as precious relics, and added that of all the saints' bodies he had seen this seemed the most entire, and withal advised them to acquaint my Lord Bishop with it, and offered himself as a messenger to carry this agreeable news. The confessor of the monastery accompanied him. The prelate with his secretary came within an hour to the convent, where according to his orders he was met by the confessor, three doctors and surgeons. The body was removed out of the dead vault, which was dark, moist, and wet, into an adjoining cellar, that it might be

S

examined more conveniently. They were all wonderfully surprised at the sight. Then his lordship went with the workmen into the vault, to examine the grave out of which it was taken. He examined also the other coffins which were not yet removed, and found those which were buried last corrupted, the others quite consumed. Being returned, he ordered the surgeon to make an incision in the pit of the stomach, through which they discovered the diaphragm perfectly sound. The prelate put his hand into the wound that was made and perceived a balsamic smell proceeding from the body, which his fingers retained two or three days after, though he washed them several times.

Upon strict examination, the doctor and surgeon declared corruption had never entered that body. The Bishop would not then let it be removed out of the coffin, neither would he permit them to remove the rotten and consumed habit, which lay very thick and moist under the body, but ordered it should be locked up, in an adjoining cellar, till he should determine what should be fit to be done. After ten days his lordship ordered another consult of four doctors and surgeons to examine the body again. The cellar in which it had been kept ten days was so moist, that everything in it turned mouldy in a night or two, yet the body received no prejudice from this place. They examined it again narrowly, opened the diaphragm, by which they found the heart, liver, lungs, and all the internal parts perfectly entire, with all the muscles, &c. They again declared that no corruption had ever entered that body, and that it must be supernatural, giving this on attestation in writing, with their own hands, that it was beyond the course of nature, leaving it to the divines to determine whether it was to be termed miraculous. They were much surprised from the beginning to find the hands out of the posture in which they are always put when dead bodies are laid out, and supplying the want of the habit, which was rotten and fallen off, lest any indecency should appear to the eyes of beholders. The religious after this had leave to remove the body to a little hermitage or oratory within the inclosure, where the religious dressed it up in a habit of silk which a devout lady was inspired to give, observing nevertheless the colours of the Order.

This holy body appears of a brownish complexion, but full of flesh, which like a living body yields to any impression made upon it, and rises again of itself when it is pressed, the joints flexible. You find a little moisture when you touch the flesh, but this is not so sensible as when the grave was first opened, and this very frequently breathes out an odoriferous balsamic smell, which is not only perceptible to those about the body, but has sometimes filled the whole room. I mentioned before that it had been observed that blood flowed out of the grave after the body had been deposited in it. This happened about six weeks after her death, and when her body was found incorrupt, they all took notice that both the sides and lid of the coffin seemed all to be tinged with blood.

It is now kept in a decent case, made for that purpose, with two locks. One key is in the hands of my Lord Bishop, and the other kept in the monastery. She died in the year 1678, on the 21st of June. Her grave was opened on the 13th of August, 1716, and at present is found as incorrupt and pliable as ever, retaining still the same agreeable balsamic scent.

This discovery of an incorrupt body was immediately published all over the town by physicians and others, who had been eye-witnesses of it. This drew vast numbers of people about the monastery, who once or twice, at the opening of the gate upon some necessary occasions, surprised the religious and rushed in in great numbers, in so much that they were several times obliged to call soldiers from the citadel to guard the inclosure. The Governor, Prince d'Escula, led the guard twice himself, and being permitted to see the body, he cast himself at her feet, kissing them with tenderness and many tears, blessing Almighty God that he had lived to see such a precious treasure in his Government. The next day he sent the Princess, his spouse, who was also wonderfully moved with devotion and piety, and in token of her respect she took the ring off her own finger and desired the director of the monastery to put it on the finger of the holy body, where it yet remains. It has a ruby in the middle, set round with diamonds. The concourse of the people who came even from the neighbouring towns was so great, that the nuns could not for some days open their gate upon any account. They cried out in the streets that God had not given the Saint for the monastery alone, but for them all; that it was the work of God, and why should they be deprived of so great a blessing? But when they saw they could not find access, they sent in such numbers of beads, medals, pictures, linens, &c., to be touched that it was sufficient employment for one or two religious for many days to comply with their request in touching the body and bringing them back. They have great numbers of testimonies, signed by the parties concerned, where they declare the great benefit received by her intercession. I shall say nothing more of this till Superiors think fit to have them published.

Authentically several have owned that the sight of the body has proved their conversion to a better life. One in particular, whose life was very disordered, acknowledged in confidence to his friend that she turned her face from him when he fixed his eyes upon her. A woman that was with child having obtained leave to see her, and apprehending that the sight of a dead body might strike her too much, to the prejudice of the infant she bore, declared afterwards that when to satisfy her devotion she looked at her in the face, she saw her countenance like that of a person young and beautiful, and resembling the sweetness of an angel. The body is kept in a little room joining to the choir of the nuns, and not in the choir itself, because they would not do anything which may seem to have the public veneration till the Superiors of the Church allow of it; yet, as they tell me, if the voice of the people may be said to be the voice of God, she has been long since canonized.

As to the matters of fact here related, concerning the state of the body in which it was found and in which it yet remains, the reader may easily satisfy his own curiosity or devotion by becoming an eye-witness of it when he pleases. I shall only add that this wonderful event, foretold by venerable Mother Xaveria, and verified in so extraordinary a manner by the discovery of the incorrupt body of venerable Mother Mary Margaret of the Angels, seems at present designed by the Divine Providence to confound the irreligion of the age, to show that His hand is not abbreviated, that He still has His saints, that He still works wonders and prodigies in the true Church. This must be the consequence which every one must naturally draw from these plain matters of fact, unless he will bear up against the conviction of his own senses (which are the only testimonies men seem now to rely on), and rank himself in the number of those whom Christ Himself blames for their obdurate incredulity, who, 'Seeing do not see, and hearing do not hear.'[1]

[1] St. Matt. xiii. 13.

Though it is not my design to write the life of this holy woman, yet the reader in this place will certainly expect some short account of her. To comply with this expectation, which seems very just, I shall add these following lines. Her name was Margaret Wake, daughter to Mr. Leonard Wake, youngest son to Sir Isaac Wake, Bart.,[2] of an ancient family in Northamptonshire. Her parents were brought up in the Protestant religion, but had the happiness to be converted to the true faith at Antwerp, where they passed most of their lives. There were several things very remarkable, both in their conversion and at their death, but I must leave this to a time more proper. After their conversion God blessed them with ten children, four sons and six daughters. The eldest of these was married to Mr. Stephens, the second to Mr. Sheldon, the third became a devout, and the fourth is the person I am speaking of. She was born on the 12th of November, 1617. From her childhood she was remarkable for her piety, at five years of age she obtained leave to fast. She entered among the English nuns at Antwerp in the year 1633, and the year following on the 11th of June, which happened to be that year the feast of the Blessed Trinity, she made her profession in the hands of the venerable Mother Anne of the Ascension (of whom I have spoken elsewhere), the first Prioress of this monastery. This virtuous Superior, a woman highly favoured by Almighty God, expressed very great esteem of this novice, and gave the Community to understand they had in her not only a fervent religious, but a superior also, who should glorify God much in this house. We have seen this prophecy fulfilled in her.

[2] [Sir Isaac Wake was born 1575, was M.P. for the University of Oxford, and Ambassador to Savoy and Venice. The present head of this ancient family is Sir Herewald Wake, Bart., of Courteen Hall, Northamptonshire.]—ED.

We find in her, as in other virtuous souls, a constant
endeavour of pleasing God in the practice of all sorts of
virtues; and, indeed, the state of perfection cannot
consist with a wilful neglect in any one point; and she
was particularly observed to go on visibly increasing in
perfection, nay, she used to tell her religious she did not
understand how it was possible for a religious person not
to go on increasing in virtue   She had a great zeal for
the glory of God, which appeared chiefly in her preparation for the principal feasts, and in her fervorous
exhortations to her religious in chapter upon these
occasions.   Her love and knowledge of God inspired
her with confidence in God.  'My God,' says she in a
paper found in her own hand, 'I have neither devotion
nor attention, nor do I desire either, yet my great and
daily defects shall not make me lose my peace of mind,
nor confidence in Your goodness.'   She had a singular
devotion to the Passion of our Blessed Saviour, conforming herself with wonderful patience to her suffering
Lord in her violent fits of the stone and other infirmities,
with which she was continually afflicted, in all which
occasions she exhorted her religious to conform themselves to the spirit of our suffering Saviour.   Her charity
to her neighbour made her industrious when she was in
office to prevent their necessities, and ease them all she
could.   When the religious asked her leave for particular
penances, her usual answer was, she would not have
them lose the merit of performing them, but that she
had rather have them demand permission to perform
humble and charitable actions in serving one another,
because this would add to the desire of penance the
more excellent virtues of charity and humility.   She often
inculcated this, as a maxim, that they should carry
themselves so that Superiors might find no difficulty in
commanding them anything, and their equals find a

pleasure in making use of their help. As to herself, though she was known to be of a choleric temper and high-spirited, she was so perfectly dead to herself, that she was never heard to raise her voice, nor ever appeared in the least discomposed.

I cannot but particularly remark two things, which, as I may say, run through her whole life. One was the means by which she arrived at so great perfection; the other aforesaid continual occasions of practising what she knew. The first was a continual and uninterrupted practice of the presence of Almighty God; the other was a constant exactness in complying with every tittle of her Rule. As to the first, when she entered upon a religious course she began to apply herself with great intenseness to this practice of the presence of God. Her Superiors soon found her indiscreet fervour would impair her health, and this truly obedient soul, always ready to hear their voice, conformed herself with submission to the more easy methods they proposed her to obtain this virtue; and God, to crown her submission and obedience, raised her to a state in which she seemed never to lose the sight of Him Who was the object of her love. From hence proceeded that evenness of temper, that perpetual recollection, that wonderful attention in composing her exterior, that nothing was ever observed disorderly in her gests, voice, or behaviour. She seemed always entirely dead to everything about her, when her duty was not concerned. This made her breathe such an air of sanctity, that several declared that her very sight was sufficient to awake in them the liveliest sentiments of the presence of Almighty God. When it was her duty to instruct, she was always inculcating thoughts of Almighty God, as of Him in Whom we live, move, and have our being, according to St. Paul. Her countenance, gesture, and all her motions were so composed, says one of her novices, that they were sufficient to mind us of this her blessed sentence. I may truly say that this practice of the presence of God was the immediate means His Providence made use of to sanctify this soul.

The other thing I mentioned was her constant exactness in complying with even the least tittle of her Rule, for which she was so remarkable, that an ancient religious speaking of her punctual observance, doubted not to say that if the Rule of St. Teresa were lost, it might be found again in her practice and conduct. 'Of twenty-seven religious,' says one yet living who was novice under her, 'whom I knew, and who had lived with her all or a considerable part of her life, and who were examined upon this subject, I could never learn of any of them,' says she, 'they had ever seen her fail in any point of our Constitution. On the contrary I heard them frequently speak of her, as of an exact model of Christian perfection. I never heard (says the same person) her raise her voice or so much as lean, or eye anything curiously, even in time of our recreation.' In sixteen years she could only twice accuse herself of casting up her eyes in the refectory. Whilst she was a private religious, she seemed not to mind what passed, according to the maxim she had fixed herself, of never minding what was not in her care. Yet when Superior she discovered and sweetly reprehended the least failings, without respect to persons. 'I once by accident (says the person above mentioned) heard one who had been lately Superior acknowledge to her some small failings in regular observance, to whom she answered with great liberty of spirit, "Dear Mother, these little things must be satisfied for."' Above all things she required of her religious the practice of these solid virtues which are only to be found in an exact observance of their Constitutions and Rules; and it was her unwearied perseverance in the practice of them for forty-five years of a religious course, which made her so pleasing in the eyes of God, and which He has been pleased to reward with the incorruption of her body upon earth and the great wonders which are daily wrought at her tomb, whilst her soul, as we have reason to believe, is in a full possession of Almighty God in heaven.

She died most piously as she had lived, the 21st of of June, 1678, the sixty-third year of her age, the forty-fifth of her religious life, and the second year after her third election for Superior. She bore her long and tedious sickness with all the patience and resignation imaginable, confirming by her practice the maxim she had always inculcated in her life, that a religious person was never to repine at sufferings, for that to fly from the Cross, was to fly from Him Who was crucified for us. She received all the Holy Sacraments, and renewed on her death-bed her vows of religion with great tenderness and sense of devotion, exhorting in the meanwhile the Community to be faithful in the observance of their Constitutions, and not to be in concern for her, for that she apprehended the passage of death no more, through the mercy of God, than she apprehended passing into the other room. She was assisted at her death by the Priest of the Society of Jesus, on which she declared that she had her sole dependance, and she procured that all under her care, should have their dependance on the Society, and took care to make her religious sensible of their happiness in being under their direction. As soon as she expired her confessor cried out in a transport, " Oh, that my soul was with hers."

THE END.

Milton Keynes UK
Ingram Content Group UK Ltd.
UKHW010111250124
436660UK00008B/67